Glimpse the entire Bible
through my
Favorite Bible Verses

Compiled by Frank Zeller

Kindle Direct Publishing

Many verses are shortened or paraphrased to keep this glimpse of the Bible reasonably short – please go to a written Bible or online Bible, to read the unmodified verses in context with other verses.

Unless otherwise indicated, all Scripture quotations are taken from the *Holy Bible*, New Living Translation, copyright © 1996, 2004, 2015 by Tyndale House Foundation. Used by permission of Tyndale House Publishers, Carol Stream, Illinois 60188. All rights reserved.

Scripture quotations taken from the Amplified® Bible (AMP), Copyright © 2015 by The Lockman Foundation. Used by permission.

Scripture quotations taken from the HOLY BIBLE: EASY-TO-READ VERSION (ERV), ©2014 by Bible League International. Used by permission.

Scripture quotations from The Authorized (King James) Version (KJV). Rights in the Authorized Version in the United Kingdom are vested in the Crown. Reproduced by permission of the Crown's patentee, Cambridge University Press

Scripture quotations marked MSG are taken from *The Message*, copyright © 1993, 2002, 2018 by Eugene H. Peterson. Used by permission of NavPress. All rights reserved. Represented by Tyndale House Publishers.

Scripture quoted by permission. Quotations designated (NET) are from the NET Bible® copyright ©1996, 2019 by Biblical Studies Press, L.L.C. http://netbible.com All rights reserved

CONTENTS

A Note from Frank
INTRODUCTION
NEW TESTAMENT

Matthew	2	Judges	101
Mark	10	Ruth	102
Luke	13	1 Samuel	102
John	23	2 Samuel	104
Acts	33	1 Kings	105
Romans	42	2 Kings	108
1 Corinthians	49	1 Chronicles	114
2 Corinthians	56	2 Chronicles	114
Galatians	58	Ezra	120
Ephesians	59	Nehemiah	120
Philippians	62	Esther	121
Colossians	63	Job	121
1 Thessalonians	65	Psalms	124
2 Thessalonians	65	Proverbs	131
1 Timothy	66	Ecclesiastes	134
2 Timothy	68	Song of Songs	136
Titus	68	Isaiah	136
Philemon	69	Jeremiah	148
Hebrews	69	Lamentations	156
James	72	Ezekiel	157
1 Peter	74	Daniel	163
2 Peter	75	Hosea	167
1 John	76	Joel	167
2 John	78	Amos	167
3 John	78	Obadiah	168
Jude	79	Jonah	168
Revelation	79	Micah	168

OLD TESTAMENT

		Nahum	168
Genesis	85	Habakkuk	168
Exodus	87	Zephaniah	169
Leviticus	89	Haggai	169
Numbers	91	Zechariah	169
Deuteronomy	94	Malachi	170
Joshua	99	**AFTERWORD**	

A Note from Frank

Note 1: Many verses are shortened or paraphrased to keep this glimpse of the Bible reasonably short – please go to a written Bible or online Bible, to read the unmodified verses in context with other verses.

Note 2: The INTENT of this book is to give a glimpse of what is in the Bible. The GOAL is for you to become interested in the entire unmodified Bible to see what God, the Creator-Owner of the universe wants to say to you.

Note 3: A FAVORITE Bible verse is, not necessarily one I emotionally like, but one that describes REALITY as it really is - not necessarily how I would desire it, because my way or desire is not likely to be God's way, see Jeremiah 17:9, Isaiah 55:8-9, Proverbs 3:5, Psalm 51:10, and Romans 12:2.

Note 4: Brackets [ ] represent the compiler's comments or definitions of words.

Note 5: CAPITALIZED WORDS represent the compiler's emphasis.

Note 6: Any internet addresses listed are offered as a resource. I cannot vouch that the content has not changed from when I added it as a resource. You may want to confirm content from other sources.

****

About the Compiler

The compiler, often with his wife, has been going on short-term mission trips around the world and in the United States since 1987. He has distributed Christian materials in 69 countries. Many of the countries he has visited multiple times.

His favorite Bible verse while on mission is 1 John 4:4, "You belong to God. The Spirit who LIVES in you is GREATER than the spirit who lives in the world."

They currently live in Wisconsin during the summer months, and Arizona during the winter months. They have two married grown sons and one granddaughter.

****

This book comes in 3 versions:

Kindle eBook
7 x 10 inch font 12 softcover book
Large Print font 16 softcover book

Search by title or "Glimpse the entire Bible" on **Amazon.com Search Bar** for the above 3 books.

****

For those who want a **PDF copy** reformatted **for cell phone** screen size, please email compiler at: hz78910@gmail.com – the PDF is ~ 2 MB.

****

Cover Photo is **Mt Sinai**, Egypt where God gave Moses the 10 Commandments.
It is a Public Domain photo taken sometime before 1914 according to Wikipedia Commons.

****

INTRODUCTION

1) Why read this book? **Why read the Bible at all?**

Ever wanted to read the Bible, but were intimidated by "Read the Bible in One Year" charts? You can read this book in 5 to 8 hours, not a year! By getting a glimpse, you will not only get an overview of the Bible, but will locate interesting verses where you may want to read in detail to learn more.

Are you aware that the Bible is unique? It consists of 66 separate "books" written by about 40 authors, written over a period of about 1500 years. The authors included kings, fishermen, farmers, shepherds, priests, government officials, and doctor. From all this diversity comes an incredible unity, with common themes woven throughout.

The Bible's unity is due to the fact that, ultimately, it has one Author – God Himself. The Bible is "inspired by God" with human authors writing what God wanted them to write, and the result was the perfect, holy, living Word of God. "Living" means that the Bible continues to speak to people today, that it continues to be relevant to today's issues, and continues to speak life into people who are truly seeking God.

A word of caution: while the Bible was written FOR us, it was not written TO us, which means we have to be careful how we "interpret" and apply what we read. Reading the Bible has been likened to traveling to a distant country, we are over 2,000 years removed from the various cultures found in the Bible. "Misreading Scripture with Western Eyes: Removing Cultural Blinders to Better Understand the Bible" by E R Richards & B J O'Brien is a book that helps to overcome our cultural biases.

The Bible is a historically accurate book, has the most historical evidence of any book, and archeology continues to find confirming evidence even to this year. The Bible is about 27 percent predictive (contains prophecies of the future) of which over half of the prophecies have already happened and further confirm the divine nature of the Bible.

Consider these **links**:
    Bible's historical accuracy and authority:
        https://www.gotquestions.org/Bible-prophecy.html

Archaeology Confirms the Old Testament:
https://breakpoint.org/the-rich-archaeological-corroboration-of-the-old-testament/

The God Who Speaks - evidence of the Bible's authority:
https://thegodwhospeaks.org/

Jay Smith & the British Museum Tour of the Bible in History:
https://www.youtube.com/playlist?list=PLAEF9835115110E90

Discover app: Discovery Bible Study:
https://play.google.com/store/apps/details?id=org.discoverapp

The book, "Christian Beliefs, Revised Ed: 20 Basics Every Christian Should Know" by Wayne Grudem are concise summaries of what the Bible says about: What is the Bible? What is God like? What is the Trinity? What is Creation? What is Prayer? What are Angels, Satan, and Demons? What is Man? What is Sin? Who is Christ? What is Atonement? What is the Resurrection? What does it mean to become a Christian? What is Death? What is the Church? What is the Final Judgment? What is Heaven? And more.

2) **To encourage followers of Jesus.**

For those who may be too busy or distracted to read the entire Bible, to re-consider what they are missing by omitting reading God's Love Letter for us. Omitting daily reading of the Bible not only hinders intimacy with Father God, Jesus, and the Holy Spirit, but blocks one of the ways God uses to "talk" with those who seek to trust, love, serve and obey Him.

For finding freedom in Jesus, consider these **links**:
Freedom in Christ   https://www.ficm.org
Get free PDF - "Restored" - reconnecting to God at:
https://www.ficm.org/ministry-materials/free-downloads

If you are a follower of Jesus, your identity is in Jesus. You are an accepted, loved, adopted child of God, see link for Bible Verses of who you are in Jesus:
https://www.ficm.org/about-us/who-i-am-in-christ/

"The Bondage Breaker" book by Neil Anderson, may help to overcome negative thoughts and temptation.

3) **For those who have not yet considered becoming a follower of Jesus.**

For those who have not read the Bible because of cultural bias or finding it difficult to understand, this short compilation of many of the most important and favorite verses of the Bible offers a way to read some of the many verses that lead to a proper understanding of who God is, how people's choices has created such a mess of the world, and what God did to correct the situation, so that we can be reconciled back to God and begin to live the abundant life with purpose and joy in and through Jesus.

Consider these **links**:
Got Questions app https://www.gotquestions.org/apps.html
Stand to Reason app http://www.str.org

4) **For those who think they know what is in the Bible, and despise it.**

This is your chance to read the highlights of the Bible so you know what you are rejecting. But be warned, many who started to read the Bible looking to easily discredit it, found instead the God who loves them, and became a follower of Jesus – this has included atheists, extremist Muslims, Wiccan priests, Satanists, and Buddhist monks, among others.

Consider these **links**:
Cross Examine app, provide reasons and evidence
https://crossexamined.org/app/
Reasons to Believe, how science and Bible actually agree
https://reasons.org/

5a) **For those who think they are followers of Jesus, but are not.**

5b) **For those who have made a god in their own image, such as "my god is love."**

You really do not want to find out too late when you hear Jesus say, "I never knew you, depart from Me" Matthew 7:23. Please consider reading this to more fully understand what a saving, loving relationship with Jesus, the Creator-Owner of the universe really is!

We are not allowed to set the terms of our relationship with the "King of kings." Having Jesus as our Lord is to follow His terms for a loving relationship with Him. Hint: it involves more than just mental belief that Jesus saves me so I can go to heaven one day, it also involves

our repentance and actually following Jesus as the Lord of my life, with obedience to what He actually says in the Bible. "Seven Words You Never Want to Hear: How to Be Sure You Won't" by D Wilson goes into helpful detail:
https://www.amazon.com/dp/1646450280/ref=redir_mobile_desktop/132-8392182-4523112

While God is definitely Love – God also – at the same time – IS Truth, Righteous, Just, and Holy. Any person or church that makes "love" their 1 and only standard is likely following a false god. They could literally be worshiping an idol – a delusion of a person's imagination – not the God of the Bible.

Consider these **links**:
    True and False Conversion
        https://www.livingwaters.com/true-and-false-conversion/
    Free Grace Theology vs. Lordship Salvation | Which is Correct? – YouTube   https://www.youtube.com/watch?v=9TtIYG17Oe0&t=13s
    How "God is Love" compares with the 3 standards Jesus sets for His Church: https://stream.org/pastors-corner-when-and-how-to-welcome-the-same-sex-couple-or-trans-person-at-your-church/
    The Gospel According to Jesus: What Is Authentic Faith?
        https://www.gty.org/store/books/451110A

6) **For those who no longer want to follow Jesus.**

For those who cannot reconcile all the evil present in the world with a loving God, or have suffered pain or abuse, perhaps even by people in a church who claim they are "Christian," please find out who the true God of the Bible is, not just what false teachers may have told you, or having unrealistic expectations of "how I would act if I was God."

Consider these **links**:
    When Life Hurts: Pain and the Christian Walk
        https://stream.org/when-life-hurts-a-discussion-of-pain-and-the-christian-walk/
    Why Would God Want Us to Praise Him?
        https://www.str.org/w/why-would-god-want-us-to-praise-him-
    How to Think about God Promoting His Own Glory
        https://www.str.org/w/how-to-think-about-god-promoting-his-own-glory

7) For easy reading access to a Bible anytime, consider an online Bible or a **free Bible App**.

> You Version Bible App:
> https://www.youversion.com/the-bible-app
> Easy to Read Bible App:
> https://www.bibleleague.org/apps

Either ERV = Easy to Read Version or NLT = New Living Translation are easy to understand.

You may want to start by reading the book of JOHN and/or MATTHEW in the New Testament. Focus most on what did Jesus SAY and what did Jesus DO, then you can learn about the life and lordship of Jesus and His love for you. After reading John and Matthew, continue by reading books of GALATIANS, EPHESIANS, PHILIPPIANS, ROMANS and LUKE.

8) May your mind and heart be open to what God may want you to know about Him! My hope is that as you glimpse the entire Bible you will **begin to experience the Bible as a love story about God's pursuit of us**. There are many stories of redemption – in both the Old and New Testaments – and you could be next!

9) Jesus did not eat with sinners because He wanted to appear inclusive, tolerant, and accepting. Jesus ate with sinners to call them to a changed and fruitful life, to die to self, and live for Him. Jesus' call is transformation of life, not affirmation of identity. (See: Matthew 16:24, John 8:11)

10) **Apparent Contradictions**

Context is how you resolve most apparent contradictions which only appear as contradictions because the Bible may emphasize a specific point in one verse and emphasize a different, but equally important, point in another verse. In addition to reading the verse with the verses before and after the verse, you may also find a Bible commentary helpful. A **free online Bible Commentary** - BIBLE REF is: https://www.bibleref.com/ Also discuss questions and concerns with a more mature follower of Jesus who may have additional resources and understanding.

An example is **2 Corinthians 6:14-18**: "Do not team up with unbelievers ..." [new believers need time to mature in a pagan society, perhaps away from their former "friends"] with **Matthew 28:18-20**: "...

Go into all the world and make disciples ..." [mature believers are to share Jesus with others] and **1 Corinthians 7:12-13**: "... If a believer has a wife who is not a believer and she is willing to continue living with him, he must not leave her. ..." [Biblical love demonstrated is more important than merely following the letter of the law, without understanding the spirit of the law].

Consider this example in the Bible clarifying a previous letter to the Corinthian church, **1 Corinthians 5:9-12** "When I wrote to you before, I told you not to associate with people who indulge in sexual sin. But I was not talking about unbelievers who indulge in sexual sin, or are greedy, or cheat people, or worship idols. You would have to leave this world to avoid people like that. I meant that you are not to associate with anyone who claims to be a believer yet indulges in sexual sin, or is greedy, or worships idols, or is abusive, or is a drunkard, or cheats people. ... It is not my responsibility to judge outsiders, but it certainly is your responsibility to judge those inside the church who are sinning."

The last example is **Proverbs 26:4-5** "Do not answer the foolish arguments of fools, or YOU will become as foolish as they are. Be sure to answer the foolish arguments of fools, or THEY will become wise in their own estimation." The emphasis is "you" versus "they", showing the need to be careful when confronting fools.

****

5 Questions to consider for any Bible Study:

1) What was hard to understand? *Explain*

2) What did you like/not like? *Explain*

3) What did you learn about Jesus/God/Holy Spirit?

4) What did you learn about people?

5) How will you change the way you live?

    a) Is there a sin to avoid?

    b) Is there a command to obey?

    c) Is there a promise to trust?

    d) Is there an example to follow?

    e) Who will you share today's discovery?

****

Glimpse the entire Bible through my Favorite Bible Verses

Many verses are shortened or paraphrased to save space – read in a Bible for the unmodified verses. Consider reading several verses in a Bible before and after each verse listed for proper context.

The Old Testament, follows after the New Testament, on page 85.

John 3:16, 36   For God loves the world so much that He gave His One and Only Son, so that everyone who believes in Him [Biblical "believes" means ongoing wholehearted commitment – trusting AND obeying – Jesus as your Savior AND Lord] will not perish but will have eternal life. ... Anyone who does not obey the Son will never experience eternal life but remains under God's judgment.

John 3:16   [*Speak out loud YOUR name in the blanks*]   For God loves _____ so much that He gave His One and Only Son, so that if _____ believes in Him, _____ shall not perish but will have eternal life.

===============

NEW TESTAMENT
Favorite Bible Verses

Matthew 3:7-8 AMP When John the Baptist saw many Pharisees [a "religious right" group emphasizing legalistic rules without mercy, similar to "truth without love" except actually was neither] and Sadducees [a "liberal left" group with near total cultural compromise, similar to "love without truth" except actually was neither] coming to watch him baptize, he denounced them, saying, "You brood of vipers [poisonous snakes]! Who warned you to flee God's coming wrath? PROVE by the WAY you LIVE that you have REPENTED of your sins and TURNED to God."

Matthew 4:1, 4, 10 Jesus [perfect "Truth and Love" personified] was led by the Spirit into the wilderness to be tempted there by the devil. ... Jesus said, "People do NOT live by bread alone, BUT by EVERY Word that comes from God." ... Jesus told the devil, "GET OUT of here, Satan, for the Scriptures say: you must worship the Lord your God and serve ONLY Him."

Matthew 5:3-13, 17-18, 21-22 KJV, 27-28, 31-32   Jesus said, "God BLESSES [gives hope and joy, independent of outward circumstances to] those who are poor in spirit and realize their NEED for Him, for the Kingdom of Heaven is theirs. God blesses those who MOURN [realize our unworthiness before God due to our sin], for they will be comforted. God blesses those who are HUMBLE [gentle, teachable, trusting God, not pride in self], for they will inherit the earth. God blesses those who hunger and thirst for RIGHTEOUSNESS [desiring to do everything God's way, complete obedience], for they will be satisfied. God blesses those who are MERCIFUL [compassion, forgive, generous], for they will be shown mercy. God blesses those whose hearts are PURE [morally pure, honest, committed to God], for they will see God. God blesses those who work for PEACE [active reconciling to end bitterness and conflict], for they will be called the children of God. God blesses those who are PERSECUTED for DOING right, for the Kingdom of Heaven is theirs. God blesses you when people mock you and persecute you and lie about you and say all sorts of evil things against you BECAUSE you are My

Followers. Be JOYFUL about it! A great REWARD awaits you in Heaven. The prophets were persecuted the same way. ... You are the SALT of the earth. But what good is salt if it has lost its flavor? It will be thrown out as worthless. ... Do NOT misunderstand why I have come. I did NOT come to ABOLISH the law of Moses or the prophets. I came to ACCOMPLISH the law's PURPOSE. I tell you the truth, until heaven and earth disappear, NOT the smallest detail of God's law will disappear UNTIL its purpose is achieved. ... You have heard that our ancestors were told, 'You must not murder.' But I say, IF you are even angry with someone without a cause, you are subject to judgment! IF you call someone an idiot, you are in danger of being brought before the court. And IF you curse someone, you are in danger of the fires of hell. ... You have heard the commandment that says, 'You must not commit adultery.' But I say, anyone who even looks at a woman with lust has already committed adultery with her in his heart. ... You have heard the law that says, 'A man can divorce his wife by merely giving her a written notice of divorce.' But I say that a man who divorces his wife, unless she has been unfaithful, causes her to commit adultery. And anyone who marries a divorced woman also commits adultery."

Matthew 6:6-7, 19-21, 24, 33-34 Jesus said, "When you PRAY, go away by yourself, shut the door behind you, and pray to your Father in private. Then your Father, who sees everything, will reward you. ... When you pray, do NOT babble on and on as people of other religions do. They think their prayers are answered by repeating words again and again. ... Do NOT store up treasures here on earth, where moths eat them, rust destroys them, and thieves steal them. STORE your TREASURES in heaven, where moths and rust cannot destroy, and thieves do not steal. WHERE your TREASURE is, there the DESIRES of your heart will also be. ... No one can serve 2 masters. For you will hate one and love the other. You will be devoted to one and despise the other. You CANNOT serve both God and money. ... SEEK the Kingdom of God above all else, and live righteously, and He will give you everything you need. Do NOT worry about tomorrow. Today's trouble is enough for today."

Matthew 7:1-7, 13-16, 20-23 Jesus said, "Do NOT judge others, and you will NOT be judged. For you will be treated as you treat others. The STANDARD you use in judging is the STANDARD by which you will be judged. WHY worry about a speck in your friend's eye when you have a log in your own? ... HOW can you think of saying to your friend, 'Let me help you get rid of that speck in your eye,' when you cannot see past the log in your own eye? HYPOCRITE! FIRST get rid of the log in your own eye; THEN you will see well enough to DEAL with the speck in your friend's eye. Do NOT waste what is HOLY on people who are UNHOLY. Do NOT throw your pearls to pigs! They will trample the pearls, then turn and attack you. [Share the gospel, but if people are not listening or are becoming hostile, move on to others who need the gospel, and are ready to hear it.] ... Keep ASKING, and you will receive what you ask for. Keep SEEKING, and you will find. Keep KNOCKING, and the door will be opened to you. ... You can enter God's Kingdom ONLY through the NARROW gate. The HIGHWAY to HELL is WIDE for the MANY who CHOOSE that way. But the GATEWAY to LIFE is very NARROW and the road is difficult, and ONLY a FEW ever FIND it. Beware of FALSE prophets who come DISGUISED as harmless sheep but are really vicious wolves. You can identify them by the way they act. Yes, you can IDENTIFY people BY their ACTIONS. ... NOT everyone who calls out to Me, 'Lord! Lord!' will ENTER the Kingdom of Heaven. [Lord means the ruler, the boss, the master of your whole life. He cannot be Lord of only a part – He must be given control of your entire life. What does the LORD require of you? See Micah 6:8] ONLY those WHO actually DO the will of My Father in heaven will enter. On Judgment Day many will say to Me, 'Lord! Lord! We prophesied in Your Name, cast out demons in Your Name and performed miracles in Your Name.' BUT I will reply, 'I NEVER knew you, DEPART from Me, you who BREAK God's laws.'"

Matthew 9:36-38 Jesus saw the crowds, and had COMPASSION on them BECAUSE they were CONFUSED and HELPLESS, like sheep without a shepherd. He said to His disciples, "The harvest is great, but the workers are few. So PRAY to the Lord who is in charge of the harvest: ASK Him to send MORE workers into His fields."

Matthew 10:22, 28, 34-37 Jesus said, "All nations will hate you because you are My Followers. But everyone who ENDURES to the end will be SAVED. ... Do NOT be afraid of those who want to kill your body; they cannot touch your soul. Fear ONLY God, who can destroy BOTH soul and body in hell. ... I came not to bring peace, but a sword. I have come to set a man against his father, a daughter against her mother, and a daughter-in-law against her mother-in-law. ... IF you love your father or mother MORE than you love Me, you are NOT worthy of being Mine. IF you love your son or daughter MORE than Me, you are NOT worthy of being Mine."

Matthew 11:28-30   Jesus said, "COME to Me, all of you who are WEARY and carry heavy burdens, and I will GIVE you REST. Take My yoke upon you. Let Me TEACH you, because I am humble and gentle at heart, and you will find rest for your souls. For the burden I give you is light."

Matthew 12:36-37, 40-41   Jesus said, "I tell you this, you must GIVE an ACCOUNT on Judgment Day for every idle word you speak. The words you say will either acquit you or condemn you. ... For as Jonah was in the belly of the great fish for 3 days and 3 nights, so will the Son of Man be in the heart of the earth for 3 days and 3 nights. ... The people of Nineveh will stand up against this generation on Judgment Day and condemn it, for they REPENTED of their sins at the preaching of Jonah. Now someone GREATER than Jonah is here, but you REFUSE to repent."

Matthew 13:36-44, 47-51   Jesus' disciples said, "Please explain to us the story of the weeds in the field." Jesus replied, "The Son of Man is the farmer who plants the good seed. The field is the world, and the GOOD SEED represents the people of the Kingdom. The WEEDS are the people who belong to the evil one. The enemy who planted the weeds among the wheat is the devil. The HARVEST is the END of the WORLD, and the harvesters are the angels. Just as the weeds are sorted out and burned in the fire, so it will be at the end of the world. The Son of Man will send His angels, and they will REMOVE from His Kingdom everything that causes sin and ALL who do EVIL. And the angels will throw them into the fiery furnace, where there will be weeping and gnashing of teeth. Then the righteous [being right, based on God's standard, includes thoughts, words and actions] will shine like the sun in their Father's Kingdom. ... The Kingdom of Heaven is like a TREASURE that a man discovered hidden in a field. In his excitement, he hid it again and SOLD EVERYTHING he owned to get enough money to buy the field. ... The Kingdom of Heaven is like a FISHING NET that was thrown into the water and caught fish of every kind. When the net was full, they dragged it up onto the shore, sat down, and sorted the good fish into crates, but threw the bad ones away. That is the way it will be at the END of the WORLD. The angels will come and SEPARATE the WICKED people FROM the righteous, throwing the WICKED into the fiery furnace, where there will be weeping and gnashing of teeth."

Matthew 15:7-14   Jesus said, "You HYPOCRITES! Isaiah was right when he prophesied about you, for he wrote, 'These people honor Me with their lips, but their hearts are FAR from Me. Their worship is a farce, for they teach MAN-MADE ideas as commands from God.' [Isaiah 29:13] ... Listen and try to understand. It is not what goes into your mouth that defiles you; you are DEFILED BY the words that come OUT of your mouth." Then the disciples came to Jesus and asked, "Do you realize you OFFENDED the Pharisees by what you just said?" Jesus replied, "Every plant not planted by My heavenly Father will be uprooted, so IGNORE them. They are BLIND guides leading the blind, and if one blind person guides another, they will both fall into a ditch."

Matthew 16:22-27 Peter took Jesus aside to reprimand Him, "Heaven forbid, Lord, This will never happen to You!" Jesus turned to Peter and said, "GET AWAY from Me, Satan! You are a dangerous TRAP to me. You SEE things merely FROM a human point of view, NOT from God's point of view." Then Jesus said to His disciples, "IF any of you wants to be My Follower, you must TURN from your selfish ways, TAKE up your cross [die daily to pride in self], and FOLLOW Me. IF you try to hang on to your life, you will LOSE it. But IF you give up your life for My sake, you will SAVE it. What do you benefit IF you gain the whole world BUT lose your own soul? Is anything worth MORE than your soul? For the Son of Man will come with His angels in the glory of His Father and will JUDGE all people ACCORDING to their DEEDS."

Matthew 18:3-4, 6, 15-17 Jesus said, "I tell you the truth, UNLESS you TURN from your sins and become like little children, you will NEVER GET into the Kingdom of Heaven. Anyone who becomes as HUMBLE [gentle, teachable] as this little child is the GREATEST in the Kingdom of Heaven. ... IF you CAUSE one of these little ones who trusts in Me to FALL into sin, it would be better for you to have a millstone tied around your neck and be drowned in the depths of the sea. ... IF another believer sins against you, go PRIVATELY and POINT OUT the offense. IF the other person listens and confesses it, you have won that person back. But IF you are unsuccessful, take 1 or 2 others with you and go back again, so that everything you say may be confirmed by 2 or 3 witnesses. IF the person still REFUSES to listen, take your case to the church. Then IF he or she will NOT accept the church's decision, treat that person as a corrupt tax collector."

Matthew 19:29 Jesus said, "Everyone who has GIVEN UP ... father or mother or children or property, for My sake, will receive a hundred times as much in return and will INHERIT eternal life."

Matthew 22:1-2, 11-14, 29 Jesus said, "The Kingdom of Heaven can be illustrated by the story of a king who prepared a great wedding feast for his son. ... When the king came in to meet the guests, he noticed a man who was NOT wearing the proper clothes for a wedding. 'Friend,' he asked, 'how is it that you are here without wedding clothes?' But the man had no reply. Then the king said to his aides, 'Bind his hands and feet and throw him into the outer darkness, where there will be weeping and gnashing of teeth.' For MANY are called, but FEW are chosen." ... Jesus replied, "Your MISTAKE is that you do NOT know the Scriptures, and you do NOT know the power of God."

Matthew 23:9-10, 13, 15, 25, 28, 33   Jesus said, "Do NOT address anyone here on earth as 'Father,' for ONLY God in heaven is your spiritual Father. And do NOT let anyone call you 'Teacher,' for you have ONLY ONE Teacher, the Messiah. ... What SORROW awaits you teachers of religious law and you Pharisees. HYPOCRITES! For you shut the door to the Kingdom of Heaven in people's faces. You will not go in yourselves. ... What SORROW awaits you teachers of religious law. HYPOCRITES! For you cross land and sea to make one convert, and then you turn that person into twice the child of hell you are! ... HYPOCRITES! For you are so careful to clean the outside of the cup and the dish, but INSIDE you are filthy – full of greed and self-indulgence! OUTWARDLY you look like righteous people, but INWARDLY your hearts are filled with hypocrisy and lawlessness. Snakes! Sons of vipers! How will you escape the judgment of hell?"

Matthew 24:4-15, 21-27, 30-31, 35-44, 46, 48-51   Jesus said, "Do NOT let anyone MISLEAD you, for many will come in My Name, claiming, 'I am the Messiah.' They will DECEIVE many. You will hear of wars and threats of wars, but do NOT panic. There will be many famines and earthquakes in the world. Then you will be arrested, persecuted, and killed. You will be hated all over the world BECAUSE you are My Followers. Many will turn away from Me and betray and hate each other. Many FALSE prophets will appear and will DECEIVE many people. Sin will be OUT OF CONTROL everywhere, and the love of many will GROW COLD. The one who ENDURES to the end will be SAVED. The Good News about the Kingdom will be preached throughout the whole world, so that all nations will hear it; and THEN the END will COME. ... The day is coming when there will be greater anguish than at any time since the world began. Unless that time of calamity is shortened, not a single person will survive. But it will be shortened for the sake of God's chosen ones. False messiahs and FALSE prophets will rise up and perform great signs and wonders so as to DECEIVE, if possible, even

God's chosen ones. I have WARNED you about this ahead of time. So IF someone tells you, 'Look, the Messiah is out in the desert,' do NOT go and look, do NOT believe it! As the lightning flashes in the east and shines to the west, so it will be when the Son of Man comes on the clouds of heaven with power and great glory. He will send out His angels who will gather His chosen ones from all over the world. Heaven and earth will disappear, but My WORDS will NEVER disappear. When the Son of Man returns, it will be like it was in Noah's day. People did not realize what was going to happen until the flood came and swept them all away. That is the way it will be when the Son of Man comes. Two men will be working together in the field; one will be taken, the other left. Two women will be grinding flour at the mill; one will be taken, the other left. Keep watch! You do NOT know what day your Lord is coming. The Son of Man will come when least expected. ... IF the Master returns and finds that the servant has done a good job, there will be a reward. But IF the servant is evil and thinks, 'My master will not be back for a while,' and begins beating the other servants, partying, and getting drunk, the Master will return unexpected and cut the servant to pieces and assign him a place with the hypocrites, where there will be weeping and gnashing of teeth."

Matthew 25:14-23, 24-30 MSG, 41-46   Jesus said, "The Kingdom of Heaven can be illustrated by the story of a man going on a long trip. He called together his servants and entrusted his money to them while he was gone. He gave 5 bags of silver to one, 2 bags of silver to another, and 1 bag of silver to the last — dividing it in PROPORTION to their abilities. He then left on his trip. The servant who received the 5 bags of silver began to invest the money and earned 5 more. The servant with 2 bags of silver also went to work and earned 2 more. But the servant who received the 1 bag of silver dug a hole in the ground and hid the master's money. After a long time their master returned from his trip and called them to GIVE AN ACCOUNT of how they had used his money. The servant to whom he had entrusted the 5 bags of silver came forward with 5 more. ... The master said, 'WELL DONE, my good and faithful servant. You have been faithful in handling this SMALL amount, so now I will give you many MORE responsibilities. Let's CELEBRATE together!' The servant who had received the 2 bags of silver came forward ... with 2 more. The master said, 'WELL DONE, my good and faithful servant. You have been faithful in handling this SMALL amount, so now I will give you many MORE responsibilities. Let's CELEBRATE together!' Then the servant with the 1 bag of silver said, 'Master, I know you have high standards. ... I was afraid I might disappoint you, so I found a good hiding place and

8

secured your money.' The master was furious. 'To LIVE so CAUTIOUSLY is a TERRIBLE way to live! If you knew I was after the best, why did you do less than the least? The least you could have done would have been to invest the sum with the bankers, where I would have gotten a little interest. Take the 1 bag of silver and give it to the one who risked the most. And THROW this "play-it-safe" USELESS servant into utter darkness.' ... [The Final Judgment can be illustrated by:] ... The King will turn to those on the LEFT and say, 'AWAY with you, you cursed ones, into the eternal fire prepared for the devil and his demons. For I was hungry, and you did not feed Me. I was thirsty, and you did not give Me a drink. I was a stranger, and you did not invite Me into your home. I was sick and in prison, and you did not visit Me.' They will reply, 'Lord, WHEN did we ever SEE You hungry or thirsty or a stranger or naked or sick or in prison, and NOT help You?' The King will answer, 'I tell you the truth, WHEN you REFUSED to help the least of My brothers and sisters, you were REFUSING to help Me.' They will go away into eternal PUNISHMENT, but the righteous [being right, based on God's standard, includes thoughts, words and actions] will go into eternal LIFE."

Matthew 26:27-28, 63-66 Jesus took a cup of wine and gave it to them saying, "This is My BLOOD, which confirms the covenant between God and His people. It is poured out as a sacrifice to FORGIVE the sins of MANY." ... Then the high priest said to Jesus, "I demand in the Name of the living God – tell us IF you ARE the Messiah, the SON of God." Jesus answered, "You have said it. And in the future you will see the Son of Man seated in the place of power at God's right hand, coming on the clouds of heaven." Then the high priest said, "Blasphemy! You have all heard his blasphemy. What is your verdict?" "Guilty!" they said.

Matthew 27:22, 25-26, 31, 33, 35-37, 39, 41-43, 45-46, 50-53 Pilate responded, "Then what should I do with Jesus who is called the Messiah?" They shouted back, "CRUCIFY Him! ... We will take responsibility for His death!" So Pilate ... turned Him over to the Roman soldiers to be crucified. ... They led Him away ... to a place called Golgotha (means "Place of the Skull"). After they had NAILED Him to the CROSS ... they sat around and kept guard as He hung there. A sign was fastened to the cross above Jesus' head. ... It read: "This is Jesus, the King of the Jews." The people passing by shouted abuse. ... The leading priests, the teachers of religious law, and the elders also mocked Jesus. "He saved others," they scoffed, "but He cannot save Himself! So He is the King of Israel, is

He? Let Him come down from the cross right now, and we will believe in Him! ... For He said, 'I AM the SON of God.'" ... At noon, darkness fell across the land until 3 o'clock. At about 3 o'clock, Jesus called out with a loud voice, "My God, My God, why have You abandoned Me?" ... Jesus shouted out again, and He released His spirit. At that moment the curtain in the Temple was torn in two, from top to bottom. The earth shook, rocks split apart, and tombs opened. The bodies of many godly men and women who had died were raised from the dead. They left the cemetery after Jesus' resurrection, went into Jerusalem, and appeared to many people.

Matthew 28:1-10, 18-20   Early on Sunday morning, Mary Magdalene and the other Mary went out to visit the tomb. Suddenly there was a great earthquake! For an angel of the Lord came down from heaven, rolled aside the stone, and sat on it. His face shone like lightning, and his clothing was as white as snow. The guards shook with fear when they saw him, and they fell into a dead faint. Then the angel spoke to the women. "Do not be afraid!" he said. "I know you are LOOKING for Jesus, who was crucified. He is not here! He is RISEN from the dead, just AS He SAID would happen. Come, see where His body was lying. Go quickly and tell His disciples that He has RISEN from the dead" ... The women were very frightened but also filled with great JOY, and they rushed to give the disciples the angel's message. As they went, Jesus met them and greeted them. And they ran to Him, grasped His feet, and WORSHIPED Him. Jesus said to them, "Do not be afraid!" ... Jesus came and told His disciples, "I have been given all AUTHORITY in heaven and on earth. Therefore, GO and MAKE DISCIPLES of all the nations, BAPTIZING them in the Name of the Father and the Son and the Holy Spirit. TEACH these new disciples to OBEY all the commands I have given you. And be sure of this: I AM with you ALWAYS."

Mark 1:15, 17-18
Jesus announced, "The Kingdom of God is near! REPENT of your sins and BELIEVE the Good News! Come, FOLLOW Me, and I will show you how to fish for people!" And they left their nets at once and followed Him.

Mark 2:5-12   Seeing their faith, Jesus said to the paralyzed man, "My child, your sins are forgiven." But some of the teachers of religious law thought to themselves, "What is He saying? This is blasphemy! ONLY God can FORGIVE sins!" Jesus knew immediately what they were thinking, so He asked them, "Why do you question this in your hearts? Is it easier to say to the paralyzed man 'Your sins are forgiven,' or 'Stand up, pick up your mat, and walk'? So I will PROVE to you that the Son of Man has the authority on earth to forgive sins." Then Jesus turned to the paralyzed man and said, "Stand up, pick up your mat, and go home!" And the man jumped up, grabbed his mat, and walked out through the stunned onlookers.

Mark 5:19, 36, 41-42 Jesus said, "Go home to your family, and TELL them everything the Lord has DONE for you and how merciful He has been." ... Jesus said to Jairus, "Do NOT be afraid. Just have FAITH [trust]." ... Holding her [Jairus' daughter] hand, Jesus said to her, "Little girl, get up!" The dead girl immediately stood up and walked around!

Mark 6:41-42, 49-51 Jesus took the 5 loaves and 2 fish, looked up toward heaven, and blessed them. Then, breaking the loaves into pieces, he kept giving the bread to the disciples so they could distribute it to the people. He also divided the fish for everyone to share. They all ate as much as they wanted. ... Jesus came WALKING ON the water. They were terrified when they saw Him. Jesus spoke to them, "Do not be afraid. Take courage! I AM here!" He climbed into the boat, and the wind stopped.

Mark 7:6-8, 13 Jesus replied, "You HYPOCRITES! Isaiah was right when he prophesied about you, writing, 'These people honor Me with their lips, but their hearts are far from Me. Their worship is a farce, for they teach MAN-MADE ideas as commands from God.' [Isaiah 29:13] For you IGNORE God's law and SUBSTITUTE your own tradition. ... You CANCEL the Word of God to hand down your own tradition."

Mark 8:11-13, 29, 31-34, 38 The Pharisees came and started to argue with Jesus. They demanded that Jesus show them a miraculous sign from heaven to prove His authority. Jesus sighed deeply and said, "Why do these people demand a miraculous sign?" ... So He got back into the boat and left them, and He crossed to the other side of the lake. ... Jesus asked them, "WHO do you say I am?" Peter replied, "You ARE the Messiah." Jesus told them that the Son of Man must suffer many terrible things and be rejected by the elders, the leading priests, and the teachers of religious law. He would be killed, but 3 days later He would rise from the dead. Peter began to rebuke Jesus for saying such things. Then Jesus rebuked Peter: "GET AWAY from me, Satan! You are SEEING things merely FROM a human point of view, NOT from God's point of view." ... Then Jesus said, "IF any of you wants to be My Follower, you must TURN from your selfish ways, TAKE up your cross [die daily to pride in self], and FOLLOW Me. IF anyone is ashamed of Me and My message in these adulterous and sinful days, the Son of Man will BE ashamed of that person when He returns in the glory of His Father with the angels."

Mark 9:23-24, 47-48   Jesus asked, "What do you mean, 'IF I can?' Anything is possible IF a person believes." The father cried out, "I do believe, but help me OVERCOME my doubts!" ... Jesus said, "If your eye causes you to sin, gouge it out. It is better to enter the Kingdom of God with 1 eye than to have 2 eyes and be thrown into hell, where maggots NEVER die and fire NEVER goes out."

Mark 10:6, 8-9, 26-27, 45   Jesus said, "God made them MALE and FEMALE from the beginning of creation. and the 2 are united into 1. ... Since they are no longer 2 but 1, let no one split apart what God has joined together." ... "WHO in the world can be SAVED?" they asked. Jesus said, "Humanly speaking, it is IMPOSSIBLE. But not with God. Everything is POSSIBLE with God. ... The Son of Man came not to be served but to GIVE His life as a ransom for many."

Mark 11:25   Jesus said, "When you are PRAYING, first FORGIVE anyone you are holding a grudge against, so that your Father in heaven will forgive your sins, too."

Mark 12:24, 26-27, 29-31   Jesus replied, "Your MISTAKE is that you do NOT know the Scriptures, and you do NOT know the power of God. ... As to WHETHER the DEAD will be RAISED – have you ever read about this in the writings of Moses, in the story of the burning bush? Long after Abraham, Isaac, and Jacob had died, God said to Moses, 'I AM the God of Abraham, the God of Isaac, and the God of Jacob.' So God is the God of the LIVING, not the dead. You have made a serious error." ... Jesus said, "The MOST IMPORTANT commandment is this: 'The Lord our God is the One and ONLY Lord. And you must LOVE the Lord your God with all your heart, all your soul, all your mind, and all your strength.' The SECOND is equally important: 'LOVE your neighbor AS yourself.' No other commandment is greater than these."

Mark 13:11-13, 22-23, 26-27, 31-33   Jesus said, "When you are arrested and stand trial, do NOT worry about what to say. Just SAY what God tells you at that time. A brother will betray his brother to death, a father will betray his own child, and children will rebel against their parents and cause them to be killed. And everyone will HATE you BECAUSE you are My Followers. But the one who ENDURES to the end will be SAVED. ... False messiahs and FALSE prophets will rise up and perform signs and wonders so as to DECEIVE, if possible, even God's chosen ones. Watch out! I have WARNED you about this ahead of time! ... Then everyone will see the Son of Man coming on the clouds with great power and glory. And He will send out His angels to gather His chosen ones from all over the world. Heaven and earth will disappear, but My Words will NEVER disappear. No one knows the day or hour when these things will happen. Stay alert!"

Mark 14:36, 38, 61-62 "Abba, Father," Jesus cried out, "everything is possible for you. Please take this cup of suffering away from Me. Yet, I want Your will to be done, NOT my will." ... Jesus said, "Keep watch and PRAY, so that you will NOT give in to temptation. For the spirit is willing, but the body is weak." ... Then the high priest asked Jesus, "ARE YOU the Messiah, the SON of the Blessed One?" Jesus said, "I AM. And you will see the Son of Man seated in the place of power at God's right hand and coming on the clouds of heaven."

Mark 15:13-15, 24, 33-34, 37 Pilate asked them, "Then what should I do with this Man you call the King of the Jews?" They shouted back, "CRUCIFY Him!" ... So to pacify the crowd, Pilate ordered Jesus flogged with a lead-tipped whip, then turned Him over to the Roman soldiers to be crucified. ... Then the soldiers NAILED Him to the CROSS. ... At noon, darkness fell across the whole land until 3 o'clock. Then at 3 o'clock Jesus called out with a loud voice, "My God, My God, why have You abandoned Me?" Then Jesus uttered another loud cry and breathed His last.

Mark 16:1-7 Saturday evening, Mary Magdalene and Salome and Mary the mother of James went out and purchased burial spices so they could anoint Jesus' body. Very early on Sunday morning, just at sunrise, they went to the tomb. On the way they were asking each other, "Who will roll away the stone for us from the entrance to the tomb?" But as they arrived, they looked up and saw that the stone, which was very large, had already been rolled aside. When they entered the tomb, they saw a young man clothed in a white robe sitting on the right side. The women were shocked, but the angel said, "Do not be alarmed. You are LOOKING for Jesus of Nazareth, who was crucified. He is NOT here! He is RISEN from the dead! Look, this is where they laid His body. Now go and tell His disciples, including Peter, that Jesus is going ahead of you to Galilee. You will see Him there, just AS He TOLD you BEFORE He died."

Luke 1:3-4   Having carefully investigated everything from the beginning, I decided to write a careful account, Theophilus, so you can BE CERTAIN of the TRUTH of everything you were taught.

Luke 1:30-35, 45   "Do not be afraid, Mary," the angel said, "for you have found favor with God! You will conceive and give birth to a son, and you will name him Jesus. He will be great and will be called the Son of the Most High. ... His Kingdom will never end!" Mary asked the angel, "But how can this happen? I am a virgin." The angel replied, "The Holy Spirit will come upon you, and the power of the Most High will overshadow you. The baby will be HOLY and He will be called the Son of God. ... You are blessed BECAUSE you BELIEVED the Lord would DO what He SAID."

Luke 2:10-11, 34   The angel said, "Do not be afraid! I bring you good news that brings great JOY to all people. The SAVIOR – the Messiah, the LORD – has been born today in Bethlehem!" ... Simeon said to Mary, the baby's mother, "This child is destined to cause many in Israel to fall, but He will be a JOY to many others. He has been sent as a sign from God, but many will oppose Him."

Luke 3:8-11, 17, 21-22   John [the Baptist] said, "PROVE by the WAY you LIVE that you have REPENTED of your sins and TURN to God. Do not say to each other, 'We are safe, for we are descendants of Abraham.' That means nothing. The ax of God's Judgment is poised, ready to sever the roots of the trees. Every tree that does NOT produce good fruit will be chopped down and thrown into the fire." The crowds asked, "WHAT SHOULD we DO?" John [the Baptist] replied, "If you have 2 shirts, GIVE 1 to the poor. If you have food, SHARE it with those who are hungry. ... He is ready to SEPARATE the chaff from the wheat with His winnowing fork. THEN He will gather the wheat into His barn but burn the chaff with never-ending fire." ... JESUS was baptized. As He was praying, the heavens opened, and the HOLY SPIRIT descended on Him like a dove. And a VOICE [God the Father] from heaven said, "You are My dearly loved SON, and You bring Me great JOY."

Luke 4:6-8, 13, 18-19, 21, 28-30, 36   The devil said, "I will give you the glory of these kingdoms, IF you will worship me." Jesus replied, "The Scriptures say, You must WORSHIP the Lord your God and SERVE ONLY Him." ... The devil then left Jesus until the next opportunity came. ... Jesus said, "The Spirit of the Lord is upon Me, for He has anointed Me to bring Good News to the poor. He has sent Me to proclaim that captives will be released, that the blind will see, that the oppressed will be set free, and that the time of the Lord's favor has come." [Isaiah 61:1-2a] … Then Jesus said: "The Scripture you have just heard has been FULFILLED this very day!" … When they heard this, the people in the synagogue were furious. Jumping up, they mobbed Jesus and forced Him to the edge of the hill. They intended to push Him over the cliff, but Jesus passed right through the crowd and went on His way. … Amazed, the people exclaimed, "What AUTHORITY and POWER Jesus's Words possess! Even evil spirits obey Him, and they flee at His command!"

Luke 5:13, 16, 32 Jesus reached out and touched him and said, "I am willing. Be healed!" … Jesus often withdrew to the wilderness for prayer. … Jesus said, "I have come to call NOT those who THINK they are righteous, BUT those who KNOW they are sinners and need to REPENT."

Luke 6:22-23, 26-28, 31-32, 35-39, 41-42, 45-46 Jesus said, "What BLESSINGS await you when people hate you and exclude you and mock you and curse you as evil BECAUSE you follow the Son of Man. When that happens, leap for JOY! For a great reward awaits you in heaven. … What SORROW awaits you who are PRAISED by the CROWDS, for their ancestors also praised FALSE prophets. … LOVE your ENEMIES! Do GOOD to those who hate you. BLESS those who curse you. PRAY for those who hurt you. … DO to others AS you would LIKE them to do TO you. IF you love only those who love you, WHY should you get credit for that? Even sinners love those who love them! … LOVE your ENEMIES! Do GOOD to them. Lend to them without expecting to be repaid. THEN your reward from heaven will be very great, and you will truly be acting as children of the Most High, for God is KIND to those who are unthankful and wicked. You must be COMPASSIONATE, just as your Father is compassionate. Do not judge others, and you will not be judged. Do NOT condemn others, OR it will all come back against you. FORGIVE others, and you will be forgiven. GIVE, and you will receive. Your gift will return to you in full. The AMOUNT you GIVE will DETERMINE the amount you GET BACK. … Can one BLIND person LEAD another? Won't they BOTH FALL into a ditch? … WHY worry about a speck in your friend's eye when you have a log in your own? HOW can you think of saying, 'Friend, let me help you get rid of that speck in your eye,' WHEN you cannot see past the log in your own eye? HYPOCRITE! FIRST get rid of the log in your own eye; THEN you will see well enough to DEAL with the speck in your friend's eye. … A good person PRODUCES good things FROM a good heart, and an evil person PRODUCES evil things FROM an evil heart. WHAT you SAY flows FROM what is IN your HEART. So WHY do you keep calling Me 'Lord, Lord!' WHEN you do NOT DO what I say?"

Luke 7:14, 23, 44-50 Jesus walked over to the coffin and touched it. "Young man," He said, "I tell you, get up." ... Jesus said, "Blessed is the one who is NOT OFFENDED by Me." ... Jesus turned to the woman and said to Simon [a Pharisee], "Look at this woman kneeling here. When I entered your home, you did not offer me water to wash the dust from My feet, but she has washed them with her tears and wiped them with her hair. You did not greet me with a kiss, but from the time I first came in, she has not stopped kissing My feet. You neglected the courtesy of olive oil to anoint My head, but she has anointed My feet with rare perfume. I tell you, her sins – and they are many – have been forgiven, so she has shown Me MUCH love. But a person who is forgiven little shows only LITTLE love." Then Jesus said to the woman, "Your sins are forgiven. Your faith has saved you; go in peace."

Luke 8:11, 13-15, 17-18, 21, 25, 38-39 Jesus said, "This is the meaning of the parable: The SEED is God's Word. The seeds on the ROCKY soil represent those who hear the message and receive it with joy. But they believe for a while, then they FALL away when facing temptation. The seeds that fell among the THORNS represent those who hear the message, but too quickly the message is CROWDED OUT by the cares and riches and pleasures of this life. And so they NEVER mature. The seeds that fell on the GOOD soil represent honest, good-hearted people who hear and CLING to God's Word and patiently produce a huge harvest. ... For all that is SECRET will eventually be brought into the OPEN. To those who LISTEN to My teaching, MORE understanding will be given. But for those who are NOT listening, even what they think they understand will be TAKEN away from them." ... Jesus replied, "My mother and my brothers are all those who HEAR God's Word and OBEY it." ... Jesus asked, "WHERE is your faith?" The disciples were terrified and amazed. "WHO is this Man?" they asked. "When He gives a command, EVEN the wind and waves OBEY Him!" ... Jesus said to the man who was freed from the demons, "Go back to your family, and TELL them everything God has DONE for you." So he went all through the town proclaiming the great things Jesus had done for him.

Luke 9:23, 29, 35, 54-56 KJV Jesus said, "IF you want to be My Follower, you must TURN from your selfish ways, TAKE UP your cross daily [die daily to pride in self], and FOLLOW Me." ... As Jesus was praying, the appearance of His face was TRANSFORMED, and His clothes became dazzling white. ... A Voice from the cloud said, "This is My Son. LISTEN to Him." ... James and John said to Jesus, "Lord, should we call down fire from heaven to burn them up?" But Jesus turned and rebuked them saying, "The Son of Man has NOT come to DESTROY people's lives, BUT to SAVE them." So they went on to another village.

Luke 10:3, 5, 16, 19-21, 27, 36-37, 41-42   Jesus said, "Now go, and remember that I am sending you out as LAMBS among WOLVES. ... Whenever you enter someone's home, first say, 'May God's PEACE be on this house.' ... Anyone who ACCEPTS your message is also accepting Me. Anyone who REJECTS you is rejecting Me. Anyone who REJECTS Me is rejecting God, who sent Me.. ... I have given you AUTHORITY over all the power of the enemy. Do not rejoice that evil spirits obey you, be JOYFUL that your names are recorded in heaven." ... Jesus was filled with the JOY of the Holy Spirit and said, "Father, Lord of heaven and earth, thank you for HIDING these things from those who THINK themselves wise and clever, and for REVEALING them to the childlike. Yes, Father, it pleased You to do it this way." ... The man answered, "You must LOVE the Lord your God with all your heart, all your soul, all your strength, and all your mind. And LOVE your neighbor AS yourself." ... Jesus asked, "Which of these 3 would you say was a neighbor to the man who was attacked by bandits?" The man replied, "The one who showed MERCY [compassion, generous, kind]." Jesus said, "Yes, now go and DO the SAME." ... The Lord said to her, "My dear Martha, you are worried and upset over all these details! There is ONLY ONE thing worth being concerned about. Mary has discovered it."

Luke 11:2-4, 23, 28, 32, 35-36, 42, 52   Jesus said, "PRAY this way: Father, may Your Name be kept holy. May Your Kingdom come soon. Give us each day the food we need, and forgive us our sins, as we forgive those who sin against us. And do not let us yield to temptation, but deliver us from the evil one." ... Jesus said, "Anyone who is NOT with Me OPPOSES Me, and anyone who is NOT working with Me is actually working AGAINST Me. ... Blessed are all who HEAR the Word of God and DO it. ... The people of Nineveh will stand up against this generation on Judgment Day and condemn it, for they REPENTED of their sins at Jonah's preaching. Now someone GREATER than Jonah is here – but you REFUSE to repent. ... Make sure that the light you THINK you have is NOT actually darkness.   IF you are filled with light, with no dark corners, THEN your whole life will be as a floodlight is filling you. ... What SORROW awaits you Pharisees! For you are careful to tithe even the tiniest income from your herb gardens, but you IGNORE justice AND the love of God. You should tithe, yes, but do NOT neglect the MORE important things. ... What SORROW awaits you experts in religious law! You REMOVE the KEY to knowledge from people. You do NOT enter the Kingdom, and PREVENT others from entering."

Luke 12:3-9, 11-12, 15, 21, 25-26, 31, 33-34, 37, 40, 47-48, 51, 53, 56
Jesus said, "Whatever you have SAID in the dark will be HEARD in the light, for all to hear! Dear friends, do NOT be afraid of those who want to kill your body; they CANNOT do any more to you after that. FEAR God, who has the power to kill you AND then throw you into hell. ... What is the price of 5 sparrows – 2 copper coins? Yet God does NOT forget a single one of them. ... So do not be afraid; you are MORE valuable to God than a whole flock of sparrows. I tell you the truth, everyone who ACKNOWLEDGES Me publicly on earth, the Son of Man will also acknowledge in heaven. But anyone who DENIES Me on earth will be denied in heaven. ... When you are brought to trial before the authorities, do NOT worry about how to DEFEND yourself or what to SAY, for the Holy Spirit will TEACH you at that time what to say. ... Beware! Guard AGAINST every kind of GREED. Life is NOT measured by how much you own. A person is a FOOL to store up earthly wealth but NOT have a rich RELATIONSHIP with God. ... Can all your WORRIES add a SINGLE moment to your life? IF worry CANNOT accomplish a little thing like that, what is the use of worrying over bigger things?" ... Jesus said, "SEEK the Kingdom of God ABOVE ALL else, and He will give you everything you need. ... GIVE to those in need. This will store up treasure for you in heaven! WHEREVER your treasure is, the DESIRES of your heart will ALSO be. ... The servants who are ready, waiting for His return will be rewarded. He will serve them as they eat! You must be READY all the time, for the Son of Man will come when least expected. ... A servant who KNOWS what the master wants, but is not prepared and does not carry out those instructions, will be severely punished. But someone who does NOT know, and then does wrong, will be punished lightly. When someone has been GIVEN much, much will be REQUIRED in return; and when someone has been TRUSTED with much, even more will be REQUIRED. ... Do you think I have come to bring PEACE? No, I have come to DIVIDE! Father will be against son and son against father; mother against daughter and daughter against

mother. ... You fools! You do NOT know how to interpret the present times."

Luke 13:4-5, 23-25, 27, 30   Jesus said, "What about the 18 people who died when the tower in Siloam fell on them? Were they the worst sinners? No! You will PERISH, too, UNLESS you REPENT of your sins and TURN to God." ... Someone asked Him, "Lord, will ONLY a FEW be SAVED?" Jesus replied, "Work hard to enter the NARROW door to God's Kingdom, for MANY will try to enter but will FAIL. When the Master of the house has locked the door, it will be TOO LATE. You will stand outside pleading, 'Lord, open the door for us!' He will reply, 'I do NOT know you. Get away from Me, all you who do evil.' ... People will come from all over the world – from east, west, north, and south – to enter the Kingdom of God. Some who seem LEAST important now will be the GREATEST then, and some who are the GREATEST now will be LEAST important then."

Luke 14:13-14, 26-29   Jesus said, "INVITE the poor, the crippled, the lame, and the blind. THEN at the resurrection of the righteous, God will REWARD you for inviting those who could not repay you. ... IF you want to be My disciple, you must hate everyone else by comparison – your father and mother, wife and children, brothers and sisters – yes, even your own life. IF you do NOT carry your own cross [die daily to pride in self] and FOLLOW Me, you CANNOT be My disciple. So you cannot become My disciple without giving up everything you own. But do NOT begin UNTIL you count the cost. For who would begin construction of a building without first calculating the cost to see if there is enough money to finish it? Otherwise, you might complete only the foundation before running out of money, and then everyone would laugh at you."

Luke 15:7, 21-24   Jesus said, "There is JOY in heaven over one lost sinner who REPENTS and RETURNS to God! ... [The lost] son said, 'Father, I have sinned against you. I am no longer worthy of being called your son.' But his father said to the servants, 'Quick! We must CELEBRATE, for my son WAS dead and is NOW alive. He WAS lost, but NOW he is found.' So the PARTY began."

Luke 16:8, 10, 13, 15-18, 26, 29-31   Jesus said, "It is TRUE that the children of this world are MORE shrewd in dealing with the world THAN are the children of the light. ... IF you are FAITHFUL in little things, you will be FAITHFUL in large ones. But IF you are DISHONEST in little things, you will NOT be honest with greater responsibilities. ... NONE can SERVE 2 masters. NONE can serve BOTH God and money. ... You like to APPEAR righteous in public, but God KNOWS your hearts. WHAT this world HONORS is DETESTABLE to God. UNTIL John the Baptist, the law of Moses and the messages of the prophets were your guides. But NOW the Good News of the Kingdom of God is preached. But that does NOT mean that the law has lost its force. It is EASIER for heaven and earth to disappear THAN for the smallest point of God's law to be OVERTURNED. For EXAMPLE, a man who divorces his wife and marries someone else commits adultery. ... Abraham said, 'There is a great chasm separating us. NONE can cross over to us from there. ... Moses and the prophets have warned them. Your brothers can READ what they wrote.' The rich man replied, 'No, if someone is sent to them from the dead, then they will repent of their sins and turn to God.' Abraham said, 'IF they will NOT listen to Moses and the prophets, they will NOT listen even IF someone RISES from the dead.'"

Luke 17:1, 3 AMP Jesus said to His disciples, "There will always be temptations to sin, but what SORROW awaits the person who DOES the tempting! ... Watch out for each other! IF another believer sins [misses the mark], REBUKE [warn, show disapproval of the sin] that person; then IF there is REPENTANCE [sorry to disobey God and turns back to God], FORGIVE him."

Luke 18:1, 8-9, 11, 13-14, 24, 27, 29-30, 31, 41-42 Jesus told His disciples a story to show that they should always PRAY and NEVER give up. ... Jesus asked, "When the Son of Man returns, HOW many will He find on the earth who HAVE faith?" ... Jesus told this story to some with great CONFIDENCE in their OWN righteousness and scorned everyone else: "The Pharisee prayed this prayer: 'I thank you, God, that I am not a sinner like everyone else. For I do not cheat, sin, or commit adultery. I am certainly not like that tax collector!' But the tax collector stood at a distance and dared not even lift his eyes to heaven as he prayed, saying, 'O God, be merciful to me, for I am a sinner.' I tell you, this SINNER, not the Pharisee, returned home JUSTIFIED before God. For those who exalt themselves will be humbled, and those who HUMBLE [teachable about reality, trusting God, not pride in self] themselves will be EXALTED." ... Jesus said, "How HARD it is for the RICH to ENTER the Kingdom of God! ... What is IMPOSSIBLE for people is POSSIBLE with God. ... I assure you that everyone who has GIVEN UP house or wife or brothers or parents or children, for the sake of the Kingdom of God, will be REPAID many times over in this life, AND will have eternal life in the world to come." ... Jesus said, "All the prophet's PREDICTIONS about the Son of

Man will come TRUE." ... Jesus asked, "What do you want Me to do for you?" "Lord," he said, "I want to see!" Jesus said, "All right, receive your sight!" Instantly the man could see, and followed Jesus.

Luke 19:10, 26-27, 42-43, 46   Jesus responded, "For the Son of Man came to SEEK and SAVE those who are LOST. ... The King replied, 'Those who USE well what they are given, even MORE will be given. But those who do NOTHING, even what little they have will be TAKEN away. As for those who did NOT want Me to be their King – bring them in and execute them here in front of Me.' ... How I wish that you would understand the WAY to peace. But NOW it is TOO LATE, and peace is hidden from your eyes, because you did NOT recognize when God visited you." ... Jesus said, "My Temple is for PRAYER, but you have turned it into a den of thieves."

Luke 20:17-18, 25   Jesus said, "The stone that the builders rejected has now become the cornerstone. Everyone who stumbles over that stone will be broken to pieces." ... Jesus said, "GIVE to Caesar what belongs to Caesar, and GIVE to God what belongs to God."

Luke 21:2-4, 13-15, 22, 25-28, 33-36   Then a poor widow came by and dropped in 2 small coins. "I tell you the truth," Jesus said, "this poor widow has GIVEN MORE than all the rest of them. For they have given a tiny part of their surplus, but she, poor as she is, has given everything she has." ... Jesus said, "This will be your OPPORTUNITY to tell them about Me. So do NOT worry in advance about how to ANSWER the charges against you, for I will GIVE you the right words and such wisdom that none of your opponents will be able to refute you! ... Those will be days of God's vengeance, and the PROPHETIC WORDS of the Scriptures will be FULFILLED. ... The nations will be in turmoil, perplexed by the roaring seas and strange tides. People will be terrified at what they see coming, for the powers in the heavens will be shaken. THEN everyone will see the Son of Man coming on a cloud with power and great glory. When all these things begin to happen, stand and look up, for your salvation is near! ... Heaven and earth will disappear, but My Words will NEVER disappear. Watch out! Do NOT let your hearts be DULLED by drunkenness AND by the worries of this life. Do NOT let that day catch you UNAWARE, like a trap. Keep alert. PRAY that you might be strong enough to ESCAPE these coming horrors and STAND before the Son of Man."

Luke 22:3-4, 7, 17-20, 26, 29-32, 37, 40, 42, 48, 66-67, 69-71   Satan ENTERED Judas Iscariot, and he went to the leading priests to BETRAY

Jesus. ... Now the Festival of Unleavened Bread arrived, when the Passover lamb is sacrificed. ... Jesus took some bread and gave thanks to God for it. Then He broke it in pieces and gave it to the disciples, saying, "This is My BODY, which is given for you. Do this to REMEMBER Me." After supper He took another cup of wine and said, "This cup is the NEW covenant between God and His people – confirmed with My BLOOD, which is poured out as a sacrifice for you." ... Jesus said, "But among you it will be DIFFERENT. ... The LEADER should be like a SERVANT. ... And just as My Father has granted Me a Kingdom, I now grant you the right to eat and drink at My table in My Kingdom. ... Simon, Satan has asked to sift each of you like wheat. But I have pleaded in prayer for you, Simon, that your faith should NOT fail. So when you REPENT and TURN to Me again, STRENGTHEN your brothers. ... Yes, everything WRITTEN about Me by the prophets will come TRUE." ... Jesus told them, "PRAY that you will NOT give in to temptation." ... Jesus prayed, "Father, if You are willing, please take this cup of suffering away from Me. Yet I want Your will to be done, NOT my will." ... Jesus said, "Judas, would you BETRAY the Son of Man with a kiss?" ... The elders of the people said, "Tell us, are You the Messiah?" Jesus replied, "If I tell you, you will not believe Me. ... But from now on the Son of Man will be seated in the place of power at God's right hand." They all shouted, "So, are You CLAIMING to be the Son of God?" Jesus replied, "You say that I AM." They said, "We ourselves heard Him say it."

Luke 23:3, 23-24, 33-34, 40-46 ERV Pilate asked Him, "Are You the King of the Jews?" Jesus replied, "You have said it." ... The mob shouted louder, demanding that Jesus be crucified, and their voices prevailed. So Pilate sentenced Jesus to die as they demanded. When they came to a place called The Skull, they NAILED Him to the CROSS. The criminals were also crucified – one on His right and one on His left. Jesus said, "Father, forgive them, for they do NOT know what they are doing." ... The other criminal ... [rebuked the mocking criminal] saying, "You should fear God. All of us will die soon. You and I are guilty. We deserve to die because we did wrong. But this Man has done nothing wrong." Then he said, "Jesus, REMEMBER me when You begin ruling as King." Jesus replied, "I promise you, TODAY you will be WITH Me in paradise." By this time it was noon, and darkness fell throughout the land until 3 o'clock. Suddenly, the curtain in Temple was torn into 2 pieces. Jesus shouted, "Father, I put My Life in Your hands!" After Jesus said this, He died.

Luke 24:1-9, 15-16, 25-27, 31-32, 36, 38-39, 41-49 Very early on Sunday morning the women went to the tomb. ... They found that the stone had been rolled away from the entrance. So they went in, but they did NOT find the body of the Lord Jesus. As they stood there puzzled, 2 men suddenly appeared to them, clothed in dazzling robes. The women were terrified and bowed with their faces to the ground. Then the men asked, "WHY are you LOOKING among the dead for someone who is ALIVE? He is NOT here! He is RISEN from the dead! Remember what He TOLD you back in Galilee, that the Son of Man must be betrayed into the hands of sinful men and be crucified, and that He would RISE again on the third day." Then they remembered that He had said this. So they rushed to tell His 11 disciples – what had happened. ... Jesus suddenly came and began walking with 2 of Jesus' followers on the road to Emmaus. But God kept them from recognizing Him. ... Jesus said, "You foolish people! You find it so hard to believe all that the prophets WROTE in the Scriptures. Wasn't it clearly PREDICTED that the Messiah would have to SUFFER all these things BEFORE entering His glory?" Then Jesus took them THROUGH the writings of Moses and the prophets, explaining from ALL the Scriptures the things CONCERNING Himself. ... Suddenly, their eyes were opened, and they recognized Him, and He disappeared! They said to each other, "Didn't our hearts feel set on fire as He EXPLAINED the Scriptures to us?" ... And just as they were telling about it, Jesus was suddenly standing there among them, saying, "PEACE be with you. WHY are you frightened? WHY are your hearts filled with doubt? LOOK at My hands. Look at My feet. You can SEE that it is really Me. TOUCH Me and make sure that I am not a ghost, because ghosts do not have bodies, as you see that I do." Still they stood there in disbelief, filled with JOY and wonder. Then He asked them, "Do you have anything here to eat?" They gave Him a piece of broiled fish, and He ate it as they watched, then said, "When I was with you before, I told you that everything WRITTEN about Me in the law of Moses and the prophets and in the Psalms must be FULFILLED." [Psalms 16:10, Isaiah 53:10-11] Then He opened their minds to understand the Scriptures. And He said, "It was WRITTEN long ago that the Messiah would suffer and die and rise from the dead on the third day. [Jonah 1:17, Matthew 12:40] It was also WRITTEN that this message would be proclaimed in the authority of His Name to all the nations, beginning in Jerusalem: 'There is FORGIVENESS of sins for all who REPENT.' You are WITNESSES of all these things. And I will send the Holy Spirit."

John 1:1-4, 9-10, 12-14, 17-18, 29-30, 51

In the BEGINNING the Word [Jesus] already EXISTED. The Word was with God, and the Word WAS God. He existed in the beginning with God. God created everything through Him. [There is only one God who eternally exists as 3 distinct Persons – the Father, Son: Jesus, and Holy Spirit. God, the Creator-Owner of all things, is one in essence and 3 in person.] The Word gave life to everything that was created, and His life brought light to everyone. ... The One who is the True Light, who gives light to everyone, was coming into the world. He came into the very world He created, but the world did NOT recognize Him. To all who believed Him and accepted Him, He gave the right to become children of God. They are REBORN – not with a physical birth, but a birth that comes from God. The Word became human and made His home among us. He was full of unfailing love and faithfulness. We have SEEN His glory, the glory of the Father's One and Only Son. ... For the law was given through Moses, but God's unfailing love and faithfulness came through Jesus Christ. No one has ever seen God. But the One and Only Son IS Himself God. ... He has REVEALED God to us. ... John [the Baptist] saw Jesus coming and said, "Look! The Lamb of God who takes away the sin of the world! He is the one I was talking about when I said, 'A Man is coming after me who is far greater than I am, for He existed long before me.'" ... Jesus said, "I tell you the TRUTH, you will all see heaven open and the angels of God going up and down on the Son of Man, the One who is the STAIRWAY between heaven and earth."

John 2:16, 18-19, 21-22, 24 Jesus told them, "Get these things out of here. STOP turning My Father's house into a marketplace!" ... The Jewish leaders demanded, "What are you doing? If God gave you authority, show us a miraculous sign to PROVE it." Jesus replied, "Destroy this temple, and in 3 days I will raise it up." When Jesus said "this temple," He meant His own body. After He was raised from the dead, His disciples remembered this, and they believed both the Scriptures and what Jesus had said. ... Jesus did NOT trust them, because He knew human nature.

John 3:2-3, 5-6, 12-20, 30-36 After dark one evening, Nicodemus came to speak with Jesus. "Rabbi," he said, "we all KNOW that God has sent You to teach us. Your miraculous signs are EVIDENCE that God is with You." Jesus replied, "I tell you the truth, unless you are BORN AGAIN, you cannot see the Kingdom of God. ... No one can enter the Kingdom of God without being born of water and the Spirit. Humans can reproduce only human life, but the Holy Spirit gives birth to spiritual life. ... If you do not believe Me when I tell you about earthly things, how can you possibly believe if I tell you about heavenly things? NO one has ever gone to heaven and returned. But the Son of Man has COME DOWN from heaven. And as Moses lifted up the bronze snake on a pole in the wilderness, so the Son of Man must be lifted up, so that everyone who believes in Him will have eternal life. For God LOVED the world so much that He GAVE His One and Only Son, so that everyone who BELIEVES in Him will not perish but will HAVE eternal life. God sent His Son into the world not to judge the world, but to SAVE the world THROUGH Him. There is NO judgment against anyone who believes in Him. But anyone who does NOT believe in Him has ALREADY been judged for not believing in God's One and Only Son. And the JUDGMENT is based on this fact: God's Light came into the world, BUT people loved the darkness more than the Light, for their actions were evil. All who do evil hate the Light and REFUSE to go near Jesus for fear their sins will be exposed." ... John [the Baptist] said, "Jesus must become GREATER and greater, and I must become LESS and less. Jesus has come from above and is greater than anyone else. We are of the earth, and we speak of earthly things, but He has COME from heaven and is greater than anyone else. He testifies about what He has seen and heard, but how few believe what He tells them! Anyone who accepts His testimony can affirm that God is true, for He is sent by God. He speaks God's Words, for God gives Him the Spirit without limit. The Father loves His Son and has put everything into His hands. Anyone who BELIEVES [understands what God's Word says about Jesus is true, is loyal and committed to obeying Jesus, trusts Jesus with their life] in God's Son HAS eternal life. Anyone who does NOT obey the Son will NEVER experience eternal life but remains under God's judgment."

John 4:7, 9-10, 23-24, 26, 28-30, 34-36 A Samaritan woman came to draw water, and Jesus said to her, "Please give Me a drink." ... The woman was surprised, for Jews refuse to have anything to do with Samaritans. She said to Jesus, "You are a Jew, and I am a Samaritan woman. Why are you asking me for a drink?" Jesus replied, "IF you only knew the gift God has for you and WHO you are speaking to, you would ask Me, and I would give you living water. ... The time is coming – indeed it's here now – when true worshipers will worship the Father in spirit and in truth. God is Spirit, so WORSHIP Him in SPIRIT and in TRUTH." ... Jesus told her, "I AM the Messiah!" ... The woman ran back to the village, telling everyone, "Come, see a Man who told me everything

I ever did! Could He possibly be the Messiah?" The people came quickly to see Him. ... Jesus explained: "My nourishment comes from doing the will of God, who sent Me, and from finishing His work. Look around. The fields are already ripe for harvest. The harvesters are paid good wages, and the fruit they harvest is people brought to eternal life. What JOY awaits both the planter and the harvester!"

John 5:6-9, 14, 17-19, 23, 34-36, 39, 41-44, 46 Jesus asked him, "WOULD you LIKE to GET WELL?" "I cannot, sir," the sick man said. Jesus told him, "Stand up, pick up your mat, and walk!" Instantly, the man was healed! Jesus told him, "Now you are well; so STOP sinning, OR something even worse may happen to you." ... Jesus replied, "My Father is always working, and so am I." So the Jewish leaders tried all the harder to find a way to kill him. For He not only broke the Sabbath, He called God His Father, thereby making Himself EQUAL with God. So Jesus explained, "Whatever the Father does, the Son also does. ... So that everyone will honor the Son, just as they honor the Father. Anyone who does NOT honor the Son is certainly NOT honoring the Father who sent Him. ... I have a greater witness than John – My teachings and My miracles. The Father gave Me these works to accomplish, and they PROVE that He sent Me. ... You SEARCH the Scriptures because they give you eternal life. The Scriptures POINT to Me! ... Your approval means NOTHING to Me, because I know you do NOT have God's love within you. For I have come to you in My Father's Name, and you have REJECTED Me. For you gladly HONOR each other, BUT you do NOT care about the HONOR that comes FROM the One who ALONE is God. ... IF you really BELIEVED Moses, you would BELIEVE Me, because Moses WROTE about Me."

John 6:27, 29, 33, 35, 45, 51, 53, 61, 63, 67-69 Jesus told them, "Do NOT be so concerned about perishable things like food. Spend your energy SEEKING the eternal life that the Son of Man can give you. This is the ONLY work God wants from you: Believe in the One He has sent." ... Jesus said, "The true bread of God is the One who comes down from heaven and gives life to the world. I AM the bread of life. Whoever comes to Me will never be hungry again. ... As written in the Scriptures, 'They will all be TAUGHT by God.'" [Isaiah 54:13] ... Jesus said, "I AM the living bread that came down from heaven. I tell you the truth, unless you eat the flesh of the Son of Man and drink His blood, you cannot have eternal life." ... Jesus said, "Does this OFFEND you? ... The Spirit ALONE gives eternal life. Human effort accomplishes NOTHING." ...

At this point many of His disciples turned away and deserted Him. Jesus turned to the Twelve and asked, "Are you also GOING to LEAVE?" Peter replied, "Lord, to WHO would we GO? You have the Words that give eternal LIFE. We believe, and we know You ARE the Holy One of God."

John 7:7-8 KJV, 18, 24, 38-39 Jesus said, "The world cannot hate you, but it does hate Me because I ACCUSE it of doing evil. You go on. I am not yet going to this festival, because My time has not yet come. ... Those who speak for themselves want glory only for themselves, but a person who SEEKS to honor the One who sent Him SPEAKS Truth, NOT lies. ... Look BENEATH the surface so you can judge CORRECTLY. ... Anyone who believes in Me may come and drink! For the Scriptures declare, 'Rivers of living water will flow from His heart.'" (When He said "living water," He was speaking of the Spirit, who would be given to everyone believing in Him.)

John 8:4-8, 10-12, 23-24, 28, 31-32, 34, 36, 42-45, 47, 58-59 "Teacher," they said to Jesus, "this woman was caught in the act of adultery. The law of Moses says to stone her. What do You say?" They were trying to trap Him into saying something they could use against Him, but Jesus stooped down and wrote in the dust with His finger. They kept demanding an answer, so He stood up again and said, "All right, but let the one who has never sinned throw the first stone!" When the accusers heard this, they slipped away one by one, beginning with the oldest, until only Jesus was left in the middle of the crowd with the woman. Jesus said to the woman, "Where are your accusers? Did not even one of them condemn you?" "No, Lord," she said. Jesus said, "Neither do I. Go and sin NO MORE." ... Jesus said, "I AM the Light of the world. IF you FOLLOW Me, you will NOT have to walk in darkness, because you will have the Light that leads to life." ... Jesus continued, "You are from below; I AM from above. You belong to this world; I do not. That is WHY I said that you will DIE in your sins; for UNLESS you BELIEVE that I AM who I claim to be, you will die in your sins." ... Jesus said, "When you lift the Son of Man on the cross, you will understand that I AM." ... Jesus said, "You are TRULY My disciples IF you REMAIN FAITHFUL to My teachings. And you will KNOW the TRUTH, and the TRUTH will SET you FREE. ... Everyone who sins is a slave of sin. ... So IF the Son sets you free, you are TRULY free." ... Jesus told them, "IF God were your Father, you would LOVE Me, because I have come to you from God. WHY can't you understand what I am saying? It is because you cannot even hear Me! For you are the children of your father the devil, and you love to do the evil things he does. He was a murderer from the beginning. He has always hated the Truth, because there is no truth in him. When he lies, it is consistent with his character; for he is a LIAR and the father of lies. So when I tell the truth, you just naturally do not believe Me! ... Anyone who BELONGS to God LISTENS gladly to the Words of God. But you do NOT listen because you do NOT belong to God." ... Jesus answered, "I tell you the Truth, BEFORE Abraham was even born, I AM!" At that point they picked up stones to throw at Him.

John 9:2-3, 38-39 The disciples asked, "Why was this man born blind? Was it because of his own sins or his parents' sins?" Jesus answered: "It was not because of his sins or his parents' sins, this happened so the power of God is seen in him." ... "Yes, Lord, I believe!" the [blind] man [now healed] said. And he worshiped Jesus. Jesus told him, "I entered this world to render judgment – to give sight to the blind and to SHOW those who THINK they SEE that they are BLIND."

John 10:9-14, 24, 30-31, 33, 36-38 Jesus said, "Yes, I AM the door. Those who come in through Me will be saved. The thief's PURPOSE is to steal and kill and destroy. My PURPOSE is to give them a full and satisfying life. The Good Shepherd sacrifices His life for the sheep. A hired hand will run when he sees a wolf coming, because he is working only for the money and does not care about the sheep. I AM the Good Shepherd: I know My own sheep, and they know Me." ... The people asked Jesus, "IF you are the Messiah, tell us plainly." Jesus replied, "... The Father and I are One." Once again the people picked up stones to kill him. ... They replied, "We are stoning you not for any good work, but for blasphemy! You, a mere man, CLAIM to be God." Jesus said, "... Why do you call it blasphemy when I say, 'I AM the SON of God'? After all, the Father set Me apart and sent Me into the world. Do NOT believe Me UNLESS I carry out My Father's work. But IF I do His work, BELIEVE in the EVIDENCE of the miraculous works I have done, even if you do not believe Me. Then you will know and understand that the Father is in Me, and I AM in the Father."

John 11:23-25, 27, 35, 41-44, 49-52 Jesus told her, "Your brother will rise again." Martha said, "Yes, he will rise when everyone else rises, at the last day." Jesus told her, "I AM the RESURRECTION and the LIFE. Anyone who believes in Me will live, even after dying." Martha told Jesus, "Yes, Lord, I have always believed You are the Messiah, the Son of God, the One who has come into the world from God." ... Jesus wept. ...

They rolled the stone aside. Jesus looked up to heaven and said, "Father, thank you for hearing Me. You always hear Me, but I said it out loud for the sake of all these people standing here, so that they will believe You sent Me." Jesus shouted, "Lazarus, COME out!" The dead man CAME out, he was bound in grave clothes, his face wrapped in a head cloth. Jesus said, "Unwrap him and let him go!" ... Caiaphas said, "You do NOT know what you are talking about! You do not realize that it is BETTER for you that One Man should die for the people than for the whole nation to be destroyed." He did not say this on his own; as high priest he was led to prophesy that Jesus would die not only for the nation, but to unite all the children of God scattered around the world.

John 12:25-26, 31, 35-37, 42-46, 48 Jesus replied, "Those who love their life in this world will lose it. Those who care nothing for their life in this world will keep it for eternity. Anyone who wants to be My disciple must FOLLOW Me, because My servants must be WHERE I am. And the Father will honor anyone who serves Me. ... The time for judging this world has come, when Satan, the ruler of this world, will be cast out." ... Jesus replied, "My Light will shine for you just a little longer. Walk IN the Light while you can, so the darkness will NOT overtake you. Those who walk in the darkness cannot see where they are going. TRUST in the Light while there is STILL TIME; then you will BECOME children of the Light." Despite all the miraculous signs Jesus had done, most still would not believe in Him. Many people did believe in Him, however some of the Jewish leaders could not admit it for fear that the Pharisees would expel them from the synagogue. For they loved human praise more than the praise of God. ... Jesus shouted to the crowds, "IF you TRUST Me, you are trusting not only Me, but also God who sent Me. For WHEN you SEE Me, you are SEEING the One who sent Me. I have come as a Light to shine in this dark world, so that all who put their TRUST in Me will no longer remain in the dark. ... But all who REJECT Me and My message will be JUDGED on the Day of Judgment by the TRUTH I have spoken."

John 13:7, 13-15, 17-20, 34-35 Jesus replied, "You do not understand now what I am doing, but someday you will. ... You call Me 'Teacher' and 'Lord,' and you are right, because that is what I am. And since I, your Lord and Teacher, have washed your feet, you ought to wash each other's feet. I have given you an example to follow. DO as I have DONE to you. ... Now that you KNOW these things, God will BLESS you for DOING them. ... This fulfills the Scripture that says, 'The one who eats my food has turned against Me.' I tell you this beforehand, so when it happens you will BELIEVE that I AM the Messiah. I tell you the truth, anyone who welcomes My messenger is welcoming Me, and anyone who welcomes Me is welcoming the Father who sent Me. ... I am giving you a new commandment: LOVE each OTHER. Just AS I have LOVED you, you should love each other. Your love for one another will PROVE to the world that you are My disciples."

John 14:1, 3, 6, 9, 14-15, 19, 21, 23-24, 26-27, 29   Jesus said, "Do NOT let your hearts be troubled. TRUST in God, and TRUST also in Me. When everything is ready, I will come and get you, so that you will always be WITH Me where I am." ... Jesus told him, "I AM the WAY, the TRUTH, and the LIFE. No one can COME to the Father EXCEPT through Me." ... Jesus replied, "Anyone who has seen Me has seen the Father!" ... Jesus said, "Yes, ask Me for anything in My Name, and I will do it! IF you LOVE Me, OBEY My commandments. Because I live, you also will live. Those who ACCEPT My commandments and OBEY them are the ones who LOVE Me. All who LOVE Me will DO what I say. My Father will love them, and We will come and make Our home with each of them. Anyone who does NOT love Me will NOT obey Me. … When the Father sends the Advocate as My Representative – the Holy Spirit – He will teach you everything and will remind you of everything I have told you. I am leaving you with a gift – PEACE of mind and heart. And the peace I give is a gift the world cannot give. So do NOT be troubled or afraid. … I have told you these things BEFORE they happen so that when they DO happen, you will BELIEVE."

John 15:1-3, 5-8, 10-14, 16-21, 23, 25-27   Jesus said, "I AM the true grapevine, and my Father is the gardener. He CUTS OFF every branch of Mine that does NOT produce fruit. He prunes the branches that do bear fruit so they produce even more. You have already been pruned and purified through the Word I have given you. ... Yes, I AM the vine; you are the branches. Those who remain in Me, and I in them, will produce much fruit. For APART FROM Me you can DO NOTHING. Anyone who does not remain in Me is thrown away like a useless branch. Such branches are gathered into a pile to be burned. When you produce much fruit, you are My true disciples. ... When you OBEY My commandments, you REMAIN in My love, just as I obey My Father's commandments and remain in His love. I told you these things so you will be FILLED with My JOY. Your JOY will overflow! This is My commandment: LOVE each OTHER in the SAME way I have LOVED you. There is no greater love than to lay down one's life for one's friends. You are My friends IF you DO what I command. ... I appointed you to GO and produce LASTING fruit, so that the Father will GIVE you WHATEVER you ASK for, USING My Name. This is My command: LOVE each other. IF the world hates you, REMEMBER that it hated Me first. The world would love you as one of its own IF you belonged to it, BUT you are no longer part of the world. I chose you to COME OUT of the world, so it hates you. Since they persecuted Me, naturally they will persecute you. And if they listened to Me, they will listen to you. They have rejected the One who sent Me. Anyone who hates Me also hates My Father. This fulfills what is written in their Scriptures: 'They hate Me without cause.' [Psalm 69:4] I will send you the Advocate – the Spirit of TRUTH. He will testify all about Me. And you must also TESTIFY about Me."

John 16:1-3, 8-9, 11, 13, 15, 23-25, 27, 33 AMP Jesus said, "I have told you these things SO that you will NOT abandon your faith. For the time is coming when those who kill you will think they are doing a holy service for God. This is because they have NEVER known the Father or Me. ... When the Holy Spirit – the Comforter, Encourager, Counselor – comes, He will CONVICT the world of its sin, and of God's righteousness, and of the coming Judgment. The world's sin is that it REFUSES to believe in Me. ... Judgment will come because the ruler of this world [Satan] has already been judged. ... When the Spirit of TRUTH comes, He will GUIDE you into all truth. ... All that belongs to the Father is Mine; this is why I said, 'The Spirit will tell you whatever He receives from Me.' ... I tell you the truth, ASK the Father directly, and He will grant your request because you use My Name. ... Ask, using My Name, and you will receive, you will have abundant JOY. I have spoken of these matters in Figures of Speech, but soon I will stop Speaking Figuratively and will tell you plainly all about the Father, ... for the Father loves you dearly because you love Me and believe that I came from God." ... Jesus said, "I told you all this so you may have PEACE in Me. Here on earth you will have trials, distress, and frustration. But be CHEERFUL and take COURAGE, because I have OVERCOME the world."

John 17:1-3, 5, 9, 15-18, 20, 23 Jesus looked up to heaven and said, "Father, the hour has come. Glorify your Son so He can give glory back to You. For You have given Him authority over everyone. He gives eternal life to each one You have given Him. And this is the WAY to have eternal life – to KNOW You, the ONLY TRUE God, and Jesus Christ, the ONE You sent to earth. ... Father, bring Me into the glory We shared before the world began. ... My prayer is NOT for the world, BUT for those You have given Me, because they belong to You. ... I am NOT asking You to take them out of the world, BUT to keep them safe from the evil one. They do NOT belong to this world any more than I do. Make them HOLY by Your TRUTH; teach them Your WORD, which is TRUTH. Just as You sent Me into the world, I am sending them into the world. ... I am praying NOT ONLY for these disciples BUT also for all who will ever believe in Me through their message. ... I am in them and You are in Me. May they EXPERIENCE such perfect UNITY that the world will know that You sent Me and that You love them as much as You love Me."

John 18:6, 36-38 As Jesus said "I AM he," they all fell to the ground! ... Jesus answered, "My Kingdom is NOT an earthly kingdom. If it were, my followers would fight to keep me from being handed over to the Jewish leaders. But my Kingdom is NOT of this world." Pilate said, "So You are a king?" Jesus responded, "You say I AM a King. I was born and came into the world to testify to the Truth. All who love the truth recognize what I say is TRUE." Pilate asked, "What is truth?"

John 19:7, 14-17, 28, 30 The Jewish leaders said, "He called Himself the SON of God." ... It was about noon on the day of preparation for the Passover. Pilate said to the people, "Look, here is your King!" ... They yelled. "CRUCIFY Him!" Pilate asked, "Crucify your King?" The leading priests shouted back "We have no king but Caesar." ... Then Pilate turned Jesus over to them to be crucified. So they took Jesus away ... to the place called Place of the Skull. There they NAILED Him to the CROSS. ... Jesus knew His mission was now finished, and to fulfill Scripture He said, "I am thirsty." ... When Jesus had tasted it, He said, "It is FINISHED!" Then He released His Spirit [and died].

John 20:1-4, 6-16, 18-22, 27-29, 30-31 Early on Sunday morning, Mary Magdalene came to the tomb and found that the stone had been rolled away from the entrance. She ran and found Peter and the other disciple, the one whom Jesus loved. ... Peter and the other disciple started out for the tomb. They were both running. ... Peter went inside. He noticed the linen wrappings lying there, while the cloth that had covered Jesus' head was folded up and lying apart from the other wrappings. Then the [other] disciple ... also went in, and he SAW and BELIEVED – for UNTIL THEN they still had NOT understood the Scriptures that SAID Jesus must RISE from the dead. Then they went home. Mary was standing outside the tomb crying, and as she wept, she stooped and looked in. She saw 2 white-robed angels, one sitting at the head and the other at the foot of the place where the body of Jesus had been lying. "Dear woman, why are you crying?" the angels asked her. "Because they have taken away my Lord," she replied, "and I do not know where they have put Him." She turned to leave and saw someone standing there. It was Jesus, but she did not recognize Him. "Dear woman, why are you crying?" Jesus asked her. ... "Mary!" Jesus said. She turned to Him and cried out, "Teacher." ... Mary Magdalene told the disciples, "I have SEEN the Lord!" That Sunday evening the disciples were meeting behind locked doors because they were afraid of the Jewish leaders. Suddenly, Jesus came and was standing there among them! Jesus said, "PEACE be with you." He showed them the wounds in His hands and His side. They were filled with JOY when they SAW the Lord! Jesus said, "PEACE be with you. As the Father has sent Me, so I am SENDING you." Then He breathed on them and said, "Receive the Holy Spirit." ... Jesus said to Thomas, "Put your finger here, and look at My hands. Put your hand into the wound in My side. Do NOT be faithless any longer. Believe!" Thomas exclaimed, "MY LORD and MY GOD!" Jesus told him, "You believe because you have seen Me. Blessed are those who believe WITHOUT seeing Me." ... The disciples saw Jesus do many other miraculous signs in addition to the ones recorded in this book. But these are WRITTEN so that you may CONTINUE to BELIEVE that Jesus IS the Messiah, the SON of God, and that by believing in Jesus you will have LIFE by the POWER of His Name.

John 21:22 Jesus said to Peter, "If I want him to remain alive until I return, what is that to you? AS FOR you, FOLLOW Me."

Acts 1:1-3, 6-10
In my first book [book of Luke] I told you, Theophilus, about everything Jesus began to do and teach until the day He was taken up to heaven after giving His chosen apostles further instructions through the Holy Spirit. During the 40 days after His crucifixion, He appeared to the apostles from time to time, and He PROVED to them in many ways that He was actually ALIVE. And He talked to them about the Kingdom of God. ... The apostles kept asking Jesus, "Lord, has the time come for you to restore our kingdom?" He replied, "The Father alone has the authority to set those dates and times, and they are NOT for you to know. You will receive POWER when the Holy Spirit comes upon you. You will be My WITNESSES, telling people about Me everywhere – in Jerusalem, throughout Judea, to the ends of the earth. After saying this, He was taken up into a cloud while they were watching. Two white robed men suddenly stood among them. "Men

of Galilee," they said, "why are you staring into heaven? Jesus has been taken from you into heaven, but someday He will RETURN from heaven in the SAME way you saw Him go!"

Acts 2:1, 4, 11, 14, 17, 21, 28, 32, 36-38, 40-42, 46 On Pentecost all the believers were meeting together in one place. ... Everyone present was filled with the Holy Spirit and began speaking in other languages. ... They were completely amazed. "Here we are – people from Libya ... and Arabs. We all hear these people speaking in our own languages about the wonderful things God has done!" ... Peter shouted to the crowd, "Listen carefully! ... Make no mistake about this. ... 'In the last days,' God says, 'I will pour out My Spirit upon all people. Your sons and daughters will prophesy. Your young men will see visions, and your old men will dream dreams. ... Everyone who CALLS on the Name of the LORD will be SAVED.' [Joel 2:28-32] King David said this about Jesus: 'I see that the LORD is always WITH me. I will NOT be shaken, for He is right beside me. My tongue shouts His praises! You have shown me the Way of Life, and fill me with the JOY of Your Presence.' [Psalm 16:8-11] God raised Jesus from the dead, and we are all WITNESSES of this. Let everyone KNOW for certain that God has made this Jesus to be BOTH Lord and Messiah!" Peter's words pierced their hearts, and they said to him, "Brothers, WHAT SHOULD we DO?" Peter replied, "You must REPENT of your sins, TURN to God, and be BAPTIZED in the Name of Jesus Christ to show that you have received FORGIVENESS for your sins. THEN you will receive the gift of the Holy Spirit. Peter continued preaching for a long time, strongly urging all his listeners, "Save yourselves from this crooked generation!" About 3,000 believers were added to the church that day. The believers were devoted to apostles' TEACHING, FELLOWSHIP, sharing in meals (including the Lord's Supper), and PRAYER with great JOY and GENEROSITY.

Acts 3:6-8, 16, 19, 22-23 Peter said, "I do NOT have any silver or gold for you. BUT I will give you what I have. In the Name of Jesus Christ the Nazarene, get up and walk!" Then Peter took the lame man and helped him up. As he did, the man's feet and ankles were instantly healed. He jumped up and began to walk! ... Peter said, "Faith in Jesus' Name has healed him. Now REPENT of your sins and TURN to God, so that your sins may be wiped away. ... Moses said, 'The LORD your God will raise up for you a Prophet like me from among your own people. LISTEN carefully to everything He tells you.' [Deuteronomy 18:15] Then Moses said, 'Anyone who will NOT listen to that Prophet will be CUT OFF from God's people.'"

Acts 4:7-12, 17-20, 29-31   They demanded of the 2 disciples, "By what power, or in whose name, have you done this?" Peter, filled with the Holy Spirit, said, "Rulers and elders, are we being questioned today because we have done a good deed for a crippled man? Do you want to know how he was healed? Let me clearly state that he was HEALED BY the powerful Name of Jesus Christ the Nazarene, the man you crucified but whom God RAISED from the dead.   For Jesus is the one REFERRED to IN the Scriptures, where it says, 'The stone that you builders rejected has now become the cornerstone.' There is SALVATION in NO ONE else! God has given NO OTHER name by which we must be SAVED."   ... They said, "We must warn them not to speak to anyone in Jesus' Name again." They called the apostles back in and commanded them never again to speak or teach in the Name of Jesus. Peter and John replied, "Do you THINK God WANTS us to OBEY you RATHER than Him? We cannot stop TELLING about everything we have seen and heard."   ... The believers prayed, "Lord, hear their threats, and give us, Your servants, great BOLDNESS in preaching Your Word. Stretch out Your hand with healing power, may miraculous signs be done through the Name of Jesus." After this prayer, the meeting place shook, and they were all filled with the Holy Spirit. Then they preached the Word of God with boldness.

Acts 5:3-5, 29-32, 34-35, 38-39, 41-42   Peter said, "Ananias, why have you let Satan fill your heart? You LIED to the Holy Spirit, and you kept some of the money for yourself. After selling the property, the money was yours to keep or give away, as you desired. You were not lying to us but to God!" As Ananias heard these words, he fell to the floor and died. Everyone who heard about it was terrified. ... Peter and the apostles replied, "We must OBEY God RATHER THAN any human authority. God RAISED Jesus from the dead after you killed Him on a cross. God put Him in the place of honor at His right hand as Prince and Savior. He did this so people would REPENT of their sins and be FORGIVEN. We are WITNESSES of these things and so is the Holy Spirit, who is given by God to those who OBEY Him."   ... Gamaliel, a respected expert in religious law, said, "Men of Israel, take care what you are planning to do to these men! My advice is, leave these men alone. Let them go. If they are planning and doing these things merely on their own, it will soon be overthrown. But if it is from God, you will not be able to overthrow them. You may even find yourselves fighting against God!" ... The apostles left the high council FULL of JOY that God had counted them worthy to suffer disgrace for the Name of Jesus. And every day, in the Temple and from house to house, they CONTINUED to teach and preach this message: "Jesus IS the Messiah."

Acts 7:51, 53-60   Stephen said, "You STUBBORN people! You are heathen at heart and DEAF to the truth. Must you forever RESIST the Holy Spirit? ... You DELIBERATELY DISOBEYED God's law." ... The Jewish leaders were infuriated, shaking their fists in rage. Stephen, full of the Holy Spirit, gazed into heaven and SAW the glory of God. He told them, "Look, I see the heavens opened and the Son of Man standing in the place of honor at God's right hand!" ... They rushed and dragged him out of the city. ... As they stoned him, Stephen prayed, "Lord Jesus, receive my spirit." He fell to his knees, shouting, "Lord, do NOT charge them with this sin!" And with that, he died.

Acts 8:4, 20-23, 29-31, 36-38 KJV   The believers who were scattered, PREACHED the Good News about Jesus WHEREVER they went. ... Peter replied, "May your money be destroyed with you for thinking you can buy God's gift! You can have NO part in this, for your heart is NOT right with God. REPENT of your wickedness and PRAY to the Lord. Perhaps He will forgive your evil thoughts, you are full of bitter jealousy and are captive by sin." ... The Holy Spirit said to Philip, "Go over and walk along beside the carriage." Philip ran over and heard the man reading from the prophet Isaiah. Philip asked, "Do you UNDERSTAND what you are reading?" The man replied, "HOW can I, unless someone INSTRUCTS me?" And he urged Philip to sit with him. As they rode along, they came to water, and the eunuch [the treasurer of Ethiopia] said, "Look! There is water! Can I be BAPTIZED?" Philip answered, "You can, IF you believe with all your heart." The eunuch replied, "I BELIEVE that Jesus is the Son of God." ... They went down into the water, and Philip baptized him.

Acts 9:4-5, 20, 22-23, 26-31   He fell to the ground and heard a Voice say to him, "Saul! Saul! WHY are you persecuting Me?" "WHO are you, Lord?" Saul asked. The Voice replied, "I am JESUS, the One you are persecuting!" ... Saul began preaching about Jesus, saying, "He is indeed the Son of God!" Saul's preaching became more and more powerful, and the Jews in Damascus could NOT refute his proofs that Jesus was the Messiah. After a while some of the Jews plotted together to kill him. ... When Saul arrived in Jerusalem, he tried to meet with the believers, but they were all afraid of him. They did not believe he had truly become a believer! Then Barnabas brought him to the apostles and told them how Saul had seen the Lord and how the Lord had spoken to Saul. He said that Saul preached boldly in the Name of Jesus in Damascus. Saul stayed with the apostles and went around Jerusalem with them, preaching boldly in the Name of the Lord. He debated some Jews, but they tried to murder him. When the believers heard about this, they ... sent him away to Tarsus, his hometown. The church then had peace and became stronger as the believers lived in the fear [respect God's power and authority, not because He is angry with us, but because we desire to please Him] of the Lord. With the encouragement of the Holy Spirit, it grew in numbers.

Acts 10:15, 25-26, 34-36, 43 The Voice spoke again: "Do NOT call something unclean IF God has made it clean." ... As Peter entered his home, Cornelius fell at his feet and worshiped him. But Peter pulled him up and said, "Stand up! I'm a human being just like you!" [Only worship the one God who eternally exists as 3 distinct Persons – the Father, Son: Jesus, and Holy Spirit. God, the Creator-Owner of all things, is one in essence and 3 in person.] ... Peter replied, "God shows NO favoritism. In every nation He ACCEPTS those who fear Him and do what is right. This is the message of GOOD NEWS – there is PEACE with God THROUGH Jesus Christ, who is LORD of all [Lord means the ruler, the boss, the master of your whole life. He cannot be Lord of only a part – He must be given control of your entire life. What does the LORD require of you? See Micah 6:8]. He is the One all the prophets testified about, saying everyone who believes in Him will have their sins forgiven through His Name.

Acts 11:16-18 Peter said, "I thought of the Lord's Words when He said, 'You will be baptized with the Holy Spirit.' And since God GAVE these Gentiles the SAME gift He gave us when we believed in the Lord Jesus Christ, who was I to stand in God's way?" When the others heard this, they STOPPED objecting and BEGAN praising God. They said, "God has also given the Gentiles the privilege of REPENTING of their sins and RECEIVING eternal life."

Acts 12:5, 7, 9, 11, 14-16 While Peter was in prison, the church PRAYED very earnestly for him. The night before Peter was to be placed on trial, he was asleep, fastened with 2 chains between 2 soldiers. Others stood guard at the prison gate. Suddenly, there was a bright light in the cell, and an angel of the Lord stood before Peter. The angel struck him on the side to awaken him and said, "Quick! Get up!" And the chains fell off his wrists. "Now put on your coat and follow me," the angel ordered. So

Peter left the cell, following the angel. But all the time he thought it was a vision. He did not realize it was actually happening. They passed the first and second guard posts and came to the iron gate and it opened all by itself. So they passed through and the angel suddenly left him. Peter said. "The Lord has SENT His angel and SAVED me from Herod!" ... When Rhoda recognized Peter's voice, she was so overjoyed that, instead of opening the door, she ran back inside and told everyone, "Peter is standing at the door!" "You're out of your mind!" they said. Peter continued knocking. When they finally opened the door and saw him, they were amazed.

Acts 13:1, 9-12, 38-41, 45-46, 48, 50-52 Among the teachers of the church at Antioch were Simeon (called "the black man"). ... Paul, filled with the Holy Spirit, looked the sorcerer in the eye. Paul said, "You son of the devil, full of every sort of DECEIT and FRAUD, and enemy of all that is good! Will you never stop PERVERTING the True Ways of the Lord? The Lord lays His hand of punishment upon you, and you will be struck blind." Instantly he became blind and began begging for someone to take his hand and lead him. When the governor saw this, he became a believer, for he was astonished at the teaching about the Lord. ... We proclaim THROUGH Jesus there is forgiveness for your sins. Everyone who believes in Him is declared RIGHT with God – something the law of Moses could never do. Be careful! Do NOT LET the prophets' words APPLY to you: "Look, you MOCKERS, be amazed and die! For I am doing something in your own day, something you will NOT believe even IF someone told you about it." ... When some of the Jews saw the crowds, they were jealous; so they slandered Paul and argued against whatever he said. Then Paul and Barnabas spoke out boldly and declared, "It was necessary that we first preach the Word of God to you Jews. But since you REJECTED it and JUDGED yourselves UNWORTHY of eternal LIFE, we will offer it to the Gentiles." ... When the Gentiles heard this, they were glad and thanked the Lord for His message; and all who were chosen for eternal life became believers. ... The Jews incited a mob and ran them out of town. Paul and Barnabas shook the dust from their feet as a sign of rejection and the believers were filled with JOY and the Holy Spirit.

Acts 14:15, 17, 19-20, 22 We are merely human beings — just like you! We have come to bring you the Good News that you should TURN FROM these worthless things and TURN TO the living God, who made heaven and earth and everything in them. God left you with EVIDENCE of Himself and His goodness. For instance, God sends you rain and good crops and gives you food and JOYFUL hearts. ... Some Jews arrived and won the crowds to their side. They stoned Paul and dragged him out of town, thinking he was dead. But as the believers gathered around him, he got up. They ENCOURAGED the believers to CONTINUE in the faith, reminding them that we must SUFFER many hardships to ENTER the Kingdom of God.

Acts 15:8, 10-11, 19, 23-24, 27-29, 36 Peter said, "God knows people's hearts, and He confirmed that He accepts Gentiles by giving them the Holy Spirit. We believe that we are all SAVED the SAME way, by the UNDESERVED grace of the Lord Jesus." ... James said, "My judgment is that we should NOT make it difficult for the Gentiles who are turning to God." ... This letter is from the apostles and elders: "We understand that some men from here have troubled you and upset you with their teaching, but we did not send them! We are sending Judas and Silas to confirm what we have decided concerning your question. For it seemed good to the Holy Spirit and to us to lay no greater burden on you than these few requirements: You must ABSTAIN FROM eating food offered to idols, from consuming blood or the meat of strangled animals, and from SEXUAL IMMORALITY. If you do this, you will do well. Farewell." ... Paul said to Barnabas, "Let's go back and visit each city where we previously preached the Word of the Lord, to see how the new believers are doing."

Acts 16:18, 23, 25-34 Paul got so exasperated that he turned and SAID TO the demon within her, "I COMMAND you IN the Name of Jesus Christ to COME OUT of her." And instantly it left her. ... They were severely beaten and were thrown into prison. Around midnight Paul and Silas were praying and singing hymns to God, and the other prisoners were listening. Suddenly, there was a massive earthquake, and the prison doors flew open, and the chains of every prisoner fell off! The jailer woke up to see the prison doors wide open. He assumed the prisoners had escaped, so he drew his sword to kill himself. But Paul shouted, "Stop! Do not kill yourself! We are all here!" ... The jailer ran to the dungeon and fell down trembling before Paul and Silas. He asked, "Sirs, WHAT must I DO to be SAVED?" They replied, "BELIEVE in the LORD Jesus." And they SHARED the Word of the Lord with him and his household. The jailer washed their wounds. THEN he and everyone in his household were baptized. He brought them into his house and set a meal before them, and he and his entire household were FULL of JOY because they all believed in God.

Acts 17:11, 22-23, 26-27   The people of Berea were more open-minded than those in Thessalonica, and they listened eagerly to Paul's message. They SEARCHED the Scriptures day after day to SEE IF Paul and Silas were TEACHING the TRUTH. ... Paul, at Mars Hill, said: "Men of Athens, I notice that you are very religious in every way. One of your altars had this: 'To an Unknown God.' This God is the One I'm telling you about. ... God created all the nations, deciding when they should rise and fall. God determined their boundaries. God's PURPOSE was for people to SEEK after God and perhaps FEEL their way toward Him and FIND Him – God is NOT FAR from any one of us."

Acts 18:5-6, 9-10, 24-26   Paul spent all his time preaching that Jesus IS the Messiah. But when they opposed and insulted him, Paul shook the dust from his clothes and said, "Your blood is upon your own heads – I am innocent. From NOW on I will go preach to others." ... The Lord spoke to Paul in a vision, "Do NOT be afraid! SPEAK OUT! Do NOT be silent! For I am WITH you, and no one will attack and harm you, for many people in this city belong to Me." ... Apollos, an eloquent speaker who knew the Scriptures well, had been taught the way of the Lord, and he taught others about Jesus with enthusiasm and accuracy. However, he knew only John's baptism. When Priscilla and Aquila heard him, they took him aside and explained the way of God even more accurately.

Acts 19:2-6, 13, 15-16, 18-19, 26, 32   "Did you receive the Holy Spirit when you believed?" Paul asked. "No, we have not even heard that there is a Holy Spirit." the believers replied. "What baptism did you experience?" Paul asked. The believers replied, "The baptism of John." Paul said, "John's baptism called for REPENTANCE from sin. But John told the people to BELIEVE in the One who would come later, meaning Jesus." They were BAPTIZED in the Name of the Lord Jesus. Then the Holy Spirit came on them, and they spoke in other tongues and prophesied. ... A group of Jews was traveling casting out evil spirits. They tried to use the Name of the Lord Jesus in their incantation, saying, "I command you in the Name of Jesus, whom Paul preaches, to come out!" One time when they tried it, the evil spirit replied, "I know Jesus, and I know Paul, BUT who are you?" Then the man with the evil spirit attacked them and they fled from the house, naked and battered. ... Many became believers, confessing their sinful practices. A number of them who had been practicing sorcery brought their incantation books and burned them at a public bonfire. The value of the books was several million dollars. ... Paul has persuaded many that handmade gods are NOT really gods at all. ... Inside, the people were all shouting, some one thing and some another. Everything was in confusion. In fact, most did not even know why they were there.

Acts 20:20-21, 23-24, 26-31, 33, 35   Paul said, "I never stopped telling you what you needed to hear. I have ONE MESSAGE – the necessity of REPENTING from sin, TURNING to God, and having FAITH in our Lord Jesus. ... The Holy Spirit tells me that jail and suffering lie ahead. But my life is worth NOTHING to me UNLESS I use it for finishing the work assigned me by the Lord Jesus – the work of TELLING others the Good News about the wonderful grace of God THROUGH Jesus. ... IF anyone suffers eternal death, it's NOT my fault, for I did NOT shrink from declaring ALL that God wants you to KNOW. Guard yourselves and God's people. Feed and shepherd God's flock – His church, purchased with His own blood – over which the Holy Spirit has appointed you as elders. I know that FALSE TEACHERS will come in among you after I leave. Even some men from your own group will DISTORT the truth in order to draw a following. Watch out! ... I have never coveted anyone's silver or gold or fine clothes. You know that these hands of mine have worked to supply my own needs and even the needs of those who were with me. I have been a constant EXAMPLE of how you can help those in need by working hard. You should remember the words of the Lord Jesus: 'It is MORE blessed to give THAN to receive.'"

Acts 21:13-14   Paul said, "Why all this weeping? I am ready not only to be jailed, but even to die for the Lord Jesus." When we could not persuade him, we gave up and said, "The Lord's will be done."

Acts 22:15-16, 18-21   You are to be His WITNESS, telling everyone what you have seen and heard. WHAT are you WAITING for? Get up and be BAPTIZED. Have your sins washed away by CALLING on the Name of the Lord. ... I saw a vision of Jesus saying to me, "Hurry! LEAVE, for the people here will NOT accept your testimony about Me. GO, I will send you far away to the Gentiles!"

Acts 23:3, 6, 11   Paul said to him, "God will slap you, you corrupt hypocrite!" ... Paul shouted, "I am on trial because my HOPE is in the RESURRECTION of the dead!" ... The Lord appeared to Paul and said, "Be encouraged, Paul. Just as you have been a witness to Me here in Jerusalem, you must preach the Good News in Rome as well."

Acts 24:15, 25   Paul said, "I have the same HOPE in God ... that He will RAISE both the righteous [being right, based on God's standard, includes thoughts, words and actions] and the unrighteous." As he reasoned about righteousness and self-control and the coming Day of Judgment, Felix became frightened, saying, "Go away for now. When it is more convenient, I will call for you again."

Acts 26:17-18, 20, 26, 28-29   Jesus said to Paul, "I am sending you to the Gentiles to OPEN their eyes, so they may turn FROM darkness TO light and FROM the power of Satan TO God. They will RECEIVE forgiveness for their sins and be GIVEN a place AMONG God's people." ... Paul said, "All must REPENT of their sins, TURN to God, and PROVE they changed by DOING good. ... King Agrippa knows about these things. I am sure these events are all familiar to him, for they were not done in a corner!" Agrippa interrupted him. "Do you think you can PERSUADE me to BECOME a Christian so quickly?" Paul replied, "Whether quickly or not, I PRAY to God that both you and everyone here might BECOME a FOLLOWER of Jesus."

Acts 27:25   Paul said, "Take COURAGE! For I BELIEVE God. It will be just AS He said."

Acts 28:30-31   Paul lived in Rome at his own expense. He welcomed all who visited him, boldly proclaiming the Kingdom of God and teaching about the Lord Jesus. And no one tried to stop him.

Romans 1:2-5, 7, 9, 12, 16-22, 24-32
God PROMISED this Good News long ago through His prophets in the Holy Scriptures. The Good News is about His Son, Jesus. He was shown to be the Son of God when He was RAISED from the dead by the power of the Holy Spirit. He is JESUS Christ our LORD. Through Christ, God has given us the PRIVILEGE and AUTHORITY to TELL Gentiles everywhere what God has DONE for them, so that they will BELIEVE and OBEY Him. May God our Father and the Lord Jesus Christ give you GRACE and PEACE. ... I often PRAY for you. Day and night I bring you and your needs in prayer to God. ... I want to ENCOURAGE you in your faith, but I also want to be encouraged by your faith. ... For I am NOT ashamed of this Good News of Jesus. It is the power of God at work, saving everyone who believes. ... This is accomplished from start to finish by FAITH. [Faith is trusting in God, committing to a life-changing reliance on following God, based on a true understanding of who God is, as revealed

in the Bible. We are not allowed to accept the attributes of God that we prefer and reject the ones we don't. If we do not accept God as He is revealed in the Bible, then we are putting our faith in a false god of our own making.] God shows His ANGER AGAINST all sinful, wicked people who SUPPRESS the TRUTH by their wickedness. They KNOW the TRUTH about God BECAUSE He has made it OBVIOUS to them. Through everything God made, they can CLEARLY SEE His eternal power and divine attributes. So they have NO EXCUSE for not knowing God. ... They knew God, but they would NOT worship Him as God NOR EVEN give Him thanks. They began to think up FOOLISH IDEAS of what God was like. As a result, their minds BECAME dark and CONFUSED. Claiming to be wise, they instead BECAME utter FOOLS. ... So God ABANDONED them to do whatever shameful things their hearts desired. As a RESULT, they did vile and degrading things with each other's bodies. They TRADED the TRUTH about God FOR a LIE. They WORSHIPED and served the THINGS God created INSTEAD of the Creator Himself! That is why God abandoned them to their SHAMEFUL DESIRES. Even the women indulged in sex with each other. And the men burned with lust for each other. Men did SHAMEFUL things with other men, and as a RESULT of this sin, they suffered within themselves the penalty they deserved. Since they thought it foolish to acknowledge God, He abandoned them to their FOOLISH thinking and let them do things that should never be done. Their lives became full of every kind of wickedness, sin, greed, hate, envy, murder, quarreling, deception, malicious behavior, and gossip. They are backstabbers, haters of God, insolent, proud, and boastful. They invent new ways of sinning, and they disobey their parents. They refuse to understand, break their promises, are heartless, and have no mercy. They KNOW God's justice requires those who do these things DESERVE to die, YET they DO them anyway. WORSE yet, they ENCOURAGE others to do them, too.

Romans 2:1, 4-8, 11, 13, 16, 21-24, 29 You think you can condemn such wicked people, but YOU ARE just AS BAD, and have NO excuse! As you judge others for doing wicked things, WHY do you think you can avoid God's judgment WHEN you DO the SAME things? ... Do you see how wonderfully kind, tolerant, and patient God is with you? Does this mean NOTHING to you? Can you SEE that His KINDNESS is intended to TURN you FROM your sin? But IF you REFUSE to turn from your sin, you are storing up terrible punishment for yourself. For a day of God's righteous judgment is coming. God will JUDGE everyone

ACCORDING to WHAT they DID. Eternal life TO those doing good AND seeking God. His anger TO those who live FOR themselves, REFUSING to OBEY the TRUTH and live lives of wickedness. ... God does NOT show favoritism. ... For merely LISTENING to the law does NOT make us right with God. It is OBEYING the law that makes us right with Him. ... The day is coming when God, through Jesus, will JUDGE everyone's SECRET life. ... IF you teach others, TEACH yourself. You say it is wrong to commit adultery, but DO you commit adultery? You condemn idolatry, but DO you have idols? You are so proud of knowing the law, but you DISHONOR God BY breaking it. They show CONTEMPT of God because of you. ... A person with a CHANGED heart SEEKS praise from God, NOT from people.

Romans 3:3-4, 8, 20, 23, 25, 27-28, 31 Just because some "believers" are unfaithful, does that mean God is unfaithful? NO! Even if everyone is a liar, God IS TRUE. ... Some say, "The more we sin, the better it is!" They deserve to be condemned. ... NO one can be made right with God by doing what the law commands. The law simply SHOWS us how sinful we are. ... As the Scriptures say, "NO one is righteous – for everyone has sinned; we all fall short of God's glorious standard [perfect]." ... You are made RIGHT [acceptable] with God when you BELIEVE [confident trust] that Jesus sacrificed His life, shedding His blood. ... Can we boast that we did anything to be accepted by God? NO, our acquittal is based on FAITH [trust, loyalty] that we are made right with God through Jesus and NOT by obeying the law. IF we emphasize faith, does this mean that we can FORGET about the law? NO! ONLY when we have faith do we TRULY fulfill the law.

Romans 4:5, 7, 13-17, 21, 24-25 People are counted as righteous, NOT because of their work, BUT because of their faith [trust, loyalty] in God who forgives sinners. ... What JOY for those whose disobedience is forgiven. ... Clearly, God's promise to give the whole earth to Abraham and his descendants was based NOT on his obedience to God's law, BUT on a RIGHT RELATIONSHIP with God that comes by faith. IF God's promise is only for those who obey the law, THEN faith is not necessary and the promise is pointless. For the law ALWAYS brings punishment on those who try to obey it. (The only way to avoid breaking the law is to have no law to break!) The promise is received by faith. It is given as a FREE gift. We are all certain to receive it, whether or not we live according to the law of Moses, IF we have faith like Abraham's. For Abraham is the father of all who believe. That is what the Scriptures mean when God told him, "I have made you the father of many nations." This happened because Abraham believed in the God who brings the dead back to life and who creates new things out of nothing. ... He was fully convinced that God is able to do His promises. ... God WILL count us as righteous [being right, based on God's standard, includes thoughts, words and actions] IF we believe Him, who raised Jesus our Lord from the dead, to make us right with God.

Romans 5:1-4, 8, 11, 17 Since we have been made right with God by faith, we have PEACE with God because of what Jesus Christ our Lord has DONE for us. Christ brings us UNDESERVED privilege and we CONFIDENTLY and JOYFULLY look forward to sharing God's glory. Be full of JOY when we run into PROBLEMS and trials, they help us develop ENDURANCE, which develops strength of CHARACTER, which strengthens our confident HOPE of salvation. ... God showed His great LOVE for us by sending Christ to die for us WHILE we were still sinners. ... Be FULL of JOY in a NEW RELATIONSHIP with God because Lord Jesus has made us FRIENDS of God. ... The sin of one man, Adam, caused death to rule over many. But God's grace and GIFT of righteousness, for all who receive it will live in triumph over sin and death THROUGH one man, Jesus.

Romans 6:11-16, 23 Consider yourselves to be DEAD to the power of sin and ALIVE to God through Jesus. Do NOT let sin control the way you live. Do NOT give in to sinful desires. Give yourselves completely to God, for you were dead, but now you have new life. DO what is RIGHT for the glory of God. Sin is NO longer your MASTER. Live under the freedom of God's grace. Since God's grace has set us free from the law, does that mean we can go on sinning? NO! You become the SLAVE of WHATEVER you CHOOSE to OBEY! You can be a slave to sin, which leads to death, or you can CHOOSE to OBEY God, which leads to morally correct living. ... The WAGES of sin is DEATH. The FREE GIFT of God is eternal LIFE through Jesus our Lord.

Romans 7:6, 7, 12, 14, 24-25 Now we can SERVE God, NOT obeying the letter of the law, BUT in living in the Spirit. ... The law SHOWS me my sin. ... The law's commands ARE holy and right and good. The trouble is not the law, for it is spiritual and good. The TROUBLE is me, a SLAVE to sin. WHO will FREE me FROM this life dominated by sin and death? The ANSWER: Jesus our Lord.

Romans 8:1-2, 4-9, 11-18, 26, 28, 31-32, 35-36, 38-39 There is NO condemnation for those who BELONG to Christ Jesus. And because you belong to Him, the power of the life-giving Holy Spirit has FREED you FROM the power of sin that leads to death. ... NO longer follow our sinful nature BUT instead follow the Holy Spirit. Those dominated by the sinful nature THINK about sinful things, but those controlled by the Holy Spirit THINK about things that please the Holy Spirit. Letting your sinful nature control your mind LEADS to death. But letting the Holy Spirit control your mind LEADS to life and peace. The sinful nature is always hostile to God. It never did obey God's laws, and it never will. Those who are still under the CONTROL of their sinful nature can NEVER please God. But you are NOT controlled by your sinful nature. You are controlled by the Holy Spirit IF you have the Spirit of God living in you. Those who do NOT HAVE the Spirit of Christ living in them do NOT BELONG to Him at all. ... The Spirit of God, who raised Jesus from the dead, lives in you. You now have NO obligation to do what your sinful nature URGES you to do. IF you live BY sinful desires, you will DIE. But IF through the power of the Holy Spirit you put to death the deeds of your sinful nature, you will LIVE. All who are LED by the Spirit of God ARE children of God. So you have NOT received a spirit that makes you FEARFUL slaves. Instead, you received God's Spirit when He adopted you as His own children. Now we call Him, "Abba, Father." For His Spirit joins with our spirit to affirm that we are God's children. Since we are His children, we are heirs of God's glory. But IF we are to SHARE His glory, we must also SHARE His suffering. Yet what we suffer NOW is NOTHING COMPARED to the glory He will reveal to us LATER. ... The Holy Spirit helps us in our weakness. The Holy Spirit prays for us. ... We know that God causes everything to work together for the good of those who love God and are called according to His purpose for them. ... IF God is FOR us, WHO can ever be AGAINST us? Since God did NOT spare even His own Son but gave Him up for us all, will He not also give us everything else? Can anything ever separate us from Christ's love? ... Does it mean He no longer loves us IF we HAVE trouble or calamity, or are persecuted, or hungry, or destitute, or in danger, or threatened with death? ... I am convinced that NOTHING can ever SEPARATE us FROM God's love. Neither death nor life, neither angels nor demons, neither our fears for today nor our worries about tomorrow – not even the powers of hell can separate us from God's love. NOTHING in all creation will ever be able to separate us from the LOVE of God that is REVEALED in Christ Jesus our Lord.

Romans 9:14-16, 19-21, 27, 31-32 Is God unfair? NO! God said, "I will show mercy to anyone I choose, and I will show compassion to anyone I choose." It is God who decides to show mercy. We neither choose nor work for it. ... Do you say, "Why does God blame people for not responding? Have they simply done what He makes them do?" No, don't say that. WHO ARE you, a mere human being, to ARGUE WITH God? Should the thing that was created say to the One who created it, "Why have you made me like this?" When a potter makes jars out of clay, does not he have a right to use the same lump of clay to make one jar for decoration and another to throw garbage into? ... Isaiah said, "Though Israel's people are numerous as sand, ONLY a REMNANT will be SAVED." ... The people of Israel, who tried hard to get right with God by keeping the law, NEVER succeeded, because they were trying to get right with God by keeping the law INSTEAD of by TRUSTING Him.

Romans 10:2-3, 9-10, 14 What enthusiasm they have, but it is MISDIRECTED zeal. They do NOT understand God's way of making people right with Himself. REFUSING to accept GOD'S WAY, they CLING to their OWN WAY. ... IF you CONFESS with your mouth saying, "Jesus is [my] LORD" and BELIEVE in your heart that God raised Jesus from the dead, you will be SAVED. For it is by believing in your heart that you are made right with God, and it is by confessing with your mouth that you are saved. ... HOW can they call on Jesus to save them IF they have NEVER heard about Him? And HOW can they hear about him UNLESS someone TELLS them about Jesus.

Romans 11:22, 33-34 God is both kind and severe. He is SEVERE TOWARD those who disobeyed, but KIND TO you IF you CONTINUE to TRUST in Him. IF you STOP trusting, you will be CUT OFF. ... How great is God's wisdom! How impossible it is for us to understand His decisions! Who can know the LORD's thoughts? WHO KNOWS enough to GIVE God ADVICE?

Romans 12:1-3, 9, 11-21 I plead with you to give your BODIES to God because of all He has done for you. Let them be a living and holy SACRIFICE – the kind He will find acceptable. This is truly the way to worship Him. Do NOT copy the behavior and customs of this world, but let God TRANSFORM you into a new person by CHANGING the WAY you THINK. Then learn to KNOW God's will for you, which is good, pleasing and perfect. ... Do NOT think you are better than you really are. Be honest in your evaluation of yourselves. ... Do NOT pretend to love others. Really LOVE them. HATE what is WRONG. HOLD tightly to what is GOOD. ... Never be lazy, but work hard and serve the Lord enthusiastically. Be JOYFUL in our confident HOPE. Be PATIENT in trouble, and keep on PRAYING. When God's people are in need, be ready to HELP them. ... Do NOT curse those who persecute you. PRAY that God will BLESS them. Be HAPPY with those who are happy, and WEEP with those who weep. Live in HARMONY with each other. Do NOT be too proud to ENJOY the company of ordinary people. Do NOT think you know it all! NEVER pay back evil with more evil. Do all you can to live in PEACE with everyone. Dear friends, NEVER take revenge. Leave that to the righteous anger of God. For the Scriptures say, "I will take revenge; I will pay them back," says the Lord. Instead, "IF your enemies are hungry, feed them. IF they are thirsty, give them a drink." Do NOT let evil conquer you, but CONQUER evil by DOING good.

Romans 13:1, 4, 6-10, 14   SUBMIT to governing authorities. For all authority comes from God. ... The authorities are God's servants, sent for your good. [If governing authorities are no longer doing good, then Acts 5:29 applies: Obey God rather than human authority.] They are God's servants for the purpose of punishing those who do what is wrong. ... Pay your taxes for these same reasons. Give respect and honor to those in authority. Owe nothing to anyone — except for your obligation to LOVE one ANOTHER. IF you love your neighbor, you will FULFILL the requirements of God's law. For the commandments say, "You must not commit adultery. You must not murder. You must not steal. You must not covet." These – and other such commandments – are summed up in this one commandment: "LOVE your neighbor AS yourself." Love does NO wrong to others, so LOVE fulfills the requirements of God's law. ... STAY in the Presence of the Lord Jesus. Do NOT think about ways to INDULGE your evil desires.

Romans 14:1, 4, 7-10, 12-13, 17, 19, 22-23   ACCEPT other believers who are weak in faith, and do NOT argue with them about what they think is right or wrong. ... WHO are you to condemn God's servants? They are responsible to the Lord, so let Him JUDGE whether they are right or wrong. And with the Lord's HELP, they will do what is right and will receive His APPROVAL. ... For we do NOT live for ourselves OR die for ourselves. IF we live, we live FOR the Lord. And IF we die, we die FOR the Lord. So whether we live or die, we BELONG to the Lord. So WHY do you condemn another believer? WHY do you look down on another believer? Remember, we will ALL stand before the judgment seat of God. ... Yes, each of us will GIVE a PERSONAL ACCOUNT to God. So let's STOP condemning each other. Decide instead to live in such a way that you will NOT cause another believer to stumble and fall. ... The Kingdom of God is living a life of GOODNESS and PEACE and JOY in the Holy Spirit. ... Aim for HARMONY in the church and try to build each other up. ... You may believe there's nothing wrong with what you are doing, but keep it between yourself and God. Blessed are those who do not feel guilty for doing something they have decided is right. But if you have doubts about whether or not you should eat something, you are sinning if you go ahead and do it. Follow your convictions. If you do anything you believe is not right, you are sinning.

Romans 15:2, 7, 13, 20, 33 Help others do what is right and build them up in the Lord. ... ACCEPT each other. ... I pray that God, the source of HOPE, will fill you completely with JOY and PEACE because you TRUST Him. Then overflow with confident HOPE through the POWER of the Holy Spirit. ... My ambition has been to preach the Good News where the Name of Jesus has never been heard, rather than where a church has already been started by someone else. ... May God, who gives us His PEACE, be with you all. Amen.

Romans 16:17-20, 25 AMP Watch out for people who cause DIVISIONS and upset people's faith by TEACHING things CONTRARY to God. STAY away FROM them. Such people are NOT serving Christ our Lord. They are serving their own personal interests. By SMOOTH TALK and FLATTERING words they DECEIVE innocent people. Be OBEDIENT to the Lord. Be WISE in doing right and stay INNOCENT of any wrong. The God of peace will crush Satan under your feet. May the grace of our Lord Jesus be with you. ... All glory to God, who is able to make you strong.

1 Corinthians 1:18, 20, 23-25, 27, 31
The message of the cross is FOOLISH to those who are headed for destruction! But we who are being SAVED know it is the very Power of God. Where does this leave the philosophers, the scholars, and the world's brilliant debaters? God makes the wisdom of this world look foolish. When we preach that Christ was crucified, the Jews are OFFENDED and the Gentiles say it's all NONSENSE. To those called by God to salvation, Jesus is the POWER of God and the WISDOM of God. God chose things the world considers foolish to shame those who think they are wise. God chose powerless things to shame the powerful. As a result, NO one can ever boast in the Presence of God. IF you want to boast, boast ONLY about the LORD.

1 Corinthians 2:1-2, 4-5, 9, 11, 14, 16 AMP   I did not use human eloquence to tell you God's plan. I decided that I would know nothing except Jesus Christ, the One who was crucified.   My message and my preaching were plain. RATHER than using clever, persuasive speeches, I relied ONLY on the POWER of the Holy Spirit. I did this so you would trust NOT human wisdom BUT the power of God. ... No eye has seen, no ear has heard, and no mind has imagined what God has prepared for those who love Him. ... No one can know a person's thoughts except that person's own spirit, and no one can know God's thoughts except God's own Spirit. ... Natural, NON-SPIRITUAL people do NOT accept or understand TRUTH from God's Spirit. It is meaningless nonsense to them. For ONLY SPIRITUAL people can UNDERSTAND what the Holy Spirit means. Those who are spiritually MATURE can DISCERN all things, but they themselves cannot be evaluated by non-believers. "Who can know the LORD's thoughts? WHO knows enough to teach Him?" [Isaiah 40:13]

1 Corinthians 3:1, 3-4, 6-7, 11, 13-20   I could NOT talk to you as to spiritually MATURE people. I had to talk to you as belonging to this world or as BABIES in the Christian life. ... For you are STILL controlled by your sinful nature. You are jealous of one another and QUARREL with each other. Are you living LIKE people of the world? When one of you says, "I am a follower of Paul," and another says, "I follow Apollos," are you ACTING just LIKE people of the world? ... I planted the seed in your hearts, and Apollos watered it, but it was God who made it grow. It's not important who does the planting, or who does the watering. What is IMPORTANT is that God makes the seed grow. ... There is NO foundation other than – Jesus Christ. ... On Judgment Day, fire will show if a person's work has any value. IF the work survives, that builder receives a reward. IF the work is burned up, the builder will suffer loss. The builder will be SAVED, like one escaping through a wall of flames. Realize that ALL of you TOGETHER are the Temple of God and the Spirit of God lives in you! God will destroy anyone who destroys this temple.   God's temple is holy, and you are that temple.   STOP DECEIVING yourselves. IF you think you are "wise" by this world's standards, you need to become a "fool" to be truly wise.   For the WISDOM of this world is FOOLISHNESS to God.   ... "The LORD knows the THOUGHTS of the 'wise' are WORTHLESS." [Psalm 94:11]

1 Corinthians 4:3-5, 7, 12-14, 18, 20   It matters little how I am evaluated by you or by any human authority. I do NOT even trust my own judgment on this point. My conscience is clear, but that does NOT prove I am right. The Lord will examine me and DECIDE. So do NOT make judgments about anyone ahead of time – before the Lord returns. For Jesus will bring our darkest secrets to light and REVEAL our private MOTIVES. Then God will GIVE to EACH one WHATEVER praise is DUE. ... What do you have that God has not given you? IF everything you have is from God, WHY boast as though it were not a gift? ... We work to earn our living, BLESSING those who curse us, and PATIENT with those who abuse us. We appeal GENTLY when evil things are said about us. I am writing this to warn you. ... Some of you have become arrogant. The Kingdom of God is NOT just a lot of TALK. ... The Kingdom of God is LIVING by God's POWER.

1 Corinthians 5:9-13 I told you NOT to associate with people who INDULGE in sexual sin. I was NOT talking about unbelievers. You would have to leave this world to avoid people like that. I meant that you are NOT to associate with anyone WHO CLAIMS to be a believer yet INDULGES in sexual sin, or is greedy, or worships idols, or is abusive, or is a drunkard, or cheats people. It is NOT my responsibility to judge outsiders, BUT it is your responsibility to JUDGE those INSIDE the church who are sinning. God will judge those on the outside. The Scriptures say, "You must remove the evil person from among you." [Deuteronomy 17:7]

1 Corinthians 6:1, 7-12, 17-20 When one of you has a dispute with another believer, how dare you file a lawsuit! To have lawsuits with one another is a defeat for you. Why NOT just accept the injustice and leave it at that? You are the ones who do wrong and cheat even your fellow believers. Do you REALIZE that those who [deliberately continue to] DO WRONG will NOT inherit the Kingdom of God? Do NOT fool yourselves. Those WHO INDULGE in sexual sin, or who worship idols, or commit adultery, or are male prostitutes, or practice homosexuality, or are thieves, or greedy people, or drunkards, or are abusive, or cheat people — NONE of these will inherit the Kingdom of God. SOME of you WERE once LIKE that. BUT you were made right with God by CALLING on the Name of the Lord Jesus Christ and by the Spirit of our God. You say, "I am allowed to do anything" — but NOT everything is good for you. Even though "I am allowed to do anything," I must NOT become a SLAVE to anything. The person who is joined to the Lord is one spirit with Him. RUN FROM sexual sin! No other sin so clearly affects the body as this one does. For sexual immorality is a sin against your own body. REALIZE that your BODY is the Temple of the Holy Spirit, who lives in you and was given to you by God! You do NOT belong to yourself, for God BOUGHT you with a HIGH price. So HONOR God with your BODY.

1 Corinthians 7:1-3, 5-6, 9-12, 17, 21, 23, 31-32, 35 Regarding the questions you asked [about marriage]. It is good to live a celibate life. But because there is so much sexual immorality, each man should have his own wife, and each woman should have her own husband. Do NOT deprive each other of sexual relations, so Satan will NOT be able to tempt you because of your lack of self-control. I say this as a concession, NOT as a command. IF they do NOT control themselves, they should marry. It's better to marry than to burn with lust. For those who are married, I have a command from the Lord. A wife must NOT leave her husband. But if she does leave him, let her remain single or else be reconciled to him. The husband must NOT leave his wife. Though I do not have a direct command from the Lord, IF a Christian man has a wife who is not a believer and she is willing to continue living with him, he must NOT leave her. ... Each of you should continue to live in whatever situation the Lord has placed you. Are you a slave? Do NOT let that worry you – but IF you get a chance to be free, TAKE it. God paid a high price for you, so do NOT be a SLAVE to the world. Do NOT become ATTACHED to the things of the world. I want you to be FREE from the CONCERNS of this life. I am saying this for your benefit, NOT to place restrictions on you. I want you to do whatever will help you serve the Lord best, with as few DISTRACTIONS as possible.

1 Corinthians 8:1-2, 4-6, 9, 12, 16 "We all have knowledge." But while KNOWLEDGE makes us FEEL important, it is LOVE that BUILDS up the church. Anyone who CLAIMS to know ALL the answers does NOT really KNOW very much. ... We know an idol is NOT a god. There are MANY FALSE gods, and some people actually worship them. There is ONLY ONE God, the Father, who created everything, and we live for Him. There is ONLY ONE Lord, Jesus Christ, through whom God made everything and we have been given life. ... Be careful so that your freedom does NOT cause others with a weaker conscience to STUMBLE. When you sin against other believers by encouraging them to do something they believe is wrong, you are sinning against Jesus. ... Preaching the Good News is not something I can boast about. Woe to me if I do not preach the Good News!

1 Corinthians 10:1, 6, 8-14, 19-20, 24, 31-33 Do NOT forget. These things are a warning to us: do NOT crave evil things as they did, or worship idols as some of them did. Do NOT indulge in sexual immorality as some of them did, causing 23,000 of them to die in one day. Nor should we put Jesus to the test, as some of them did and then died from snakebites. Do NOT complain as some of them did, and then were destroyed. IF you THINK you are standing strong, be careful NOT to fall. The temptations in your life are NO different from what others experience. God is faithful. He will NOT allow the temptation to be more than you can stand. He will SHOW you a way out. So, my dear friends, FLEE from the worship of idols. Am I saying that food offered to idols has some significance, or that idols are real gods? NO! I am saying that these sacrifices are OFFERED to demons, NOT to God. I do NOT want you to participate with demons. Do NOT be only concerned for your own good but FOR the good of others. Whatever you do, do everything for the glory of God. Give NO offense to people or the church of God. I do NOT just do what is best for me. I DO what is best for others so that many may be saved.

1 Corinthians 11:16, 17, 20, 28, 32 If anyone wants to argue about this, I simply say: we have no other custom than this, and neither do God's other churches. I cannot praise you. It appears more harm than good is done when you meet together, you are NOT really interested in the Lord's Supper. You should EXAMINE yourself BEFORE eating the bread and drinking the cup. When we are judged by the Lord, we are being disciplined so that we will not be condemned along with the world.

1 Corinthians 12:2-3, 10, 25-27, 29-31 When you were pagans, you were led astray worshiping speechless idols. I want you to know that NO ONE speaking by the Spirit of God will curse Jesus, and NO ONE can say, "Jesus is [my] LORD," except by the Holy Spirit. … A spiritual GIFT is given to each of us so we can HELP each OTHER. To one person the Holy Spirit gives the ability to give wise advice; to another a message of special knowledge, to another great faith, and to someone else the gift of healing. The Holy Spirit gives a person power to perform miracles, another ability to prophesy, someone else ability to DISCERN IF a message is FROM the Spirit of God or FROM a demon, another is given ability to speak in unknown languages, while another is given the ability to interpret what is being said. … This makes for HARMONY among the members, so that all the members CARE for each other. If one part suffers, all the parts suffer with it, and if one part is honored, all the parts are glad. ALL of you TOGETHER are Christ's body, and each of you is a part of it. ... Are we ALL apostles? Are we ALL prophets? Are we ALL teachers? Do we ALL do miracles? Do we ALL do healing? Do we ALL speak in unknown languages [tongues] ? Do we ALL interpret unknown languages? NO! ... Earnestly desire the most helpful gifts.

1 Corinthians 13:1-10, 13 IF I could speak all languages, but NOT love others, I would be a NOISY gong. IF I possessed all knowledge, and IF I had faith to move mountains, but NOT love others, I would be NOTHING. IF I gave everything to the poor, but NOT love others, I would gain NOTHING. Love is PATIENT, KIND and keeps NO record of being wronged. Love is NOT jealous, boastful, proud, rude, demand its own way, irritable. Love does NOT rejoice with injustice BUT is FULL of JOY when TRUTH wins. Love NEVER gives up, never loses faith, IS always HOPEFUL, and ENDURES through every circumstance. Love LASTS forever! Our knowledge is partial, and prophecy reveals only part of the picture! When full understanding comes, these partial things become useless. These 3 will LAST forever – FAITH, HOPE, LOVE – the greatest is LOVE.

1 Corinthians 14:1-4, 9, 12-13, 16, 18-20, 24-25, 27-33, 39-40 Let LOVE be your highest goal! But ALSO DESIRE the special abilities the Spirit gives. If you speak in tongues, you will be talking only to God, since people will not be able to understand you. But one who prophesies strengthens others, encourages them, and comforts them. A person who speaks in tongues is strengthened personally, but one who speaks a word of prophecy strengthens the entire church. If you speak to people in words they do not understand, how will they know what you are saying? You might as well be talking into empty space. Since you are so eager to have the special abilities the Spirit gives, SEEK those that will strengthen the whole church. So anyone who speaks in tongues should pray also for the ability to interpret what has been said. For if you praise God only in the spirit, how can those who do not understand you praise God along with you? I thank God that I speak in tongues more than any of you. But in a church meeting I would rather speak 5 understandable words to help others than 10,000 words in an unknown language. Do NOT be CHILDISH in your understanding of these things. BE innocent as BABIES when it comes to evil, BUT be MATURE in understanding matters of this kind. If you are prophesying, and unbelievers come into your meeting, they will be convicted of sin and judged by what you say. As they listen, their secret thoughts will be exposed, and they will worship

God, declaring, "God is truly here among you." No more than 2 or 3 should speak in tongues. They must speak one at a time, and someone must interpret what they say. But if no one is present who can interpret, they must be silent in your church meeting and speak in tongues to God privately. Let 2 or 3 people prophesy, and let the others evaluate what is said. But if someone is prophesying and another person receives a revelation from the Lord, the one who is speaking must stop. In this way, all who prophesy will have a turn to speak, one after the other, so everyone will learn and be encouraged. Remember that people who prophesy are in control of their spirit and can take turns. God is NOT a God of DISORDER, BUT of PEACE, as in all the meetings of God's holy people. Be eager to prophesy, and do not forbid speaking in tongues. Be sure everything is done properly and in order.

1 Corinthians 15:2-8, 12-13,17, 19, 23, 32-34, 55-58 This Good News that SAVES you IF you CONTINUE to believe the message I told you – UNLESS, of course, you believed SOMETHING that was NEVER true in the first place. I passed on to you what is MOST IMPORTANT. Jesus died for our sins, just as the Scriptures said. He was buried, and He was raised from the dead on the third day, just as the Scriptures said. He was seen by Peter and then by the Twelve. After that, He was seen by more than 500 of His followers at one time, most of whom are still alive, though some have died. Then He was seen by James. Last of all, I also saw Him. ... Since we preach that Christ rose from the dead, why are some of you saying there will be no resurrection of the dead? For if there is no resurrection of the dead, then Christ has not been raised either. And if Christ has not been raised, then your faith is useless and you are still guilty of your sins. And if our hope in Christ is only for this life, we are more to be pitied than anyone. But in fact, Christ has been raised from the dead, as the first of the harvest; then all who belong to Christ will be raised when He comes back. ... If there is no resurrection, "Let's feast and drink, for tomorrow we die!" Do NOT be FOOLED by those who say such things, for "BAD company CORRUPTS good character." THINK carefully about what is right, and STOP sinning. To your shame, I say that SOME of you do NOT know God at all. ... O death, where is your victory? For sin is the sting that results in death. But thank God! He gives us VICTORY over sin and death THROUGH our Lord Jesus Christ. So be STRONG and IMMOVABLE. Work eagerly for the Lord, for NOTHING you do for the Lord is USELESS.

1 Corinthians 16:1-4, 13-14, 22-23   Regarding your question about the MONEY being collected for God's people in Jerusalem. Follow the same procedure I gave to the churches in Galatia. On the first day of each week, each of you should put aside a portion of the money you have earned. Do not wait until I get there. I will write letters of recommendation for the messengers you choose to deliver your gift to Jerusalem. If it seems appropriate for me to go along, they can travel with me. ... Be on guard. STAND FIRM [lean neither left or right] in the faith.   Be COURAGEOUS. Do everything with LOVE. If anyone does not love the Lord, that person is cursed. May the Lord Jesus be with you.

2 Corinthians 1:11, 20   You are HELPING us by PRAYING for us. God has answered many prayers for our safety. ... For all of God's promises have been fulfilled in Christ with a resounding "Yes!" And through Christ, our "Amen" (which means "Yes") ascends to God for His glory.

2 Corinthians 2:9, 17   I wrote to you as I did to test you and see if you would comply with my instructions. We are NOT like the many hucksters who preach for personal profit. We preach the Word of God with sincerity and with Christ's authority, knowing that God is WATCHING us.

2 Corinthians 3:17   The Lord is Spirit, and wherever the Spirit of the Lord is, there is FREEDOM.

2 Corinthians 4:3-5, 8-10, 14, 16-18   The Good News we preach is hidden only from people who are perishing. Satan, who is the god of this world, has BLINDED the minds of those who do not believe. They do NOT understand this message about the glory of Christ JESUS, who is the EXACT LIKENESS of God. ... We preach that Jesus Christ is LORD. ... We are pressed on every side by troubles, but we are NOT crushed. We are perplexed, but NOT driven to despair. We are hunted down, but NEVER abandoned by God. We get knocked down, but we are NOT destroyed. Through suffering, our bodies continue to share in the death of Jesus so that the life of Jesus may also be seen in our bodies. We know that God, who raised the Lord Jesus, will also raise us with Jesus and present us to Himself together with you. That is why we NEVER give up. Though our bodies are dying, our spirits are being RENEWED every day. For our present troubles are small and will NOT last long. Yet they produce for us a GLORY that will last FOREVER! So we do NOT look at the troubles we can see now; rather, we fix our GAZE on things that cannot be seen [Jesus in heaven waiting for us]. The things we see now will SOON be GONE, but the things we cannot see will LAST FOREVER.

2 Corinthians 5:8, 10, 17-21   ABSENT from the body, then we will be PRESENT with the Lord. ... For we must ALL stand before Christ to be JUDGED. We will each RECEIVE whatever we DESERVE for the good or evil we have DONE in this earthly body. ... All who belong to Christ become a NEW person. The old is gone, a new life has begun! This is a gift from God, who brought us back to Himself through Jesus. God has GIVEN us this task of RECONCILING people to Him. God was in Jesus, reconciling the world to Himself, no longer counting people's sins against them. He gave us this WONDERFUL message of reconciliation. We are Christ's AMBASSADORS. We speak for Jesus when we plead, "COME BACK to God!" For God made Jesus, who NEVER sinned, to be the OFFERING for our sin, so that we could be made RIGHT with God THROUGH Jesus.

2 Corinthians 6:2, 14-18; 7:1   God says, "At the right time, I heard you." The "right time" is NOW. TODAY is the day of salvation. ... Do NOT team up WITH unbelievers who reject God. How can you make partners out of right and wrong? Can light live with dark? What harmony can there be between Christ and the devil? How can a believer be a partner with an unbeliever? What union is between God's temple and idols? We are God's temple. The LORD Almighty said: "I will live in them and walk among them. I will be their God, and they will be My people. [Leviticus 26:12, Ezekiel 37.27] Now, separate from unbelievers. Do not touch their filthy things. [Isaiah 52:11, Ezekiel 20:34] I will be your Father, and you will be My sons and daughters." [2 Samuel 7:14] Because we have these promises, let us clean ourselves from all filth of body and spirit. Let us work toward complete HOLINESS because we fear [respect God's power and authority, because we desire to please] God.

2 Corinthians 7:9-10   I am glad I sent that severe letter, ... because the PAIN caused you to REPENT and CHANGE your ways. It was the kind of sorrow God wants His people to have, to lead us AWAY FROM sin and RESULTS IN salvation. There is NO regret for that kind of sorrow. WORLDLY sorrow, which LACKS repentance, RESULTS in spiritual DEATH.

2 Corinthians 8:1-3, 8, 12-13   The churches in Macedonia are being tested by many troubles, and they are very poor. But they are also filled with abundant JOY, which has overflowed in GENEROSITY. They gave not only what they could afford, but far more. And they did it of their own free will. I am not commanding you to do this. But I am testing how genuine your love is by comparing it with the eagerness of the other churches. WHATEVER you give is acceptable IF you give it CHEERFULLY. And give according to WHAT you HAVE, not what you do not have. Of course, I do NOT mean your giving should make life easy for others and hard for yourselves. I ONLY mean that there should be SOME equality.

2 Corinthians 9:8 God will provide all you need and PLENTY left over to SHARE with others.

2 Corinthians 10:4-5, 18 We USE God's mighty weapons, NOT worldly weapons, to DESTROY the STRONGHOLDS of human reasoning, false arguments and rebellious thoughts. We DESTROY every proud obstacle that keeps people FROM knowing God. We TEACH them to OBEY Christ. ... When people commend themselves, it does NOT count for much. The IMPORTANT thing is for the Lord to commend them.

2 Corinthians 11:13-15 These people are FALSE apostles, LYING workers who only PRETEND to be apostles of Christ. But I am not surprised! Even Satan DISGUISES himself as an angel of light. In the end they will get the punishment their evil deeds deserve.

2 Corinthians 12:8-10 I begged the Lord to take it away 3 times. Each time God said, "My grace is all you need. My power works BEST in weakness." Now I am glad about my weaknesses, so the power of Christ can work through me. That is why I take pleasure in my weaknesses, and in insults, hardships, persecutions, and troubles that I suffer for Jesus. For when I am weak, then I am strong.

2 Corinthians 13:5, 14 EXAMINE yourselves to see IF your FAITH is GENUINE. Test yourselves. You know IF Jesus is AMONG you. IF NOT, you have FAILED the test of genuine faith. ... May the grace of the Lord JESUS Christ, the love of GOD, and the fellowship of the HOLY SPIRIT be with you all.

Galatians 1:6-8, 10
I am shocked you are TURNING away FROM God, who called you to Himself through the loving mercy of Christ. You are FOLLOWING a DIFFERENT way that PRETENDS to be the Good News but is NOT the Good News at all. You are being FOOLED by those who deliberately TWIST the truth concerning Christ.

Let God's curse fall on anyone, including us, who preaches a DIFFERENT kind of Good News than the one we preached to you. ... I am NOT trying to win the APPROVAL of people, BUT of God.

Galatians 2:20-21 My old self was crucified with Christ. It is no longer I who live, but Christ lives in me. I live in this body by TRUSTING in the Son of God, who loved me and gave Himself for me. IF keeping the law can make us right with God, THEN there is NO need for Christ to die for us.

Galatians 3:28 There is NO longer Jew or Gentile, slave or free, male and female. You are all ONE in Jesus.

Galatians 5:13-17, 19-24 Live in FREEDOM, but do NOT use your freedom to satisfy your sinful nature. Instead, USE your freedom to SERVE one another in love. The whole LAW is summed up in ONE command: LOVE your neighbor AS yourself. Watch out! Beware of destroying one another. Let the Holy Spirit GUIDE your lives. THEN you will NOT be doing what your sinful nature craves. The sinful nature wants to do evil, the OPPOSITE of what the Holy Spirit wants. The Holy Spirit gives us desires that are the OPPOSITE of what the sinful nature desires. These 2 are constantly fighting each other. ... When you follow the desires of your SINFUL nature, the RESULTS are clear: sexual immorality, impurity, lustful pleasures, idolatry, sorcery, hostility, quarreling, jealousy, outbursts of anger, selfish ambition, dissension, division, envy, drunkenness, wild parties, and other sins. Anyone living that sort of life will NOT inherit the Kingdom of God. The Holy Spirit produces this fruit in our lives: LOVE, JOY, PEACE, PATIENCE, KINDNESS, GOODNESS, FAITHFULNESS, GENTLENESS, and SELF-CONTROL. There is NO law AGAINST these things! Those who belong to Christ Jesus have nailed the passions and desires of their sinful nature to His cross and crucified them there.

Galatians 6:1-5, 7 ERV IF another believer is OVERCOME by some sin, you who are godly [committed to obeying God] should GENTLY and HUMBLY HELP that person back onto the RIGHT path. Be careful NOT to FALL INTO the SAME temptation yourself. SHARE each other's burdens, and in this way obey the law of Christ. IF you THINK you are too important to HELP someone, you are only FOOLING yourself. You are NOT that important. Pay careful attention to your OWN work, for then you will get the satisfaction of a job well done, and you will NOT need to COMPARE yourself to anyone else. For we are each RESPONSIBLE for our OWN conduct. ... Do NOT be misled – IF you think you can FOOL God, you are only FOOLING yourself. You will always HARVEST what you PLANT.

Ephesians 1:3, 17 All PRAISE to God who blesses us with every spiritual blessing because we are WITH Jesus. ... I PRAY for you constantly asking God, the Father of our Lord Jesus Christ, to GIVE you spiritual wisdom and insight so that you may GROW in your intimate knowledge of God.

Ephesians 2:1-2, 8-10, 19 Once you were DEAD because you used to live IN sin, just like the rest of the world, OBEYING the devil – the spirit at work in the hearts of those who REFUSE to obey God. ... God SAVED you by His grace WHEN you TURNED and TRUSTED Jesus. It is a GIFT from God. Salvation is not a reward for the good things we have done, so none of us can boast about it. For we are God's masterpiece. He has created us anew in Jesus, so we can DO the GOOD things He planned for us long ago. ... Now you are NO longer strangers and foreigners. You are MEMBERS of God's Family.

Ephesians 3:14-20 PRAY to the Father, the Creator of everything in heaven and on earth, that from His unlimited resources He will empower you with inner STRENGTH through His Spirit. Then Christ will make His home in your hearts AS you TRUST in Him. Your roots will GROW into God's love and keep you strong. May you have the power to understand how wide, how long, how high, and how deep His love is. May you EXPERIENCE the LOVE of Jesus, though it is too great to fully understand. THEN you will be made complete with all fullness of life and power that comes from God. All glory to God, who through His power in us, can accomplish MORE than we ask or think.

Ephesians 4:11-19, 22-29, 31-32 These are the GIFTS Christ gave to the church: apostles, prophets, evangelists, and pastors and teachers. Their responsibility is to EQUIP God's people to DO His work and BUILD UP the church, the body of Christ, until we all come to UNITY, becoming MATURE in the Lord. NO LONGER be immature like children. We will NOT be tossed by new teaching. We will NOT be influenced when people try to TRICK us with LIES. Instead, speak the TRUTH in LOVE, growing more LIKE Christ. He makes the whole body fit together perfectly. As each part does its own special work, it helps the other parts grow, so that the whole body is healthy and growing and full of love. Live NO LONGER as the Gentiles do, who are hopelessly CONFUSED. Their minds are full of darkness; they wander far from the life God gives because they have CLOSED their minds and HARDENED their hearts against Him. They have NO SENSE of shame. They live for lustful pleasure and eagerly practice every kind of impurity. THROW OFF your former way of life, which is CORRUPTED by lust and DECEPTION. Let the Holy Spirit RENEW your thoughts and attitudes. BE like God – TRULY righteous and holy. STOP telling LIES. Do NOT let ANGER control you, for anger gives an OPENING to the devil. QUIT stealing, use your hands for good hard work, and then GIVE generously to others in need. Do NOT use foul or abusive language. Let everything you say be good, HELPFUL, an ENCOURAGEMENT to those who hear them. Get RID of all bitterness, rage, anger, harsh words, slander, and all types of evil behavior. Be KIND to each other, FORGIVING, just as God through Christ has forgiven you.

Ephesians 5:3-11, 15-19, 21-22, 25-27 Let there be NO sexual immorality, impurity, or greed among you. Such sins have NO place AMONG God's people. Foolish talk, and coarse jokes – are NOT for you. Be THANKFUL to God. NO immoral, impure, or greedy person will INHERIT the Kingdom of Jesus. For a greedy person is an idolater, worshiping the things of this world. Do NOT be fooled by those who try to EXCUSE these sins, for the anger of God will fall on all who DISOBEY Him. Do NOT participate in the things these people do. Now you have Light from the Lord. So live as people of Light! Produce ONLY what is good and right and true. Carefully determine what pleases the Lord. Take NO part in the worthless deeds of evil, instead, EXPOSE them. Be careful, do NOT live like fools, BUT be wise. Make the most of every OPPORTUNITY in these evil days. Do NOT act thoughtlessly, but understand what the Lord wants you to DO. Be filled with the Holy Spirit, singing to the Lord in your hearts. ... SUBMIT to one another out of reverence for Christ. For wives, this means submit to your husband AS to the Lord. For husbands, this means love your wife, AS Christ loved the church. He gave up His life for her to make her holy and clean, by the cleansing of God's Word. He did this to present her to Himself as a glorious church without a spot or any other blemish. She will be HOLY and without fault.

Ephesians 6:1, 4, 7, 10-19 Children, OBEY your parents because you belong to the Lord. Fathers, do NOT provoke your children to ANGER by the way you treat them. Bring them up with the discipline and instruction that comes from the Lord. ... Work with enthusiasm, as you were working for the Lord rather than for people. ... Be STRONG in the Lord and in His mighty power. Put on all of God's armor so that you will be able to STAND firm [lean neither left or right] AGAINST all strategies of the devil. We are NOT fighting against flesh-and-blood enemies, BUT against evil authorities of the unseen world, against mighty powers in this dark world, and AGAINST evil spirits in the heavenly places. Put on every piece of God's armor to RESIST the enemy in the time of evil. Stand your ground, PUTTING ON the belt of TRUTH and the body armor of God's RIGHTEOUSNESS. For shoes, put on the PEACE that comes from the Good News. Hold up the shield of FAITH to stop the devil's fiery arrows. Put on SALVATION as your helmet, and take the sword of the Spirit, which is the WORD of God. Stay alert and be persistent in PRAYERS for all believers. ASK God to give me the right words to boldly EXPLAIN God's Good News to people.

Philippians 1:6, 11-12, 14, 27-30
God BEGAN a good work in you, and CONTINUES until it is finished when Jesus returns. Be filled with the FRUIT of your salvation – the RIGHTEOUS CHARACTER produced by Jesus – for this will bring praise to God. Everything that has happened to me here has helped to spread the Good News. For everyone here, including the whole palace guard, knows that I am in chains because of Jesus. And because of my imprisonment, most of the believers here have gained confidence and boldly SPEAK God's message WITHOUT fear. ... Live as CITIZENS of HEAVEN, in a manner worthy of the Good News about Christ. Do NOT be INTIMIDATED by your enemies. This will be a sign that they will be destroyed, but that you will be saved, by God. For you have been given not only the privilege of TRUSTING in Jesus but also the privilege of SUFFERING for Him. We are in this struggle TOGETHER.

Philippians 2:3-7, 12-16 Do NOT be selfish; do NOT try to impress others. Be HUMBLE [gentle, teachable, trusting God], think others as better than you. Do NOT look out only for your own interests, but TAKE an INTEREST in others, too. Have the same attitude that Jesus had. Though Jesus is God, He gave up His divine privileges. He took the humble position of a slave and was born as a human being. ... Work hard to SHOW the RESULTS of your salvation, OBEYING God with deep reverence. God HELPS you WANT to DO what PLEASES Him, and He GIVES you the POWER to DO it. Do everything WITHOUT complaining and arguing. Live as children of God, offering the Truth of the Good News, shining like bright lights in a world full of perverse people.

Philippians 3:1-3, 10-11, 13, 16, 18-20 Be JOYFUL in the Lord. Watch out for those people who do evil, those mutilators who say you must be circumcised to be saved. We RELY ON what Christ Jesus has DONE for us. We put NO confidence in human effort. I want to KNOW Christ and EXPERIENCE the mighty power that raised Him from the dead. I want to suffer with Him, sharing in His death, so that one way or another I will experience the resurrection from the dead! I FOCUS on this 1 thing: FORGETTING the past and LOOKING forward to what lies ahead. Hold on to the progress we have already made. There are MANY whose CONDUCT shows they are really ENEMIES of Jesus. They are headed for destruction. Their god is their appetite, they brag about shameful things, and they THINK only about WORLDLY things. BUT we are CITIZENS of HEAVEN, and we are eagerly WAITING for Jesus our Lord, to RETURN as our Savior.

Philippians 4:3-9, 11-13 MSG, 19-20 My coworkers [whose] ... NAMES are written IN the BOOK of LIFE. Always be FULL of JOY in the Lord. Be JOYFUL! Be CONSIDERATE in all you do. Do NOT worry about anything; instead, PRAY about everything. Tell God what you need. THANK God for all He has done. Then experience God's PEACE, which exceeds anything we understand. His peace will GUARD your hearts and minds AS you LIVE in Christ Jesus. Fix your THOUGHTS on what is true, honorable, right, pure, lovely, and admirable – if anything is excellent or praiseworthy – THINK about such things. Keep PUTTING into PRACTICE all you learned – everything you heard from me and saw me doing. Then the God of peace will be WITH you. ... I have learned how to be CONTENT with whatever I have. I have learned the secret of living in every situation, whether it is with a full stomach or empty, with plenty or little. WHATEVER I have, WHEREVER I am, I am able to be CONTENT in all these circumstances BY Jesus who gives me STRENGTH. ... This same God who takes care of me will supply all your needs from His glorious riches, which have been given to us in Christ Jesus. All glory to God our Father forever and ever!

Colossians 1:9-14, 21-23, 29
We ASK God to give you complete knowledge of His will and to give you spiritual WISDOM. Then the way you live will always please the Lord, and your lives will produce every kind of good fruit. You will GROW as you learn to

KNOW God better and better. We also PRAY that you will be strengthened with all His glorious POWER so you will have all the ENDURANCE and PATIENCE you need. May you be filled with JOY, always THANKING the Father. For God has rescued us from the kingdom of darkness and transferred us into the Kingdom of His dear Son, who purchased our freedom and forgave our sins. This INCLUDES you who were ONCE FAR away from God. You were His enemies, separated from Him by your evil thoughts and actions. Yet NOW God has RECONCILED you to Himself THROUGH the death of Christ in His physical body. As a result, He has brought you into His Presence, and you are holy and blameless as you stand before Him without a single fault. But you must CONTINUE to believe this TRUTH and STAND FIRMLY in it. Do NOT drift away from the ASSURANCE you received when you heard the Good News. DEPEND on Christ's mighty POWER.

Colossians 2:8, 13-14, 18-23 Do NOT let anyone capture you with EMPTY philosophies and high-sounding NONSENSE that come from human thinking and from the evil spiritual powers of this world, rather than from Jesus. ... You were DEAD because of your sins. Then God made you ALIVE with Christ, for He forgave ALL our sins. He CANCELED the record of the charges against us and took it away by nailing it to the cross. So do NOT let anyone condemn you by insisting on pious self-denial, saying they had visions about these things. Their sinful minds have made them proud, and they are NOT connected to Christ, the Head of the body. The body GROWS as it FEEDS on God's WORD. You have died with Christ, and He has SET you FREE from the evil spiritual powers of this world. So WHY do you keep on following the rules of the world, such as, "Do not handle! Do not taste! Do not touch!"? Such rules are mere human teachings. These rules may SEEM wise because they require strong devotion and pious self-denial. But they provide NO help in conquering a person's evil desires.

Colossians 3:1-3, 5, 8-11, 16-17 You have been raised to NEW life with Jesus, set your SIGHTS on heaven, where Christ sits in the place of honor at God's right hand. THINK about the things of heaven, NOT the things of earth. For you died to this life, and your real life is hidden with Christ in God. Put to death the sinful things lurking within you. Have NOTHING to do WITH sexual immorality, impurity, lust, and evil desires. A greedy person is an idolater, worshiping the things of this world. NOW is the time to get RID of anger, rage, malicious behavior, slander, lying, and dirty language. Be RENEWED as you learn to KNOW your Creator and BECOME LIKE Him. In this new life, it does NOT matter IF you are a Jew or a Gentile, [black or white, female or male], uncivilized, slave, or free. Christ is ALL that matters. Let the message of Jesus fill your lives. Teach and counsel each other with the wisdom He gives. Sing psalms and hymns and spiritual songs to God with thankful hearts. WHATEVER you DO or SAY, do it as REPRESENTING the Lord Jesus, giving THANKS, through Jesus, to God the Father.

Colossians 4:2   Devote yourselves to PRAYER with an ALERT mind and a THANKFUL heart.

1 Thessalonians 2:2
You know how badly we had been treated at Philippi just before we came to you and how much we suffered there. Yet our God gave us the COURAGE to declare His Good News to you BOLDLY, in spite of great opposition.

1 Thessalonians 4:3-5, 7-8, 13, 16   God's will is for you to be HOLY, so STAY away FROM all SEXUAL sin. Each of you CONTROL your own BODY and live in HOLINESS – NOT in lustful passion like the pagans who do NOT know God and His ways. God has called us to live HOLY lives, NOT impure lives. Anyone who REFUSES to live by these rules is not disobeying human teaching but is REJECTING God, who gives His Holy Spirit to [guide and empower] you. ... We want you to know what will happen to the believers who have died so you will not grieve like people who have no hope. For the Lord will come from heaven with a commanding shout and with the trumpet call of God. First, the Christians who have died will rise from their graves.

1 Thessalonians 5:2, 8, 16-23 MSG   The day of the Lord's RETURN will come unexpectedly, like a thief in the night. ... Let us who live in the light be clearheaded, protected by the armor of FAITH and LOVE, and wearing as our helmet the CONFIDENCE of our salvation. ... Always be JOYFUL. Never stop PRAYING. Be THANKFUL in all circumstances, for this is God's will for you who belong to Christ Jesus. Do NOT suppress the Holy Spirit. Do NOT scoff at prophecies. Do NOT be gullible. TEST EVERYTHING that is said, and KEEP ONLY what is GOOD. THROW OUT anything TAINTED with EVIL. Now may the God of PEACE make you HOLY in every way, and may your whole spirit and soul and body be kept blameless until our Lord Jesus Christ comes again.

2 Thessalonians 1:6, 9, 11-12   In His justice God will PAY BACK those who persecute you. ... They will be PUNISHED with ETERNAL destruction, forever SEPARATED from the Lord. ... We keep on praying for you, asking God to enable you to live a life worthy of His call. May He give you the POWER to accomplish all the good things your faith prompts you to do. Then our Lord Jesus will be honored because of the way you live.

2 Thessalonians 2:3, 7-12, 15   Do NOT be fooled BY what they say. For that day will NOT come UNTIL there is a GREAT REBELLION against God and the man of lawlessness is revealed — the one who brings destruction. ... For this lawlessness is already at work secretly, and it will remain secret until the One who is holding it back steps out of the way. Then the man of lawlessness will be revealed, but the Lord Jesus will kill him with the breath of His mouth and destroy him by the splendor of His coming. This man of lawlessness will come to do the work of Satan with COUNTERFEIT power and signs and miracles. He will use every kind of EVIL DECEPTION to FOOL those on their way to destruction, because they REFUSE to love and ACCEPT the TRUTH that would save them. So God will cause them to be greatly DECEIVED, and they will believe these LIES. Then they will be condemned FOR enjoying evil RATHER than believing the truth. ... STAND FIRM and keep a strong grip on the teaching we passed on to you.

2 Thessalonians 3:1-3, 5-6, 10, 13-16   Pray for us. PRAY that the Lord's message will SPREAD rapidly and be HONORED wherever it goes. Pray, too, that we will be rescued from wicked and evil people, for not everyone is a believer. The Lord is faithful, He will strengthen you and guard you from the evil one. ... May the Lord lead you into a FULL understanding and expression of the love of God and the PATIENT endurance that comes from Christ. STAY away FROM all "believers" who live idle lives and do NOT follow Jesus. ... Those unwilling to work will not get to eat. ... Dear brothers and sisters, NEVER get tired of doing good. Note those who REFUSE to obey what we say in this letter. STAY away FROM them so they will be ashamed. Do NOT think of them as enemies, but WARN them as a brother or sister. May the Lord of Peace give you His PEACE in every situation.

1 Timothy 1:8-11   We know that the LAW is good WHEN used CORRECTLY.   For the law is FOR people who are lawless and rebellious, who are ungodly and sinful, who consider nothing sacred and defile what is holy, who kill their father or mother or commit other murders. The law is for people who are sexually immoral, or who practice homosexuality, or are slave traders, liars, promise breakers, or who do anything else that CONTRADICTS the wholesome teaching that comes from the glorious Good News entrusted to me by our blessed God.

1 Timothy 2:1-2, 5-6 PRAY for all people. ASK God to help them, intercede on their behalf, and give thanks for them. PRAY this way for kings and all who are in authority so we can live peaceful, quiet godly [committed to obeying God] lives. ... For there is ONLY ONE God and ONE Mediator who can RECONCILE God and people — the man Christ Jesus. He gave His life to purchase FREEDOM for everyone.

1 Timothy 3:2-6 An ELDER must be a man whose life is above reproach. He must be faithful to his wife. He must exercise self-control, live wisely, and have a good reputation. He must enjoy having guests in his home, and he must be able to teach. He must NOT be a heavy drinker or be violent. He must be gentle, NOT quarrelsome, and NOT love money. He must manage his own family well, having children who respect and obey him. For if a man cannot manage his own household, how can he take care of God's church? An elder must NOT be a new believer, because he might become proud, and the devil would cause him to fall.

1 Timothy 4:1-2 MSG, 12-13 The Holy Spirit tells us that as time goes on, some will TURN away FROM the true faith and FOLLOW deceptive demonic teachings put forth by hypocritical LIARS. These liars have lied so well and for so long that they have LOST their capacity for TRUTH. ... Do NOT let anyone think less of you because you are young. Be an EXAMPLE to all believers in what you say, in the way you live, in your love, your faith, and your purity. ... Devote yourself to the public reading of Scripture and to teaching.

1 Timothy 5:8, 22 Those who will NOT care for their relatives, especially those in their own household, have denied the true faith. Such people are WORSE THAN unbelievers. ... NEVER be in a hurry to appoint a church leader. Do NOT share in the sins of others.

1 Timothy 6:3-8, 10-12 Some people may CONTRADICT our teachings of the Lord Jesus Christ, that promote a godly life. Anyone who teaches something DIFFERENT is arrogant, LACKS understanding, and has an unhealthy desire to QUIBBLE over the meaning of words. This STIRS up arguments ending in jealousy, DIVISION, slander, and evil suspicions.

These people always CAUSE TROUBLE. Their minds are CORRUPT, turning from the TRUTH. To them, "godliness" is a way to become wealthy. ... True godliness WITH contentment is great wealth. We brought nothing with us when we came into the world, and we cannot take anything with us when we leave it. So if we have enough food and clothing, let us be CONTENT. ... For the love of money is the ROOT of all kinds of evil. And some people, craving money, have WANDERED from the true faith and pierced themselves with many sorrows. ... So RUN FROM all these evil things. PURSUE righteousness and a godly life, along with faith, love, perseverance, and GENTLENESS. Fight for the TRUE faith.

2 Timothy 1:6-7 AMP

I remind you to fan into flames the spiritual gift God gave you. God does NOT give us a spirit of cowardice or fear, but God GIVES us a spirit of POWER, LOVE, CALM, WELL-BALANCED mind, and SELF-CONTROL.

2 Timothy 2:15, 19, 23-26 Work hard so you can present yourself to God and receive His approval. Be a good worker who CORRECTLY explains the Word of Truth. ... God's Truth stands firm like a foundation stone with this inscription: "The LORD knows those who are His." and "All who BELONG to the LORD must TURN away FROM evil." ... Again I say, do NOT get involved in foolish, ignorant arguments that only start fights. A servant of the Lord must NOT quarrel but must be KIND to everyone, be able to TEACH, and be PATIENT with difficult people. GENTLY instruct those who oppose the Truth. Perhaps God will CHANGE those people's hearts, and they will LEARN the Truth. Then they will come to their senses and ESCAPE from the devil's TRAP. For they have been held CAPTIVE by the devil to DO whatever he wants.

2 Timothy 3:11-17 You know how I was persecuted — but the Lord rescued me from all of it. EVERYONE living a godly [committed to obeying God] life in Jesus will suffer PERSECUTION. But evil people and IMPOSTERS will flourish. They will DECEIVE others and will themselves be DECEIVED. Remain faithful to the things you have been taught. ... You have been taught the Holy Scriptures from childhood, and they have given you the wisdom to receive the salvation that comes by TRUSTING in Christ Jesus. ALL Scripture is INSPIRED by God and is USEFUL to teach us what is TRUE and to make us REALIZE what is WRONG in our lives. It CORRECTS us WHEN we are wrong and

TEACHES us to DO what is right. God uses it to prepare and EQUIP His people to DO every GOOD work.

2 Timothy 4:3-4   For a time is coming when people will NOT listen to TRUE teaching. They will FOLLOW their OWN desires and will LOOK for teachers who will tell them WHATEVER their itching ears WANT to hear. They will REJECT the TRUTH and CHASE after LIES.

Titus 1:15-16
Everything is pure to those whose hearts are pure. But NOTHING is pure to those who are CORRUPT and unbelieving, because their minds and consciences are corrupted. Such people CLAIM they know God, but they DENY Him BY the WAY they LIVE. They are DETESTABLE and DISOBEDIENT, WORTHLESS for doing good.

Titus 2:12-15 TURN FROM godless living and sinful pleasures. Live in this evil world WITH wisdom, righteousness, and devotion to God, while we look forward with HOPE to when the glory of our great God and Savior, Jesus Christ, will be revealed. He gave His life to FREE us FROM every kind of sin and to make us His very own people, totally COMMITTED to DOING good deeds. Teach these things and ENCOURAGE the believers to DO them. CORRECT them when necessary.

Titus 3:1, 9   REMIND the believers to be OBEDIENT, always ready to DO what is GOOD. Do NOT get involved in FOOLISH discussions about spiritual pedigrees OR in quarrels and fights about obedience to Jewish laws. These things are USELESS and a WASTE of time.

Philemon 1:6
I am PRAYING that you will be active in SHARING your faith, so that you will understand and experience all the good things we have in Christ.

Hebrews 1:2-3, 14
In these LAST DAYS, God has spoken to us through His Son. He made the whole world through His Son. Jesus is the PERFECT COPY of God's nature. He holds everything together by His powerful command. The Son made people clean from their sins. He sat down at the right side of God. Angels are servants – spirits sent to care for people who will inherit salvation.

Hebrews 3:6-13, 18-19   Jesus, as the Son, is in charge of God's entire house. We are God's house, IF we KEEP our courage and REMAIN confident in our HOPE in Christ. The Holy Spirit says, "TODAY when you HEAR His voice, do NOT harden your hearts AS Israel did when they rebelled, when they tested Me in the wilderness. Your ancestors tested and tried My patience, even though they saw My miracles for 40 years. So I was angry and I said, 'Their hearts always TURN away FROM Me. They REFUSE to DO what I tell them. They will NEVER enter My place of rest.'" Be careful. Make sure that your own hearts are NOT evil and unbelieving, TURNING you away FROM the living God. WARN each other every day, while it is "TODAY," so NONE of you will be DECEIVED by sin and hardened against God. ... Who was God speaking when He took an oath that they would never enter His rest? Wasn't it the people who disobeyed Him?   So we see that BECAUSE of their UNBELIEF [not trusting, disloyal] they were NOT able to enter His rest.

Hebrews 4:12, 15-16   The WORD of God is ALIVE and POWERFUL. It EXPOSES our innermost THOUGHTS and DESIRES. ... Our High Priest understands our weaknesses, for Jesus faced all of the SAME testings we do, YET He did NOT sin. So let us COME boldly to the throne of our gracious God. There we will RECEIVE His mercy, and find HELP when we need it most.

Hebrews 5:8-9, 11, 13-14   Though Jesus was God's Son, He learned obedience from the things He suffered. God qualified Him as a perfect High Priest. He is the SOURCE of eternal salvation for all those who OBEY Him. There is much more we would like to say, but it is difficult to explain, since you are SPIRITUALLY DULL and do NOT seem to listen. For those who live on milk are still BABIES and do NOT know how to DO what is right. Solid food is for those who are MATURE, who through TRAINING can RECOGNIZE the DIFFERENCE between RIGHT and WRONG.

Hebrews 6:1, 3-6, 9, 11-12   STOP going over the BASIC teachings about Christ again and again. Let us go on and BECOME MATURE in our understanding. We do not need to start again with the fundamental IMPORTANCE of REPENTING from evil deeds and placing our FAITH in God. And so, God willing, we will move forward to further understanding. ... It is impossible to bring back to repentance those who were once enlightened – those who have experienced the good things of heaven and shared in the Holy Spirit, who have tasted the goodness of the Word of God and the power of the age to come – and who then turn away from God, by rejecting the Son of God. ... Dear friends, even though we are talking this way, we really do NOT believe it applies to you. We are confident that you are meant for the better things that come with salvation. God is not unjust. Our great desire is: you will KEEP ON loving others, making certain your HOPE comes true. Then you will NOT BECOME spiritually dull and INDIFFERENT. Follow the example of those who are going to inherit God's promises because of their FAITH [grateful, loyal, obedient trust] and ENDURANCE.

Hebrews 9:14-15, 22, 27-28 For by the power of the eternal Spirit, Christ offered Himself to God as a PERFECT sacrifice for our sins. That is why Jesus is the One who MEDIATES a new covenant between God and people, so that all who are called can receive the eternal inheritance God has promised them. ... WITHOUT the shedding of blood, there is NO forgiveness. Just as each person is destined to DIE ONCE and after that COMES Judgment, so also Christ died ONCE for all time as a sacrifice to take away the sins of MANY people.

Hebrews 10:22-27, 32-36 Let us go right into the PRESENCE of God with sincere hearts fully TRUSTING Him. For our guilty consciences have been cleaned with Christ's blood. ... Let us hold tightly without wavering to the HOPE we affirm, for God can be TRUSTED to keep His promise. Let us think of ways to motivate one another to ACTS of love and good works. And let us NOT neglect our meeting together, as some people do, but ENCOURAGE one another, especially now that the day of His return is drawing near. ... Dear friends, IF we DELIBERATELY CONTINUE sinning after we have received knowledge of the Truth, there is NO LONGER any sacrifice that will COVER these sins. There is ONLY the terrible expectation of God's Judgment and the raging fire that will consume His enemies. ... Think back on those early days when you first learned about Christ. Remember how you remained faithful even though it meant terrible suffering. Sometimes you were EXPOSED to public ridicule and were beaten, and sometimes you HELPED others who were suffering the same things. You suffered along with those who were thrown into jail, and when all you owned was taken from you, you accepted it with JOY. You knew there were BETTER things WAITING for you that will LAST FOREVER. So do not throw away this confident TRUST in the Lord. Remember the great reward it brings you! Patient ENDURANCE is what you need now, so that you will CONTINUE to DO God's will. Then you will receive all that He has promised.

Hebrews 11:6 It is IMPOSSIBLE to please God WITHOUT faith [grateful, loyal, obedient trust in Jesus who died to pay our sin penalty and rose from the dead to be our Lord]. Anyone who wants to come to Him must believe that God exists and that He rewards those who sincerely SEEK Him.

Hebrews 12:1-3, 14-15, 23-25 ERV   We have many faithful people as examples. Run the race and NEVER quit. REMOVE the sin that easily makes us fall. LOOK to Jesus. He PATIENTLY ENDURED the angry insults of sinful people. He accepted the shame of the cross because of the JOY waiting for Him. Now He is sitting at the right side of God's throne. THINK about Jesus so that you will NOT get discouraged and stop trying. … Work at living in PEACE with everyone, and work at living a HOLY life, for those who are NOT holy will NOT see the Lord. … Watch out that NO poisonous root of BITTERNESS grows up to trouble you, CORRUPTING many. … COME to God, who is the judge over all things. You have come to Jesus, the One who BROUGHT the new agreement between God and people. Be careful that you do NOT refuse to listen when God speaks. If the people of Israel did NOT escape WHEN they refused to listen to Moses, the earthly messenger, we will certainly NOT escape IF we REFUSE to listen when God speaks to us from heaven!

Hebrews 13:1-6, 8-9, 15-16   Keep on LOVING each other AS brothers and sisters. Do NOT forget to show hospitality to strangers. Do NOT forget those who are in prison. Remember them as though you are in prison with them. Do NOT forget those who are suffering. Remember them as though you are suffering with them. Give HONOR to marriage, and REMAIN faithful to one another in marriage. God will surely JUDGE people who are IMMORAL. Do NOT love money; be SATISFIED with what you have. For God has said, "I will NEVER fail you. I will NEVER abandon you." [Deuteronomy 31:6, 8] Say with confidence, "The Lord is my HELPER, so I will have NO fear. What can MERE people do to me?" [Psalm 118:6] ... Jesus Christ is the SAME yesterday, today, and forever. … Do NOT be attracted by STRANGE, new IDEAS. Your strength comes from God's grace, NOT from rules, which do NOT help. ... Therefore, let us OFFER through Jesus a CONTINUAL sacrifice of PRAISE to God, proclaiming our ALLEGIANCE to His Name. Do not forget to DO good and to SHARE with those in need. These are the sacrifices that PLEASE God.

James 1:2-5, 13-14, 19-22, 26-27
When troubles come your way, consider it an OPPORTUNITY for great JOY. When your faith is TESTED, your ENDURANCE has a chance to GROW. Let it grow, when your endurance is fully developed, you will be perfect, needing nothing.

IF you NEED wisdom, ASK our generous God, and He will give it to you. When you are being tempted, do NOT say, "God is tempting me." God NEVER tempts anyone. TEMPTATION comes FROM our own DESIRES, which entice us and drag us away. ... You must be QUICK to listen, SLOW to speak, and SLOW to get angry. Human anger does NOT produce the righteousness God desires. So get RID of all the filth and evil in your lives, and humbly ACCEPT the WORD God has planted in your hearts, for it has the POWER to save your souls. But do NOT just LISTEN to God's Word. You must DO what it says. Otherwise, you are ONLY FOOLING yourselves. ... IF you CLAIM to be religious but do NOT CONTROL your tongue, you are fooling yourself, and your religion is WORTHLESS. Pure and genuine religion in the sight of God the Father means CARING for orphans and widows in their distress and REFUSING to let the world CORRUPT you.

James 2:17, 26 Unless faith PRODUCES good DEEDS, it is dead and useless. Just as the body is dead without breath, so faith is DEAD WITHOUT good works.

James 3:10, 13, 15-17, 18 ERV Blessing and cursing come out of the SAME mouth ... this is NOT right! ... IF you are wise and understand God's ways, PROVE it by living an honorable life, doing good works with humility. ... JEALOUSY and SELFISH ambition are NOT God's kind of wisdom. Such things ARE earthly and demonic. ... There you will FIND disorder and EVIL of every kind. ... The WISDOM from God is first PURE, then PEACEFUL, GENTLE, HELPING others who have trouble and DOING good for others. It shows NO favoritism and is ALWAYS fair and honest. People working for PEACE in a PEACEFUL way get the blessings that come from right living.

James 4:4, 6-8, 17 Do you not REALIZE that FRIENDSHIP with the world makes you an ENEMY of God? ... God OPPOSES the proud but FAVORS the humble. So HUMBLE [teachable, trusting God, not pride in self] yourselves before God. RESIST the devil, and he will FLEE from you. Come CLOSE to God, and God will come CLOSE to you. You sinners, your LOYALTY is DIVIDED between God and the world. It is sin to KNOW what you ought to do and NOT do it.

James 5:1-6, 16, 20 You rich people: WEEP and groan in anguish because of all the terrible troubles ahead. The very wealth you were counting on will eat away your flesh like fire. This TREASURE you have accumulated will stand as EVIDENCE against you on the Day of Judgment. Listen! Hear the cries of those who you have cheated of their pay. You have spent your life in luxury. You have condemned and killed innocent people, who do not resist you. ... CONFESS your sins to each other and PRAY for each other SO that you may be healed. The earnest PRAYER of a righteous [being right, based on God's standard, includes thoughts, words and actions] person has great POWER and produces wonderful RESULTS. ... Whoever brings a sinner back will save that person from death.

1 Peter 1:1-7, 15, 24-25 To God's CHOSEN people who are STRANGERS in this world. His Spirit has made you HOLY, by the blood of Jesus Christ. May God give you more and more grace and peace. ALL PRAISE to God, the Father of our Lord Jesus Christ. It is by His great MERCY that we have been born again, because God raised Jesus Christ from the dead. Now we live with GREAT expectation, and we have a PRICELESS inheritance – that is kept in heaven for you, pure and undefiled, beyond the reach of change and decay. And through your faith, God is PROTECTING you by His POWER until you receive this salvation, which is ready to be revealed on the last day for all to see. So be truly GLAD. There is wonderful JOY ahead, even though you have to ENDURE many trials for a little while. These trials will SHOW that your faith is GENUINE. So when your faith REMAINS STRONG through many trials, it will bring you much praise and glory and honor on the day when Jesus Christ is revealed to the whole world. ... Now you must be HOLY in everything you DO, just as God who chose you is HOLY. ... People are like grass; their beauty is like a flower. The grass withers and the flower fades. But the WORD of the Lord REMAINS FOREVER.

1 Peter 2:1-3, 9 KJV Get RID of all evil behavior. Be DONE with all deceit, hypocrisy, jealousy, and unkind speech. Like babies, CRAVE pure spiritual milk of God's WORD so that you will grow into a full experience of salvation. ... You are God's very own possession. As a result, you can SHOW others the GOODNESS of God, for He called you OUT of the darkness INTO His Light.

1 Peter 3:8 ERV, 9, 12, 14-16 Live together in PEACE. Try to UNDERSTAND each other. LOVE each other as brothers and sisters. Be KIND and HUMBLE [gentle, teachable, trusting God, not pride in self]. Do NOT repay evil for evil. ... Instead, pay them back with a BLESSING. ... The Lord WATCHES over those who DO right, and He is OPEN to their PRAYERS. But the Lord turns against those who do evil. ... IF you suffer for doing what is right, God will reward you for it.

Do NOT worry OR be afraid of threats. Worship Jesus as LORD of your life. IF someone asks about your HOPE in Jesus, ... explain in a GENTLE and RESPECTFUL way.

1 Peter 4:1, 3-4, 10, 12, 14 Since Christ suffered physical pain, you must arm yourselves with the same attitude He had, and be READY to SUFFER, too. For if you have suffered physically for Christ, you are finished with sin. You had ENOUGH in the past of the evil things that godless people enjoy — their immorality, lust, their feasting and drunkenness and wild parties, and their terrible worship of idols. Your former friends are surprised when you NO longer plunge into the destructive things they do. So they slander you. ... God has given you a gift from His variety of spiritual gifts. Use them to SERVE one another. Dear friends, do NOT be surprised at the fiery trials you are going through, AS IF something strange were happening to you. So be FULL of JOY when you are insulted for being a FOLLOWER of Jesus, for THEN the glorious Spirit of God rests upon you.

1 Peter 5:1-3, 5, 7-9 You who are ELDERS in the churches. I appeal to you: Care for the flock that God has entrusted to you. Watch over it willingly, not grudgingly, not for what you will get out of it, but be eager to serve God. Do not lord it over the people assigned to your care, but LEAD them BY your own good EXAMPLE. You younger men must accept the authority of the elders. All of you, serve each other in humility, for God OPPOSES the proud but FAVORS the humble [gentle, teachable, trusting God, not pride in self]. ... Give all your WORRIES and DOUBTS to God, for He CARES about you. Stay alert! Watch out for your great ENEMY, the devil. He prowls around like a roaring lion, looking for someone to devour. STAND FIRM [lean neither left or right] AGAINST him, and be strong in your faith. Remember that your Christian brothers and sisters all over the world are going through the SAME kind of suffering you are.

2 Peter 1:2-3, 5-10, 16-21
May God give you more PEACE as you GROW in your knowledge of God and Jesus our LORD. God has given us everything we need for living a godly [committed to obeying God] life. We receive this by coming to KNOW Him. Make every effort to RESPOND to God's promises. SUPPLEMENT your faith WITH moral excellence, knowledge of our Lord Jesus WITH self-control, patient endurance WITH godliness [committed to obeying God], AND love for everyone. The more you GROW like this, the more PRODUCTIVE and

USEFUL you will be in our Lord Jesus. BUT those who fail to develop in this way are shortsighted or BLIND. Work hard to PROVE that you really are AMONG those God has called and chosen. DO these things, and you will NEVER fall away. ... We were NOT making up clever stories when we told you about the powerful coming of our Lord Jesus Christ. We SAW His majestic splendor with our own eyes when He received honor and glory from God the Father. The Voice from the majestic glory of God said to Jesus, "This is My dearly loved Son, who brings Me great JOY." We ourselves HEARD that Voice from heaven when we were with Jesus on the holy mountain. Because of that experience, we have even greater CONFIDENCE in the message proclaimed by the prophets. You must pay close ATTENTION to what they WROTE, for their words are like a lamp shining in a dark place — until the Day dawns, and Jesus the Morning Star shines in your hearts. REALIZE that NO prophecy in Scripture ever came from the prophet's own understanding, OR from human initiative. The prophets were moved by the Holy Spirit, and they SPOKE from God.

2 Peter 2:1, 9-10 There were FALSE prophets in Israel, just as there will be FALSE teachers among you. They will cleverly teach DESTRUCTIVE heresies and even DENY the Master. They bring destruction on themselves. ... The Lord can RESCUE godly [committed to obeying God] people from their trials, even WHILE keeping the wicked under punishment. He is ESPECIALLY hard on those who FOLLOW their own TWISTED sexual desire, and who DESPISE authority. These people are proud and arrogant, even scoffing at supernatural beings.

2 Peter 3:8, 12-14, 16 Remember: a day is as a thousand years to the Lord, and a thousand years is as a day. ... Desire the coming Day of God, when He will destroy the heavens with fire, and the earth will melt away in the flames. But we are looking forward to the NEW heavens and NEW earth He has promised, a world filled with God's righteousness. While you are WAITING for these things to happen, make every effort to be found living PEACEFUL lives that are blameless in His sight. ... Some of Paul's comments are hard to understand, and those who are ignorant and unstable have TWISTED Paul's letters to mean something quite DIFFERENT, just as they do with other parts of Scripture. And this will RESULT in their DESTRUCTION.

1 John 1:1, 5-10 NET
We proclaim the One who existed from the beginning, who we have HEARD and SEEN. We saw Him with our eyes and TOUCHED Him with our hands. He is the WORD of LIFE. ...

God is Light, and there is NO darkness in Him. So we are LYING IF we say we have fellowship with God BUT live in spiritual darkness; we are NOT practicing the TRUTH. IF we are living in the Light, as God is the Light, THEN we have FELLOWSHIP with each other. ... IF we SAY we do NOT sin [if we say OUR favorite sin is NOT really a sin], we are DECEIVING ourselves and NOT living in the TRUTH. IF we CONFESS our sins to Him, He is faithful and just to FORGIVE us our sins and to cleanse us from all wickedness. IF we CLAIM we have NOT sinned [if we claim OUR favorite sin is NOT really a sin], we are CALLING God a LIAR and showing that He has NO place in our hearts.

1 John 2:4-6, 9-10, 15-17 MSG IF someone CLAIMS, "I know God," but does NOT obey God's commandments, that person is a LIAR and is NOT living in the TRUTH. Those who OBEY God's Word SHOW they completely LOVE Him. Those who say they live in God should LIVE their lives AS Jesus did. ... IF anyone claims, "I am living in the Light," BUT hates a Christian brother or sister, that person is STILL living in darkness. Anyone who loves people, does NOT CAUSE others to STUMBLE. ... Do NOT love the world's ways. Do NOT love the world's goods. Love of the world SQUEEZES OUT love for the Father. Practically EVERYTHING in the world – wanting your own way, wanting everything for yourself, wanting to appear important – has NOTHING to do with the Father. It just ISOLATES you from Him. The world and all its wanting is on the WAY OUT – but WHOEVER DOES what God wants is SET FOR eternity.

1 John 3:2, 7-10, 16-18, 20, 23-24 Dear friends, we are already God's children, but He has not yet shown us what we will be like when Christ appears. But we do know that we will be LIKE Him, for we will SEE Him AS He really IS. ... Do NOT let anyone DECEIVE you: When people DO what is RIGHT, it shows that they are righteous, even as Christ is righteous. But WHEN people KEEP ON sinning, it shows that they BELONG TO the devil. BUT the Son of God came to DESTROY the works of the devil. Those who have been born into God's family do NOT make a PATTERN of [deliberate, continual] sinning, because God's life is in them. So they CANNOT CONTINUE sinning, BECAUSE they are children of God. We can tell WHO are children of God and WHO are children of the devil. Anyone who does NOT live righteously and does NOT love other believers does NOT belong to God. ... We know what REAL LOVE is because Jesus gave up His life for us. So we also ought to give up our lives for our brothers and sisters. IF someone has enough money to live well and SEES a brother or sister in need BUT shows NO compassion – HOW can God's love be in that person? Dear children, let's NOT merely SAY that we LOVE each other; let us SHOW the truth BY our ACTIONS. ... Even IF we FEEL guilty, God is GREATER THAN our FEELINGS, and He knows everything. ... This is God's commandment: We must BELIEVE in the Name of His Son, Jesus Christ, and LOVE one ANOTHER, just as He commanded us. Those who OBEY God's commandments REMAIN in FELLOWSHIP with Him, and He with them.

1 John 4:1, 4, 6, 9, 18-21 Do NOT believe everyone who CLAIMS to speak by the Holy Spirit. You must TEST them to see IF the spirit they have COMES from God. For there are many FALSE prophets. ... You belong to God. The Holy Spirit who LIVES in you is GREATER than the spirit who lives in the world. ... We belong to God, and those who know God listen to us. IF they do NOT belong to God, they do NOT listen to us. That is HOW we know IF someone has the Spirit of TRUTH or the spirit of deception. ... This is how God showed His love among us: He sent His ONE and ONLY Son into the world that we might live THROUGH Him [Jesus]. ... Such love has NO fear, because perfect love EXPELS all fear. We love each other BECAUSE He loved us FIRST. IF someone says, "I love God," BUT hates a Christian brother or sister, that person is a LIAR. IF we do NOT love people we can see, HOW can we love God, whom we cannot see? Those who love God must ALSO love their Christian brothers and sisters.

1 John 5:10-12, 14-16, 21 All who BELIEVE in the Son of God KNOW in their hearts that this is TRUE. Those who do NOT believe are CALLING God a LIAR because they do not believe what God has testified about His Son. God has testified: Whoever HAS the Son HAS life; whoever does NOT have God's Son does NOT have life. ... We are confident that He HEARS us whenever we ASK for anything that PLEASES Him. We know that He will give us what we ask for. IF you see a Christian sinning in a way that does not lead to death, you should PRAY, and God will give that person life. ... KEEP away FROM anything that MIGHT TAKE God's place in your hearts.

2 John 1:6, 8-9
LOVE means DOING what God commands us, to LOVE one ANOTHER. ... Do NOT lose what we have worked so hard to achieve. Be diligent to receive your full reward. Anyone who WANDERS away FROM this teaching has NO RELATIONSHIP with

God. Anyone who REMAINS in the teaching of Christ has a RELATIONSHIP with both the Father and the Son.

3 John 1:4, 11
I can have no greater JOY than to hear that my CHILDREN are FOLLOWING the TRUTH. ... Follow ONLY what is good. Those who DO good PROVE they are God's children, and those who DO evil PROVE they do NOT know God.

Jude 4, 7-8, 10-12, 16, 18-19, 20-25
Some UNGODLY people have wormed their way into your churches, SAYING that God's marvelous grace ALLOWS us to live IMMORAL lives. Their DOOM was predicted long ago, for they have DENIED our only MASTER and LORD, Jesus Christ. ... Do NOT forget Sodom and Gomorrah which were FILLED with immorality and sexual perversion. Those cities were DESTROYED by fire and serve as a WARNING of the eternal fire of God's Judgment. In the same way, these people – who CLAIM authority FROM their dreams – live IMMORAL lives, DEFY authority, and scoff at supernatural beings. ... These people scoff at things they do NOT understand. Like unthinking animals, they do whatever their instincts tell them, and so they BRING about their own DESTRUCTION. What sorrow awaits them! These people eat with you in your fellowship meals, they are like DANGEROUS reefs that can shipwreck you. ... They CARE only FOR themselves. ... These people are GRUMBLERS and COMPLAINERS, living only to satisfy their desires. They brag loudly about themselves, and they FLATTER others to get what they want. ... In the last days there would be scoffers whose purpose in life is to SATISFY their ungodly desires. These people are creating DIVISIONS among you. They follow their natural instincts because they do NOT have God's Spirit in them. ... BUILD each other up in your HOLY faith, PRAY in the power of the Holy Spirit, and await the mercy of our Lord Jesus Christ, who will bring you eternal life. Show MERCY to those whose faith is wavering. RESCUE others by snatching them from the flames of judgment. Show MERCY to others, but DO so WITH great caution, HATING the sins that CONTAMINATE their lives. All glory to God, who is able to KEEP you FROM falling away and will bring you with great JOY into His glorious Presence. All glory to Him WHO ALONE is God, our Savior through Jesus our Lord. All glory, majesty, power, and authority are His before all time, in the present, and beyond all time! Amen.

Revelation 1:3, 17-18 God blesses all who LISTEN to this message and OBEY what it says, for the time is near. ... When I saw Jesus, I fell at His feet as if I were dead. But He laid His right hand on me and said, "Do not be afraid! I AM the First and the Last. I AM the living one. I died, but look – I AM alive forever and ever! I hold the KEYS of death and the grave."

Revelation 2:2-7 [Jesus to Church of Ephesus] "I know all the things you do. I have seen your hard work and your patient endurance. I know you do NOT tolerate evil people. You have examined the CLAIMS of those who say they are apostles but are NOT. You have discovered they are LIARS. You have patiently suffered for Me WITHOUT quitting. But I have this complaint against you. You do NOT love Me or each other as you did at first! TURN BACK to Me and DO the works you did at first. IF you do NOT repent, I will come and REMOVE your lampstand. But this is in your favor: You HATE the evil deeds of the Nicolaitans, just as I do. Anyone with ears to hear must LISTEN to the Spirit and UNDERSTAND what He is saying to the churches. To everyone who is VICTORIOUS I will give fruit from the Tree of Life in the paradise of God."

Revelation 2:9-11 [Jesus to Church of Smyrna] "I know about your suffering and your poverty – but you are rich! I know the blasphemy of those opposing you. Their synagogue belongs to Satan. Do NOT be afraid of what you are about to SUFFER. The devil will throw some of you into prison to test you. You will suffer for 10 days. But IF you REMAIN faithful even when facing death, I will GIVE you the Crown of Life. Whoever is VICTORIOUS will NOT be harmed by the second death."

Revelation 2:13-16 [Jesus to Church of Pergamum] "I know that you live in the city where Satan has his throne, yet you have remained LOYAL to Me. You REFUSED to deny Me even when Antipas, my faithful witness, was martyred. BUT I have a few complaints against you. You TOLERATE some among you whose TEACHING is like that of Balaam, who taught them to sin by committing SEXUAL sin. You also TOLERATE some Nicolaitans [Nicolaitans compromised their faith to enjoy the sinful pleasures of society and perhaps to burn incense to the emperor. They compromised to peacefully coexist with Roman society. But such compromise diluted their faith; thus, Jesus said it could not be tolerated.] who follow the SAME teaching. REPENT of your sin, or I will come and fight against them with the Sword of My Mouth [God's Judgment]."

Revelation 2:19-29   [Jesus to Church of Thyatira]   "I have seen your love, your faith, your service, and your patient endurance. I can see your CONSTANT IMPROVEMENT. BUT I have this complaint against you. You are PERMITTING that woman – that Jezebel who calls herself a prophet – to TEACH them to commit SEXUAL sin. … I gave her time to REPENT, but she does NOT want to TURN away FROM her IMMORALITY. Therefore, I will throw her on a bed of suffering, and those who commit adultery WITH her will SUFFER greatly UNLESS they REPENT and TURN away FROM her evil deeds. … Then all the churches will know that I AM the One who SEARCHES the THOUGHTS and INTENTIONS of every person. I will GIVE to EACH of you WHATEVER you DESERVE. But I also have a message for the rest of you in Thyatira who have NOT followed this FALSE teaching ("deeper truths" as they call them – depths of Satan, actually). I will ask nothing more of you except that you HOLD TIGHTLY to what you have until I come. To all who are VICTORIOUS, who OBEY Me to the VERY END, they will have the same authority I received from My Father!"

Revelation 3:1-6   [Jesus to Church of Sardis]   "I know you have a reputation for being ALIVE – but you are DEAD. Wake up! Strengthen what little remains. Your ACTIONS do NOT meet the requirements of God. Go back to what you heard and believed at first. REPENT and TURN to Me again. If you do not wake up, I will come to you suddenly as a thief. Yet there are some who have NOT soiled their clothes with evil. They will WALK with Me in white, for they are WORTHY. All who are VICTORIOUS, I will never erase their names from the Book of Life."

Revelation 3:8-13   [Jesus to Church of Philadelphia]   "I have opened a door for you that no one can close. You have little strength, yet you OBEYED My WORD and did NOT deny Me. I will force those who belong to Satan's synagogue – those LIARS who say they are Jews but are not – to come and bow down at your feet. They will acknowledge that you are the ones I love. Because you have OBEYED My command to PERSEVERE, I will PROTECT you from the great time of testing that will come upon the whole world to test those who belong to this world. I am coming soon. HOLD ON to what you have, so that NO one will TAKE away your crown. All who are VICTORIOUS, they will be citizens in the city of My God."

Revelation 3:15-22   [Jesus to Church of Laodicea]   "I know all the things you do, that you are like LUKEWARM water, neither hot nor cold, I will SPIT you OUT of My mouth!   You say, 'I am rich. I have everything I want. I do not need a thing!' You do NOT realize that you are wretched and miserable and poor and blind and naked. I correct and discipline everyone I love.   So be diligent and TURN FROM your INDIFFERENCE. ... I stand at the door and knock. IF you HEAR My voice and OPEN the door, I will COME in, and we will SHARE a meal TOGETHER as friends."

Revelation 4:1-3, 5-8, 11   I saw a door standing open in heaven, and the Voice [Jesus] said, "Come up here." I saw One sitting on a throne in heaven, who was brilliant as gemstones. The glow of an emerald circled His throne like a RAINBOW.   From the throne came lightning and thunder. In front of the throne is the Spirit of God. In front of the throne was a shiny sea of glass, sparkling like crystal. Around the throne were 4 living beings, each covered with eyes, front and back. ... Each of these living beings had 6 wings, and their wings were covered all over with eyes, inside and out. They keep on saying, "HOLY, HOLY, HOLY is the Lord God, the Almighty – the One who ALWAYS was, who is, and who is still to come. You are WORTHY, O Lord our God, to RECEIVE glory and honor and power. For You CREATED all things, and they exist because You created what you pleased."

Revelation 5:1-3, 6-13   I saw a scroll in the right hand of the One who was sitting on the throne. "WHO is WORTHY to break the seals on this scroll and open it?" No one in heaven or on earth was able to open the scroll. Then I saw a Lamb that looked as if it had been slaughtered, but it was now standing between the throne and the 4 living beings. He stepped forward and took the scroll from the One sitting on the throne. The 4 living beings fell down before the Lamb. Each one had a harp, and they held gold bowls filled with incense, which are the prayers of God's people. They sang a new song: "You are WORTHY to take the scroll and open it. For You were slaughtered, and Your blood has ransomed people for God from every tribe, language, and nation. You have caused them to become a Kingdom of priests for our God. And they will reign on the earth." I heard the voices of millions of angels around the throne singing in a mighty chorus: "WORTHY is the Lamb who was slaughtered — to RECEIVE power and wisdom and strength and honor and glory and blessing." Then I heard every creature in heaven and on earth and in the sea sing: "Blessing and honor and glory and power belong to the One sitting on the throne and to the Lamb forever and ever."

Revelation 9:16-21 Their army was 200 million mounted troops. And in my vision, I saw the riders wore armor that was fiery red and dark blue and yellow. The horses had heads like lions, and fire and smoke and burning sulfur billowed from their mouths. One-third of all the people on earth were killed by these 3 plagues – by the fire and smoke and burning sulfur that came from the mouths of the horses. But the people who did not die in these plagues STILL REFUSED to REPENT of their evil deeds and TURN to God. They CONTINUED to WORSHIP demons and idols made of gold, silver, bronze, stone, and wood – idols that can neither see nor hear nor walk! And they did NOT REPENT of their murders OR their witchcraft OR their sexual immorality OR their thefts.

Revelation 13:5, 7-8, 16-18 The beast was allowed to speak great blasphemies against God. He was given authority to do whatever he wanted for 42 months. The beast was allowed to wage war against God's holy people and to conquer them. ... And all the people who belong to this world worshiped the beast. They are the ones whose NAMES were NOT written in the Lamb's Book of Life before the world was made. ... The beast required everyone – small and great, rich and poor, free and slave – to be given a MARK on the right hand or on the forehead. No one could buy or sell anything without that MARK, which was either the name of the beast or the number representing his name. ... The meaning of the number of the beast is the number of humanity. His number is 666.

Revelation 14:7 The angel shouted, "Fear [respect God's power and authority, because we desire to please Him] God. GIVE glory [honor, praise] to God. For ... He will sit as JUDGE. WORSHIP Him who made the heavens and the earth."

Revelation 17:8 The people who belong to this world, whose NAMES were NOT written in the Book of Life ...

Revelation 19:7-9, 16 Let us be GLAD and be JOYFUL, and give HONOR to Jesus. For the time has come for the wedding feast of the Lamb, and His bride has prepared herself. She has been given the finest of pure white linen to wear. For the fine linen represents the GOOD deeds of God's holy people. The angel said, "Blessed are those who are INVITED to the wedding feast of the Lamb. ... These are TRUE WORDS that come from God." ... On Jesus' robe at His thigh is written: KING of all kings and LORD of all lords.

Revelation 20:10, 15   The devil, who had DECEIVED them, was THROWN into the fiery lake of burning sulfur, joining the beast and the false prophet. There they will be tormented day and night forever and ever. ... Anyone whose NAME was NOT FOUND recorded in the Book of Life was THROWN into the lake of fire.

Revelation 21:1, 3-8, 27   Then I saw a NEW heaven and a NEW earth. ... A shout from the Throne said, "God will live WITH His people. God will WIPE every tear from their eyes. There will be NO more death, sorrow, crying, or pain." The One sitting on the Throne said, "I will make everything NEW. ... It is finished! I AM the Beginning and the End. To all who are VICTORIOUS, I will BE their God, and they will be My children. BUT cowards, unbelievers, the corrupt, murderers, the immoral, those who practice witchcraft, idol worshipers, and all liars – their FATE is in the fiery lake of burning sulfur. This is the SECOND death." ... NOTHING evil will be allowed to enter, NOR anyone who practices shameful idolatry and dishonesty – but ONLY those whose NAMES are written IN the Lamb's Book of Life.

Revelation 22:8-9, 12-15, 17-20 ERV   I, John, fell down to worship at the feet of the angel. He said, "No, do not worship me. I am a servant of God, just like you and all who OBEY what is WRITTEN in this BOOK. Worship ONLY God!" ... Jesus said, "Look, I AM coming SOON, bringing My reward with Me to REPAY all people ACCORDING to their DEEDS. I AM the First and the Last, the Beginning and the End." Blessed are those who wash their robes. They will be PERMITTED to ENTER through the gates of the city and eat the fruit from the Tree of Life.   OUTSIDE the city are the dogs – the sorcerers, the sexually immoral, the murderers, the idol worshipers, and all who LOVE to LIVE a LIE. ... The Spirit and the bride say, "COME." ... IF anyone ADDS anything to what is written here, God will ADD to that person the plagues described in this book. And IF anyone REMOVES any of the words from this book of prophecy, God will REMOVE that person's share in the Tree of Life and in the holy city that are described in this book. Jesus, the One who says that all this is TRUE, now says, "Yes, I AM coming SOON." Come, LORD Jesus!

===============

OLD TESTAMENT
Favorite Bible Verses

Genesis 1:1-2, 26-27   In the beginning God CREATED the heavens and the earth. And the Spirit of God was hovering over the surface of the waters. ... Then God said, "Let Us make human beings in Our Image." So God created human beings, MALE and FEMALE, in His own Image.

Genesis 2:18, 24   The LORD God said, "It is NOT good for the man to be ALONE. I will make a HELPER who is just RIGHT for him." ... This explains why a man leaves his father and mother and is JOINED to his wife, and the two are UNITED into one.

Genesis 3:1, 4-7, 14-15, 17, 22   The serpent [Satan] was the shrewdest of all the wild animals the Lord God had made. One day he asked the woman, "DID God REALLY SAY you must not eat the fruit from any of the trees in the garden?" [Satan distorts God's Word by misquoting what God says to get us to question the clear command of God] ... "You will NOT die!" the serpent replied [Satan outright lies to deceive us to question God's intentions] to the woman. "God knows that your eyes will be opened as soon as you eat it, and you WILL BE LIKE God, [Satan appeals to our pride to be in control, not depend on God] knowing both good and evil." The woman was convinced. She saw that the tree was beautiful and she wanted the wisdom it would give her. So she took some of the fruit and ate it. Then she gave some to her husband, who was with her, and he ate it, too. At that moment their eyes were opened, and they suddenly FELT SHAME at their nakedness. So they sewed fig leaves together to cover themselves. ... Then the LORD God said to the serpent [Satan], "Because you have done this, you are cursed. And I will cause hostility between you and the woman, and between your offspring and her offspring. He will strike your head, and you will strike His heel." And to the man God said, "Since you LISTENED to your wife and ate from the tree whose fruit I commanded you not to eat, the ground is cursed BECAUSE of you. All your life you will struggle to scratch a living from it." ... The LORD God said, "Look, the human beings have become like

Us, knowing good and evil. What if they reach out and take fruit from the Tree of Life and eat it? Then they will live forever!"

Genesis 4:6-16 "WHY are you so angry?" the LORD asked Cain. "WHY do you look so dejected? You will be ACCEPTED IF you DO what is RIGHT. But IF you REFUSE to do what is right, then watch out! SIN is … eager to CONTROL you. But you must SUBDUE it and BE its master." One day Cain said to his brother, Abel, "Let's go out into the fields." While they were in the field, Cain killed Abel. Afterward the LORD asked Cain, "Where is your brother, Abel?" Cain responded, "I don't know. Am I my brother's guardian?" But the LORD said, "What have you done? Your brother's blood cries out to Me from the ground! Now you are banished from the ground. … No longer will the ground yield good crops for you, no matter how hard you work! From now on you will be a homeless wanderer on the earth." Cain replied to the LORD, "My punishment is too great for me to bear! … Anyone who finds me will kill me!" The LORD replied, "No, for I will give a sevenfold punishment to anyone who kills you." Then the LORD put a mark on Cain to warn anyone who might try to kill him. Cain left the LORD's presence and settled in the land of Nod, east of Eden.

Genesis 6:11-13 Now God saw that the earth had become CORRUPT and was filled with violence. God observed all this corruption in the world, for everyone on earth was corrupt. So God said to Noah, "I have decided to DESTROY all living creatures, for they have filled the earth with VIOLENCE!"

Genesis 9:2-4, 13, 15 God said to Noah, "All animals, all birds, and all fish will look on you with fear. I have given them to you for FOOD, just as I have given you grain and vegetables. But never eat meat that still has BLOOD in it. … I have placed My RAINBOW in the clouds, as the sign of My promise to never again use a flood to destroy all life on earth."

Genesis 11:1, 4-7, 9 At one time all the people of the world spoke the SAME language. … They said, "Come, let's build a great city with a tower that reaches into the sky. This will keep us from being scattered all over the world." But the LORD came to look at the tower the people were building. The LORD said, "The people are united, speaking the same language. Nothing will be impossible for them! Let's confuse the people with different languages. Then they will not understand each other." That is why the city was called Babel, because that is where the LORD confused the people with DIFFERENT languages. In this way He scattered them all over the world.

Genesis 16:13 Thereafter, Hagar used another Name to refer to the LORD, who had spoken to her. She said, "You are the God who SEES me."

Genesis 18:14 The LORD said to Abraham, "Is anything too hard for the LORD? I will return about this time next year, and Sarah will have a son."

Genesis 20:6 In the dream God responded, "Yes, I know you are innocent. That is why I kept you from sinning against Me, and why I did not let you touch her."

Genesis 39:8-10 Joseph REFUSED and told her, "Look, my master trusts me with everything in his entire household. He has held back nothing from me except you, his wife. HOW could I do such a wicked thing? It would be a great SIN AGAINST God." She kept putting pressure on Joseph day after day, but he refused to sleep with her, and he kept out of her way as much as possible.

Genesis 50:20 Joseph replied, "You INTENDED to harm me, but God INTENDED it all for good. He brought me to this position so I could save the lives of many people."

Exodus 1:15-21
Pharaoh, the king of Egypt, gave this order to the Hebrew midwives, Shiphrah and Puah: "When you help the Hebrew women as they give birth, watch as they deliver. If the baby is a boy, kill him; if it is a girl, let her live." But BECAUSE the midwives feared God, they REFUSED to obey the king's orders. They ALLOWED the boys to live. So the king of Egypt demanded. "Why have you allowed the boys to live?" The midwives replied, "The Hebrew women are not like the Egyptian women. They have their babies so quickly that we cannot get there in time." So God was good to the midwives, and the Israelites continued to multiply, growing more and more powerful. And because the midwives feared God, He gave them families of their own.

Exodus 3:10-15 The LORD said, "Now go, for I am sending you to Pharaoh. You must lead My people Israel out of Egypt." But Moses protested, "Who am I to appear before Pharaoh? Who am I to lead the people of Israel out of Egypt?" God answered, "I will be WITH you." Moses protested, "If I go to the people of Israel and tell them, 'The God of your ancestors has sent me to you,' they will ask me, 'What is His Name?' Then what should I tell them?" God replied to Moses, "I AM WHO I AM. Say this to the people: I AM has sent me to you." God also said to

Moses, "Say this to the people of Israel: Yahweh, the God of your ancestors – the God of Abraham, the God of Isaac, and the God of Jacob – has sent me to you. This is My eternal Name, My Name to remember for all generations."

Exodus 6:6-7   The LORD said to Moses, "I AM the Lord. I will free you from your oppression and will rescue you from your slavery in Egypt. I will redeem you with a powerful arm and great acts of judgment. I will claim you as My own people, and I will be your God."

Exodus 15:13   With Your unfailing love You LEAD us who You have redeemed, to Your holy home.

Exodus 16:8   Moses added, "The LORD will give you meat to eat in the evening and bread to satisfy you in the morning, for He has heard all your COMPLAINTS against the LORD, not against us."

Exodus 20:1-17   [10 Commandments]   God gave the people all these instructions: "I AM the LORD your GOD, who rescued you from the land of Egypt, the place of your slavery.   [1]   You must NOT have any other god BUT Me.   [2]   You must NOT make for yourself an idol of any kind OR an image of anything in the heavens or on the earth or in the sea. You must NOT bow down to them or worship them, for I, the LORD your God, am a jealous God who will NOT tolerate your affection for any other gods. I lay the sins of the parents upon their children; the entire family is affected – even children in the third and fourth generations of those who reject Me. But I lavish unfailing love for a thousand generations on those who love Me and obey My commands.   [3]   You must NOT misuse the Name of the LORD your God. The LORD will not let you go unpunished if you misuse His Name.   [4]   Remember to observe the Sabbath day by keeping it holy. You have 6 days each week for your ordinary work, but the seventh day is a Sabbath day of REST dedicated to the LORD your God.   [5]   HONOR your father and mother. Then you will live a long, full life. ...   [6]   You must NOT murder.   [7]   You must NOT commit adultery.   [8]   You must NOT steal.   [9]   You must NOT testify falsely against your neighbor.   [10]   You must NOT covet your neighbor's house. You must NOT covet your neighbor's wife, or anything belonging to your neighbor."

Exodus 21:22-25   Now suppose 2 men are fighting, and in the process they accidentally strike a PREGNANT woman so she gives birth PREMATURELY. IF NO further injury results, the man who struck the woman must pay the amount of compensation the woman's husband demands and the judges approve. But IF there is FURTHER injury, the punishment must match the injury: a life for a life, an eye for an eye, a tooth for a tooth, a hand for a hand, a burn for a burn, a bruise for a bruise.

Exodus 22:21-25, 28   You must NOT mistreat or oppress foreigners in any way. Remember, you yourselves were once foreigners in Egypt. You must NOT exploit a widow or an orphan. IF you exploit them in any way and they cry out to me, THEN I will certainly hear their cry. My anger will blaze against you. IF you lend money to any of My people who are in NEED, do NOT charge interest AS a money lender would. ... You must NOT dishonor God, OR curse any of your rulers.

Exodus 23:1-3, 6-8, 24   You must NOT pass along FALSE rumors. You must NOT cooperate with evil people by LYING on the witness stand. You must NOT follow the CROWD in doing wrong. When you are called to testify in a dispute, do NOT be swayed by the crowd to TWIST justice. Do NOT slant your testimony in favor of a person just BECAUSE that person is poor. In a lawsuit, you must NOT deny justice to the poor. NEVER charge anyone FALSELY with evil. NEVER sentence an innocent person to death. ... Take NO bribes, for a BRIBE makes you IGNORE something that you clearly see. A bribe makes even a righteous person TWIST the truth. ... You must NOT worship the gods of these nations OR serve them in any way OR imitate their evil practices. INSTEAD, you must utterly destroy them and smash their sacred pillars.

Exodus 24:10-11, 17   On the mountain, these men SAW God, but God did not destroy them. He was standing on what looked like blue sapphires, as clear as the sky! They all ate and drank together. The glory of the LORD appeared at the summit like a consuming fire.

Exodus 32:33   The LORD said, "I will ERASE the names of everyone who sinned against Me."

Exodus 33:15-18   Moses said, "... How will anyone know that You look favorably on us, if You do not go with us? For Your Presence AMONG us sets us apart from all other people on the earth." The LORD replied, "I will indeed do what you have asked, for I look favorably on you, and I know you by name." Moses responded, "Then show me Your glorious Presence."

Leviticus 10:1-3
Aaron's sons Nadab and Abihu put coals of fire in their incense burners. They disobeyed the LORD by burning before Him the wrong kind of fire, different than He had commanded. Fire blazed

from the LORD's Presence and burned them up. Moses said to Aaron, "This is what the LORD MEANT when He said, 'I will display My Holiness THROUGH those who come near Me.'" And Aaron was silent.

Leviticus 11:44   The LORD said, "I AM the LORD your God. Be HOLY, because I am HOLY. Do NOT defile [corrupt, spoil, destroy] yourselves."

Leviticus 17:11   The LORD said, "For the life of the body is in its blood. I have given you the blood on the altar to purify you, making you right with the Lord. It is the BLOOD, given in exchange for a life, that makes purification possible."

Leviticus 18:22-28, 30, 32   The LORD said, "Do NOT PRACTICE homosexuality, having sex with another man as with a woman. It is a detestable sin. A man must NOT DEFILE himself by having sex with an animal. And a woman must NOT offer herself to a male animal to have intercourse with it. This is a perverse act. Do NOT defile yourselves in any of these ways, FOR the people I am driving out BEFORE you have defiled themselves in all THESE ways. Because the ENTIRE land has become DEFILED, I am punishing the people who live there. I will cause the land to vomit them out. You must NOT commit ANY of THESE detestable sins. All these detestable activities are PRACTICED by the people of the land where I am taking you, and this is how the land has become defiled. So do NOT defile the land and give it a reason to vomit you out, as it will vomit out the people who live there now. So OBEY My instructions, and do NOT defile yourselves by committing any of these detestable practices that were committed by the people who lived in the land before you. I AM the LORD your God. ... Stand up in the presence of the elderly, and show RESPECT for the aged. FEAR [respect God's power and authority, not because He is angry with us, but because we desire to please Him] your God. I AM the LORD."

Leviticus 20:6-8, 10, 13, 15-16, 23, 26   The LORD said, "I will also TURN AGAINST those who commit spiritual prostitution by putting their trust in mediums or in those who consult the spirits of the dead. ... SET yourselves APART to be HOLY, for I, the LORD your God, am HOLY. ... Keep all My decrees by putting them into PRACTICE, for I AM the LORD who makes you HOLY. ... IF a man COMMITS adultery with his neighbor's wife, both the man and the woman who have committed adultery must be put to death. ... IF a man PRACTICES homosexuality, having sex with another man as with a woman, both men have committed a detestable act. They must both be put to death. ... IF a man has sex with an animal, he must be put to death. IF a woman presents herself to a male animal to have intercourse with it, she must be put to death. Do NOT live according to the customs of the people I am driving out before you. It is because they do these shameful things that I detest them. You must be HOLY because I, the LORD, am HOLY. I have SET you APART from all other people to be My very OWN."

Leviticus 25:23   The LORD said, "The land must never be sold on a permanent basis, for the land BELONGS to Me. You are only foreigners and tenant farmers working for Me."

Leviticus 26:3, 12, 14-16, 27-28, 30, 37-39, 43-44   The LORD said, "IF you FOLLOW My decrees and are careful to OBEY My commands, ... I will walk AMONG you: I will be your God, and you will be My people. ... IF you do NOT listen to Me or IF you break My covenant by rejecting My decrees, treating My regulations with contempt, and REFUSING to obey My commands, I will punish you. I will bring sudden terrors upon you – wasting diseases and burning fevers that will cause your life to ebb away. ... IF in spite of all this you STILL refuse to listen and STILL remain hostile toward Me, THEN I will give full vent to My hostility. I will punish you 7 times over for your sins. I will DESTROY your pagan shrines and knock down your places of worship. I will leave your lifeless corpses piled on top of your lifeless idols, and I will despise you. Though no one is chasing you, you will stumble over each other as though fleeing from a sword. You will have NO power to stand up against your enemies. You will die among the foreign nations. Those of you who survive will waste away in your enemies' lands because of their sins. ... They have CONTINUALLY REJECTED My regulations and despised My decrees. But DESPITE all this, I will NOT utterly reject or despise them while they are in exile in the land of their enemies. I will NOT cancel My covenant with them, for I AM the LORD their God."

Leviticus 27:30   One TENTH of the produce of the land, whether grain from the fields or fruit from the trees, BELONGS to the LORD and must be set apart to Him as holy.

Numbers 5:5-7
The LORD said to Moses, "WHEN you DO something WRONG to another person. You are really sinning AGAINST God. You must CONFESS your sin and make FULL restitution for what you did, adding an additional 20 percent and returning it to the person who was wronged.

Numbers 6:24-26   May the LORD BLESS you and PROTECT you. May the LORD SMILE on you and be KIND to you. May the LORD show you His FAVOR and give you His PEACE.

Numbers 11:23   The LORD said to Moses, "Has My arm lost its power? Now you will see whether or not My Word comes TRUE!"

Numbers 12:1, 3, 8-11, 13-14   Miriam and Aaron CRITICIZED Moses because he had married a Cushite woman. But the LORD HEARD them. (Moses was very humble – more humble [gentle, teachable, trusting God, not pride in self] than any other person on earth.) "I speak to Moses face to face, clearly, and not in riddles! He sees the LORD as He is. WHY were you NOT afraid to criticize My servant Moses?" The LORD was very angry with them, and He departed. As the cloud moved from above the Tabernacle, there stood Miriam, her skin as white as snow from leprosy. When Aaron saw what had happened to her, he cried out to Moses, "Oh, my master! Please do NOT punish us for this sin we have so FOOLISHLY committed." Moses cried out to the LORD, "O God, I beg you, please heal her!" The LORD said to Moses, "Keep her outside the camp for 7 days, and then she may be accepted back."

Numbers 14:9, 22, 24, 27-30, 34   Joshua and Caleb said, "Do NOT rebel against the LORD. Do NOT be afraid of the people of the land. ... They have NO protection. The LORD is WITH us! Do NOT be afraid of them!" ... The LORD said, "NOT one of these people will ever ENTER that land. They have all seen My glorious Presence and the miraculous signs I performed both in Egypt and in the wilderness, but again and again they have tested Me by REFUSING to listen to My voice. ... But My servant Caleb has a different attitude than the others have. He has remained LOYAL to Me, so I will bring him into the land he explored. ... How long must I put up with this WICKED community and its COMPLAINTS about Me?" ... "As surely as I live," declares the LORD, "I will DO to you the VERY THINGS I heard you SAY. You will all DROP DEAD in this wilderness! BECAUSE you COMPLAINED against Me, every one of you who is 20 years old or older and was included in the registration will die. The ONLY exceptions will be Caleb son of Jephunneh and Joshua son of Nun. ... Because your men explored the land for 40 days, you must wander in the wilderness for 40 years – a year for each day, suffering the CONSEQUENCES of your sins. Then you will discover what it is like to have Me for an enemy."

Numbers 15:30-31   The LORD said, "Those who brazenly violate the LORD's will have blasphemed the LORD, and they must be cut off from the community. Since they have treated the LORD's Word with contempt and DELIBERATELY DISOBEYED His command, they must be completely CUT OFF and suffer the punishment for their guilt."

Numbers 20:7-12   The LORD said to Moses, "Speak to the rock over there, and it will pour out its water."   Moses and Aaron summoned the people to gather at the rock. "Listen, you rebels!" he shouted. "Must we bring you water from this rock?" Then Moses raised his hand and struck the rock twice with the staff, and water gushed out. So the entire community and their livestock drank their fill. But the LORD said to Moses and Aaron, "Because you did NOT trust Me enough to demonstrate My Holiness to the people of Israel, you will NOT lead them into the land I am giving them!"

Numbers 21:4-9   The people of Israel grew impatient with the long journey, and they began to speak against God and Moses.   They COMPLAINED, "There is nothing to eat here and nothing to drink. We hate this horrible manna!" So the LORD sent poisonous SNAKES among the people, and many were bitten and died. Then the people cried out, "We have sinned by speaking against the LORD and against you. Pray that the LORD will take away the snakes." So Moses prayed for the people. Then the LORD told him, "Make a replica of a poisonous snake and attach it to a pole. All who are bitten will LIVE IF they simply LOOK at it!" So Moses made a snake out of bronze and attached it to a pole. Then anyone who was bitten by a snake could look at the bronze snake and be healed!

Numbers 23:19   Balaam said, "God is NOT a man, so He does NOT lie. He does NOT change His mind. Has He ever spoken and failed to act? Has He ever promised and not carried it through?"

Numbers 24:9   Blessed are all who BLESS you, Israel. Cursed are all who CURSE you.

Numbers 30:10-12   Suppose a woman is married when she makes a vow or a pledge. IF her husband hears of it and does not object, her vow or pledge will stand. But IF her husband refuses to accept it on the day he hears of it, her vow or pledge is nullified, and the LORD will forgive her.

Numbers 35:33-34   The LORD said, "Murder POLLUTES the land. No sacrifice except the execution of the murderer can PURIFY the land from murder. You must NOT defile the land where you live, for I LIVE there Myself. I AM the LORD, who lives among the people of Israel."

Deuteronomy 1:16-17   Moses instructed the judges, "Be perfectly FAIR in your decisions and IMPARTIAL in your judgments. LISTEN to the cases of those who are POOR as well as those who are RICH. Do NOT be afraid of anyone's anger, FOR the decision you make is God's decision."

Deuteronomy 2:2-7   The LORD said, "You are wandering long enough, turn to the north. You will pass through Edom. The Edomites will feel threatened. Be careful. Do NOT bother them. IF you need food or water, pay for it. For the LORD has been WITH you, and you have lacked nothing."

Deuteronomy 3:24   Moses said to the LORD, "LORD, You have only begun to show Your greatness and strength to me, Your servant. Is there any other god who can perform such great and mighty deeds as You do?"

Deuteronomy 4:2-4, 7-9, 24-25, 29-31, 39   Moses said, "Do NOT ADD to OR SUBTRACT from these commands I am giving you. Just OBEY the commands of the LORD your God that I am giving you. The LORD your God destroyed everyone who had worshiped Baal, the god of Peor. But all of you who were faithful to the LORD your God are still alive today – every one of you. … What great nation has a god as near to them as the LORD our God is NEAR to us WHENEVER we CALL on Him? What great nation has LAWS as RIGHTEOUS and FAIR as the instructions from the Lord? Watch out! Be careful NEVER forget what you have seen. Be sure to PASS them ON to your CHILDREN and GRANDCHILDREN. … The LORD your God is a devouring fire. He is a jealous God. When you have children and grandchildren and have lived in the land a long time, do NOT corrupt yourselves by making idols of any kind. This is evil in the sight of the LORD your God and will arouse His anger. … IF you SEARCH for the LORD your God with ALL your heart and soul, you will FIND Him. In the future, when you are suffering, RETURN to the LORD your God and LISTEN to what He tells you. … Remember and KEEP FIRMLY in your mind: The LORD IS God, and there is NO OTHER God."

Deuteronomy 5:1-21 = Exodus 20:1-17 = [10 Commandments]

Deuteronomy 5:29, 33   The LORD said, "ALWAYS have hearts to FEAR [respect God's power and authority, because we desire to please] Me and OBEY all My commands! STAY on the path that I command you to FOLLOW."

Deuteronomy 6:4-7, 12-15   Moses said, "The LORD is our God, the LORD ALONE. LOVE the LORD your God with all your heart, all your soul, and all your strength. ... COMMIT yourselves wholeheartedly to these commands that I am giving you today. Repeat them again and again to your children. Talk about them when you are at home and when you are on the road, when you are going to bed and when you are getting up. ... Do NOT forget the LORD. Fear [reverential awe, honor, respect] the LORD and serve Him. You must NOT worship any gods of the nations, for the LORD your God, who lives among you, is a jealous God. He will wipe you from the face of the earth."

Deuteronomy 7:9-10, 21, 25-26   Moses said, "The LORD is the faithful God who keeps His covenant and lavishes His unfailing love on those who LOVE Him and OBEY His commands. But He does NOT hesitate to destroy those who reject Him. Do NOT be afraid, for the LORD is AMONG you. ... BURN their idols in fire. Do NOT covet the gold that covers them. Do NOT take it, as it will become a TRAP to you, for it is detestable to the LORD. Do NOT bring any detestable objects into your home, for then you will be destroyed, just like them. Utterly DETEST such things."

Deuteronomy 8:2-3, 19-20   Moses said, "Remember how the LORD led you through the wilderness, HUMBLING you and TESTING you to PROVE your character, and to find out IF you would OBEY His commands. He did it to TEACH you that people do NOT live by bread alone; rather, we LIVE by EVERY Word that comes from the LORD. ... IF you ever FORGET the LORD and follow FALSE gods, worshiping and bowing down to them, you will certainly be DESTROYED, just as the LORD has destroyed other nations in your path."

Deuteronomy 9:4   Do NOT say, "The LORD gave us this land because we are such good people!" NO, it is BECAUSE of the wickedness of the other nations that He is pushing them out of your way.

Deuteronomy 10:12, 16-21   Moses said, "What does the LORD require of you? He REQUIRES only that you FEAR [reverential awe, honor, respect] the LORD, and LIVE in a way that PLEASES Him, and LOVE [be loyal to] Him and SERVE Him with all your heart and soul. ... STOP being stubborn. GIVE your hearts to God. ... The LORD is the GOD of gods and LORD of lords. He shows NO partiality. God ensures orphans and widows receive JUSTICE. He shows love to the foreigners living among you and GIVES them food and clothing. So you must show LOVE to foreigners. You must fear, worship, and CLING to the LORD. Your oaths must be in His Name ALONE. The LORD ALONE is your God, the ONLY One who is WORTHY of your PRAISE."

Deuteronomy 11:16, 19-20, 26-28   Moses said, "Be careful! Do NOT let your heart be DECEIVED so that you turn away from the LORD and serve and worship other gods.   ... TEACH My Instructions to your CHILDREN. Talk about them WHEN you are at home and WHEN you are on the road, WHEN you are going to bed and WHEN you are getting up. Write them on the doorposts of your house. ... I am giving you the CHOICE between a blessing and a curse! You will be blessed IF you OBEY the commands of the LORD your God. But you will be cursed IF you REJECT the commands of the LORD and turn away from Him and worship gods you have not known before."

Deuteronomy 12:7-8, 15, 23, 30-32   Moses said, "Make a feast before the Lord your God, with JOY in everything to which you put your hand, because the Lord has given you His blessing. Your pattern of worship will change. ... You may eat MEAT when you want. But NEVER eat the BLOOD, because the life is in the blood. ... Do NOT fall into the TRAP of following their customs and worshiping their gods. Do NOT inquire ABOUT their gods, saying, 'How do these nations worship their gods? I want to follow their example.' You must NOT worship the LORD the way the other nations worship their gods, for they perform for their gods every DETESTABLE act the LORD hates. They even BURN their sons and daughters as sacrifices to their gods. OBEY ALL the commands. Do NOT ADD anything OR SUBTRACT anything from them."

Deuteronomy 13:1-6, 8-9   Moses said, "IF [false] prophets say, 'Come, let us worship other gods' – do NOT listen to them. The LORD is testing you to see IF you truly LOVE Him with all your heart and soul. Serve ONLY the LORD and fear [reverential awe, honor, respect] Him ALONE. OBEY His commands, LISTEN to His voice, and CLING to Him. The FALSE prophets who try to lead you astray encourage rebellion against the LORD. You must put them to death. PURGE the evil from among you. Suppose someone secretly ENTICES you – EVEN your brother, your child, your wife, or your closest friend – and says, 'Let us go worship other gods.' Do NOT listen to them!"

Deuteronomy 14:1-2, 7-8, 11   Moses said, "You are SET APART as HOLY to the LORD. IF there are any poor when you arrive in the land the Lord is giving you, do NOT be hard-hearted or tightfisted toward them. Instead, be GENEROUS and LEND them whatever they need. I am commanding you to SHARE freely with the poor and with other Israelites in need."

Deuteronomy 16:19-20, 22   Moses said, "You must NEVER TWIST justice OR show partiality. NEVER accept a BRIBE, for bribes blind the eyes of the wise and CORRUPT the decisions of the godly [committed to obeying God]. Let TRUE justice prevail. ... NEVER worship FALSE gods, for the LORD your God HATES them."

Deuteronomy 18:9-15, 17-18, 20-22   Moses continued, "Be very careful NOT to IMITATE the detestable customs of the nations living there. For example, NEVER sacrifice your son or daughter as a burnt offering. Do NOT let your people PRACTICE fortune-telling, or use sorcery, or interpret omens, or engage in witchcraft, or cast spells, or function as mediums or psychics, or call the spirits of the dead. Anyone who does these things is DETESTABLE to the LORD. It is because the other nations have done these detestable things that the LORD your God will drive them out ahead of you. But you must be BLAMELESS before the LORD. The nations you are about to displace consult sorcerers and fortune-tellers, but the LORD your God FORBIDS you to do such things. The LORD your God will raise up for you a Prophet like me from among your fellow Israelites. You must LISTEN to Him. ... Then the LORD said to me, '...I will put My Words in His mouth, and He will tell the people everything I command Him. ... Any prophet who FALSELY claims to speak in My Name or who speaks in the name of another god must die.' But you may wonder, 'HOW will we KNOW whether or not a prophecy is FROM the LORD?' IF the prophet speaks in the LORD's Name BUT his prediction does NOT happen or come true, you will KNOW that the LORD did NOT give that message ... and need NOT be feared."

Deuteronomy 19:15-16, 19-21   Moses said, "You must NOT convict anyone of a crime on the testimony of only 1 witness. The facts of the case must be established by the testimony of 2 or 3 witnesses. If a MALICIOUS witness ACCUSES someone of a crime, you must IMPOSE on the ACCUSER the sentence he intended for the other person. PURGE such evil from among you. THEN the rest of the people will hear about it and be AFRAID to do such an evil thing. ... Your rule should be life for life, eye for eye, tooth for tooth, hand for hand, foot for foot."

Deuteronomy 20:18   Moses said, "PREVENT the people of the land from teaching you to IMITATE their detestable customs in the worship of their gods, which would cause you to sin against the LORD."

Deuteronomy 22:5   Moses said, "A woman must not put on men's clothing, and a man must not wear women's clothing. Anyone who does this is DETESTABLE in the sight of the LORD your God."

Deuteronomy 23:1, 7 ERV, 15, 17-18, 21-23   Moses said, "If a man's testicles are crushed or his penis is cut off, he may not be admitted to the assembly of the LORD. … You must NOT HATE Edomites, because they are your relatives. You must NOT HATE Egyptians, because you were a stranger in their land. … IF slaves should escape from their masters and take refuge with you, you must NOT hand them over to their masters. NO man or woman, may become a temple prostitute. You must NOT bring to the house of the LORD any offering from the earnings of a prostitute, which is DETESTABLE to the LORD. … The LORD your God demands that you promptly fulfill all your vows, OR you will be guilty of sin. However, it is NOT a sin to NOT make a vow. BUT once you have VOLUNTARILY made a vow, be careful to FULFILL your promise to the LORD your God."

Deuteronomy 24:17   Moses said, "TRUE JUSTICE must be given to foreigners and to orphans."

Deuteronomy 25:16   Moses said, "All who CHEAT with dishonest measures are DETESTABLE to the LORD."

Deuteronomy 28:14, 20-21   Moses said, "You must NOT follow after other gods and worship them. … The LORD will SEND on you curses, confusion, and frustration … UNTIL you are completely destroyed for doing evil. … The LORD will afflict you with diseases UNTIL none of you are left."

Deuteronomy 29:18-20, 29   Moses said, "No one should turn away from the LORD to worship gods of other nations. Do NOT THINK, 'I am safe, even though I am [deliberately, continuously] following the desires of my own stubborn heart.' This will LEAD to utter RUIN! The LORD will NEVER pardon such people. All the curses written in this book will come down on them, and the LORD will ERASE their NAMES from under heaven. … The LORD has secrets. But we are ACCOUNTABLE for all that is REVEALED to us."

Deuteronomy 30:5, 14-15, 19-20   Moses said, "The LORD will return you to the land that belonged to your ancestors, and you will possess that land again. He will make you more prosperous and numerous than your ancestors! … The MESSAGE is very close; it is on your lips and in your heart so that you can OBEY it. LISTEN! … Today, you have the

CHOICE between life and death, between blessings and curses. CHOOSE life, and live! Make this CHOICE by LOVING the LORD, OBEYING Him, and COMMITTING firmly [being loyal] to Him. This is the KEY to your LIFE."

Deuteronomy 31:6, 8, 12, 20-21, 27, 29   Moses said, "BE strong and courageous! ... Do NOT be afraid or discouraged, do NOT panic, for the LORD will personally be WITH you. He will NEITHER fail you NOR abandon you. ... Call them together – men, women, children – so they may HEAR this Book of Instruction and LEARN to RESPECT the LORD and carefully OBEY ALL the instructions." ... The LORD said, "They will become prosperous and become fat. They will worship other gods and will despise Me. ... I KNOW your INTENTIONS, how rebellious and stubborn you are! ... You will become utterly CORRUPT. DISASTER will come on you because you will do what is evil."

Deuteronomy 32:4-6, 15-20, 37-39, 47   Moses said, "The Lord is the Rock, His deeds are perfect, just, fair, faithful, and does NO wrong! BUT they have acted corruptly and perversely toward Him, who CREATED you. They are deceitful and twisted. Is this the WAY you REPAY the LORD, you FOOLISH and SENSELESS people? ... But Israel soon became fat and unruly! Then they abandoned the God who had made them, making light of the Rock of their salvation. They provoked His fury with detestable deeds. They OFFERRED sacrifices to demons, which are NOT God. You FORGOT God who gave you birth. The LORD saw this and said, 'I will abandon them; then see what happens. For they are twisted without integrity.' ... God will ask, 'WHERE are their gods, the rocks they fled to for refuge who ate their sacrifices and drank their offerings? LET those gods arise and help you! Look now! There is NO other God BUT Me!' ... These INSTRUCTIONS are NOT empty words – they ARE your LIFE! OBEY them."

Deuteronomy 33:3, 9   Moses said, "God LOVES His people. They FOLLOW His steps and ACCEPT His teaching. ... They OBEY Your Word and are more LOYAL to You than to their children or parents."

Joshua 1:7-9

The LORD said to Joshua, "BE strong and courageous. Be careful to OBEY ALL the instructions Moses gave you. Do NOT DEVIATE, turning either right or left. STUDY this Book of Instruction continually. MEDITATE on it day and night so you will be sure to OBEY everything written in it. Then you will succeed in all you do. This is My command – BE strong and courageous! Do NOT be afraid or discouraged. For the Lord your God is WITH you wherever you go."

Joshua 2:9 Rahab said, "I know the LORD has given you this land. We are all afraid of you."

Joshua 3:9, 15-16 Joshua told the Israelites, "Come and listen to what the LORD your God says." … AS SOON AS the priests STEPPED into the river, the water STOPPED flowing.

Joshua 4:23-24 Joshua said, "The LORD your God dried up the river right before your eyes, and He kept it dry until you were all across, just as He did at the Red Sea. He did this so all the nations of the earth might know the LORD is powerful, and so you might fear [respect, honor] the LORD forever."

Joshua 5:13-14 Joshua demanded, "Are you friend or foe?" "NEITHER one," He replied. "I AM the COMMANDER of the LORD's army." At this, Joshua fell to the ground in reverence. "I am at Your command," Joshua said. "What do You want Your servant to do?"

Joshua 6:17 Joshua commanded, "… Jericho must be destroyed as an offering to the LORD. Only Rahab the prostitute and the others in her house will be spared, for she protected our spies."

Joshua 7:13 The LORD says: "Hidden among you, O Israel, are things set apart for the LORD. You will NEVER defeat your enemies UNTIL you REMOVE these things from among you."

Joshua 23:15-16 Joshua said, "As the LORD has given you the GOOD things He promised, He will bring DISASTER on you IF you DISOBEY Him BY worshiping and serving OTHER gods."

Joshua 24:15, 19-21, 23-24 Joshua said, "IF you REFUSE to serve the LORD, then CHOOSE TODAY who you will serve. Do you prefer the [false] gods of your ancestors? Or the [false] gods in the land you now live? But as for me and my family, we will SERVE the LORD. The LORD is a HOLY and jealous God. IF you abandon the LORD and serve other gods, He will turn against you and destroy you, even though He has been so good to you." But the people answered, "No, we will SERVE the LORD!" … Joshua said, "Then, DESTROY the idols among you, and TURN your hearts TO the LORD." The people said, "We will OBEY the LORD ALONE."

Judges 2:1-3, 22 The LORD said, "I brought you out of Egypt into this land ... you were NOT to make any covenants with the people living in this land; instead, you were to DESTROY their altars. But you DISOBEYED My command. ... I will no longer drive out the people living in your land. They will be thorns in your sides, and their gods will be a constant TEMPTATION to you. ... I did this to TEST Israel – whether or not they would FOLLOW the LORD."

Judges 3:5-9 The people of Israel INTERMARRIED with them, served their gods and FORGOT the LORD. Then the LORD was angry against Israel. When the people cried out to the LORD for help, the LORD raised up a rescuer to save them.

Judges 4:4, 9 Deborah, the wife of Lappidoth, was a prophet and the judge over Israel at that time. Deborah replied, "I will go with you. But you will receive no honor in this venture, for the LORD's victory over Sisera will be at the hands of a woman." So Deborah went with Barak to Kedesh.

Judges 5:15 The princes of Issachar were with Deborah and Barak. They FOLLOWED Barak, rushing into the valley. But in the tribe of Reuben there was great INDECISION.

Judges 6:31 Joash shouted to the mob, "WHY are you defending Baal? IF Baal truly is a god, LET him defend himself and destroy the one who broke down his altar!"

Judges 10:12-16 The LORD replied, "When they oppressed you, you cried out to Me for help, and I rescued you. Yet you have abandoned Me and served other gods. So I will NOT rescue you anymore. Cry out to the gods you have chosen! Let them rescue you!" BUT the Israelites pleaded with the LORD, "We have sinned. Punish us as You see fit, only rescue us." The Israelites PUT ASIDE their foreign gods and SERVED the LORD.

Judges 14:6 The Spirit of the LORD came powerfully upon Samson, and he ripped the lion's jaws apart with his bare hands.

Judges 16:15-21, 25, 28-30 Delilah pouted, "How can you tell me, 'I love you,' when you do not share your secrets with me?" She tormented him with nagging day after day until he was sick to death of it. Finally, Samson shared his secret with her. Delilah sent for the Philistine rulers who returned with the money. Delilah lulled Samson to sleep and called in a man to shave off the 7 locks of his hair. In this way she began to bring him down, and his strength left him. When he woke up, he did NOT realize the LORD had left him. So the Philistines captured him and gouged out his eyes and forced him to grind grain in the prison. ... Half drunk, the people demanded, "Bring out Samson so he can amuse us!" So he was brought from the prison to amuse them, and he stood between the pillars supporting the roof. Samson prayed to the LORD, "Sovereign LORD, remember me again. O God, please strengthen me just one more time. With one blow let me pay back the Philistines for the loss of my 2 eyes." Samson pushed his hands against the 2 center pillars that held up the temple, the temple crashed down on the Philistine rulers and the people. He killed more people when he died, than during his entire lifetime.

Judges 17:1-13   Micah returned the money to his mother, she took 200 silver coins and gave them to a silversmith, who made them into an image and an idol, and these were placed in Micah's house. In those days Israel had NO king; all the people did WHATEVER SEEMED RIGHT in their own eyes. One day a young Levite, happened to stop at Micah's house. "Where are you from?" Micah asked him. He replied, "I am a Levite from Bethlehem, and I am looking for a place to live." "Stay here with me," Micah said, "and you can be a priest to me. I will give you 10 pieces of silver a year, a change of clothes, and your food." The Levite agreed to this.

Ruth 1:16-17
Ruth said, "Wherever you go, I will go; wherever you live, I will live. Your people will be my people, and your God will be my God!" Naomi saw that Ruth was determined to go with her.

1 Samuel 2:1-3, 22-25, 27-31
Hannah prayed: "I have JOY in the Lord! The Lord has made me strong. I have JOY because You rescued me. NONE is HOLY like the Lord! There is NONE besides You. There is no Rock like our God. STOP acting proud and haughty! Do NOT speak with arrogance! For the Lord is God and KNOWS what you have DONE. He will JUDGE your ACTIONS." ... Eli was aware that his sons were seducing the young women who assisted at the entrance of the Tabernacle. Eli said to them, "I have been hearing reports about the wicked things you are doing. You must stop, my sons! If someone sins against another person, God can mediate for the guilty party. But IF someone sins against the LORD, WHO can intercede?" But Eli's sons did NOT listen to their father. ... One day a man of God came to Eli and gave

him this message from the LORD: "... WHY do you GIVE your sons more HONOR than you GIVE Me? You and they have become fat from the best offerings of my people Israel! I will HONOR those who HONOR Me, and I will DESPISE those who THINK LIGHTLY of Me. ... I will put an end to your family, so that your family will no longer serve as My priests. ... None of your family will reach old age."

1 Samuel 3:19-21 The LORD was with Samuel, and everything he said proved to be true. All Israel knew Samuel was a prophet of the LORD. The LORD continued to give messages to Samuel.

1 Samuel 7:3 Samuel said, "IF you are really SERIOUS about wanting to RETURN to the LORD, Get RID of your foreign gods and your images. Determine to OBEY ONLY the LORD."

1 Samuel 12:14-15, 20-21, 23-25 Samuel said, "IF you fear [respect God's power and authority, because we desire to please] and worship the LORD, THEN both you and your king will show that you recognize the LORD as your God. But IF you rebel against the LORD's commands, refusing to obey and listen to Him, THEN the LORD will be against you and your king." ... "Do NOT be afraid," Samuel reassured them. "You have certainly DONE wrong, but make sure NOW that you worship the LORD with all your heart, and do NOT turn your back on Him. Do NOT go BACK to worshiping WORTHLESS idols that cannot help or rescue you – they are totally USELESS! ... I will certainly NOT sin against the LORD by ending my PRAYERS for you. I will continue to TEACH you what is good and right. Be sure to fear and faithfully SERVE the LORD. THINK of all the WONDERFUL things He has DONE for you. But IF you CONTINUE to sin, you and your king will be SWEPT away."

1 Samuel 13:8-14 Saul waited 7 days for Samuel, as Samuel had instructed, but Samuel did not come. Saul's troops were slipping away. So Saul sacrificed the burnt offering himself. JUST AS Saul was finishing with the burnt offering, Samuel arrived saying, "WHAT is THIS you have DONE?" Saul replied, "They are ready to march against us, and I haven't asked for the LORD's help! I felt compelled to offer the burnt offering myself before you came." "How FOOLISH!" Samuel exclaimed. "You have NOT kept the command the LORD gave you. Now your kingdom must end, the LORD seeks a man after His own heart."

1 Samuel 14:27-29 Jonathan had not heard his father's command, and dipped his stick into a piece of honeycomb and ate the honey and felt refreshed. One of the men said, "Your father made the army take a strict oath that anyone who eats food today will be cursed. That is why everyone is weary and faint." Jonathan exclaimed. "My father has made trouble for us! Such a command only hurts us."

1 Samuel 15:22-23, 29   Samuel said, "What is MORE PLEASING to the LORD: your burnt offerings and sacrifices or your OBEDIENCE to His voice? OBEDIENCE is better than sacrifice. SUBMISSION is better than offerings. Rebellion is as sinful as witchcraft, and stubbornness as bad as worshiping idols. BECAUSE you have REJECTED the command of the LORD, God has REJECTED you as king. … The God of Israel, does NOT lie, NOR change His mind. He is NOT like a human!"

1 Samuel 16:7   The LORD said to Samuel, "Do NOT judge BY his appearance or height, for I have rejected him. The LORD does NOT see things the WAY you see them. People JUDGE by OUTWARD appearance, but the LORD LOOKS at the HEART."

1 Samuel 17:37, 45-47   David said, "The LORD who RESCUED me from the lion and the bear will RESCUE me from Goliath!" Saul consented, "May the LORD be WITH you!" ... David replied to Goliath, "You come to me with sword, spear, and javelin, but I COME to you in the NAME of the LORD, who you have defied. Today the LORD will conquer you, I will kill you, and the world will know there is a God in Israel! The LORD RESCUES His people, but NOT with sword and spear. This is the LORD's BATTLE, and He will give you to us!"

1 Samuel 24:12, 15, 19   David shouted to Saul, "May the LORD JUDGE between us. Perhaps the LORD will punish you for what you are trying to do to me, but I will NEVER harm you. May the LORD JUDGE which of us is right and punish the guilty one. He is my advocate, and He will RESCUE me from your power!" Saul called back, "Who lets his enemy get away when he had him in his power? May the LORD reward you well for the KINDNESS you have shown me today."

2 Samuel 8:15   David reigned over all Israel and did what was JUST and RIGHT for all his people.

2 Samuel 12:13-14   David confessed, "I have sinned AGAINST the LORD." Nathan replied, "The LORD has FORGIVEN you, you will NOT die for this sin, but you showed utter CONTEMPT for the LORD, your child will die."

2 Samuel 14:14   The woman from Tekoa said to King David, "All of us must DIE eventually. BUT God devises ways to BRING us BACK when we have been separated from Him."

2 Samuel 22:27-29, 31-34, 49   David sang, "… To the PURE You show Yourself pure, but to the WICKED You show Yourself hostile. You RESCUE the humble [gentle, teachable, trusting God, not pride in self], but You HUMILIATE the proud. O LORD, You are my lamp. God's way is perfect. All the LORD's promises PROVE TRUE. He is a shield for all who look to Him for protection. WHO is God except the LORD? … God is my strong fortress. … God DELIVERS me from my enemies. You SAVE me from violent opponents."

2 Samuel 23:3, 6-7   The God of Israel said: "The one who rules righteously [being right, based on God's standard, includes thoughts, words and actions], rules in the fear [reverential awe, honor, respect] of God. … But the GODLESS are like thorns to be thrown away. … They will be totally consumed by FIRE."

1 Kings 2:3
Observe the requirements of the LORD your God, and FOLLOW ALL His ways, so that you will be successful in all you do and wherever you go.

1 Kings 3:9-10, 25-28   Solomon said to the LORD, "Give me an understanding heart so that I can KNOW the DIFFERENCE between RIGHT and WRONG." The Lord was pleased Solomon ASKED for wisdom to LISTEN and MAKE the right DECISIONS. … Solomon said, "Cut the living child in 2, and give half to 1 woman and half to the other!" The woman who was the real mother, cried out, "Oh no, my lord! Give her the child!" The other woman said, "Divide him!" The king said, "Do not kill the child, but give him to the woman who wants him to live, for she is his mother!" The people were in awe as they saw the wisdom God had given him to render justice.

1 Kings 8:22-24, 39-40, 61   Solomon prayed, "LORD, there is NO God like You in all of heaven. You KEEP your promises and show unfailing love to all who walk in WHOLEHEARTED devotion to You. ... GIVE your people WHAT their ACTIONS DESERVE, for You ALONE KNOW each human heart, THEN they will fear [reverential awe, honor, respect] You. May you be FAITHFUL [trusting, loyal] to the LORD. May you always OBEY His commands, as you are doing today."

1 Kings 9:2-9   The LORD appeared to Solomon, "IF you will FOLLOW Me with DEPENDABLE HONESTY and GODLINESS [committed to obeying God], THEN I will establish your dynasty forever. But IF you or your descendants ABANDON and DISOBEY Me, and serve and worship OTHER gods, THEN I will uproot Israel, making Israel an object of mockery and ridicule. All who pass by will be appalled and ask, 'Why did the LORD do such terrible things to this land?' The answer will be, 'Because His people abandoned the LORD their God, and worshiped other gods.'"

1 Kings 11:1-13   King Solomon loved many foreign women. The LORD had clearly instructed the people, "You must NOT marry them, because they will TURN your hearts TO their gods." Yet Solomon INSISTED on loving them anyway. He had 700 wives of royal birth and 300 concubines. And they did TURN his heart away FROM the LORD. In Solomon's old age, they turned his heart to worship other gods. Solomon worshiped Ashtoreth, the goddess of the Sidonians, and Molech, the detestable god of the Ammonites. Solomon did what was evil in the LORD's sight; he REFUSED to follow the LORD COMPLETELY, as his father, David, had done. On the Mount of Olives, he even BUILT a pagan shrine for Chemosh, the detestable god of Moab, and another for Molech, the detestable god of the Ammonites. Solomon built such shrines for all his foreign wives to use for burning incense and sacrificing to their gods. The LORD was very ANGRY with Solomon, for his heart had turned away from the LORD, who had APPEARED to him TWICE. Solomon did NOT listen to the LORD's command. The LORD said, "Since you have NOT kept My covenant and have disobeyed My decrees, I will TEAR the kingdom AWAY from you. I will let your son be king of one tribe, for the sake of My servant David."

1 Kings 13:17-18, 24   The LORD gave me this command: "You must not eat or drink anything while you are there, and do not return to Judah by the same way you came." But the old prophet LIED, "An angel gave me this command from the LORD: 'Bring him home with you so he can eat.'" As the man of God was leaving, a lion came and killed him, because he disobeyed the Lord's command.

1 Kings 15:11-12   King Asa did what was pleasing in the LORD's sight, … he BANISHED the male and female shrine prostitutes from the land and got RID of all the idols his ancestors had made.

1 Kings 17:12-16   The widow said, "I have only a handful of flour and a little cooking oil. This is our last meal, and then my son and I will die."

Elijah said to her, "Do NOT be afraid! Go ahead and do just what you've said, but make a little bread for me first. Then use what's left to prepare a meal for yourself and your son. This is what the LORD says: There will always be flour and olive oil left in your containers until the time when the LORD sends rain and the crops grow again!" She DID as Elijah said, and there was ALWAYS ENOUGH flour and olive oil left in the containers, JUST AS the LORD had promised through Elijah.

1 Kings 18:21, 24, 26, 29, 37-45   Elijah said, "HOW LONG will you WAVER? IF the LORD is the TRUE God, FOLLOW Him! But IF Baal is God, then follow him!" The people were silent. Elijah continued, "Call on the name of your god, and I will call on the Name of the LORD. The God who ANSWERS by setting fire to the wood IS the TRUE God!" ... They called on the name of Baal from morning until the time of the evening sacrifice, but there was NO sound, NO reply, NO response. ... Elijah's turn came and said, "LORD, ANSWER me so these people will know that You, LORD, are God and that You have brought them back to Yourself." Immediately the fire of the LORD flashed down and burned up the young bull, the wood, the stones, and the dust! All the people saw it, they fell face down and cried out, "The LORD – He IS God! The LORD IS God!" Elijah commanded, "Seize all the prophets of Baal!" So the people seized them all, and Elijah killed them. ... Elijah said, "I hear a mighty rainstorm coming!" Elijah climbed to the top of Mount Carmel and bowed low to the ground and PRAYED with his face between his knees. Then he said to his servant, "Go and look out toward the sea." The servant went and looked, then returned to Elijah and said, "I did not see anything." Seven times Elijah told him to go and look. Finally the SEVENTH time, his servant told him, "I saw a little cloud about the size of a man's hand rising from the sea." And soon the sky was black with clouds. A heavy wind brought a terrific rainstorm.

1 Kings 19:11-16, 18   As Elijah stood there, the LORD passed by, a mighty windstorm hit the mountain, but the LORD was NOT in the wind. There was an earthquake, but the LORD was NOT in the earthquake. There was a fire, but the LORD was NOT in the fire. There was a GENTLE WHISPER. The Voice said, "WHAT are you doing HERE, Elijah?" He replied again, "I have zealously served the LORD God Almighty. But the people of Israel have broken their covenant with You, torn down Your altars, and killed every one of Your prophets. I am the only one left, and now they are trying to kill me, too." The LORD told him, "GO BACK, and anoint Hazael to be king of Aram, anoint Jehu to be king of Israel, and anoint Elisha to replace you as My prophet. I will preserve 7,000 others in Israel who have NEVER bowed down to Baal or kissed him!"

1 Kings 21:20-21, 23, 25-27, 29   "My enemy, you have found me!" King Ahab exclaimed to Elijah. Elijah answered, "I have come because you have SOLD yourself TO what is EVIL in the LORD's sight. ... The LORD says, 'I will bring disaster on you!' ... And regarding Jezebel, the LORD says, 'Dogs will eat Jezebel's body.'" ... No one so completely sold himself to what was evil in the LORD's sight as Ahab did UNDER the INFLUENCE of his wife Jezebel. His worst outrage was worshiping idols just as the Amorites had done. When Ahab heard this message, he tore his clothing, dressed in burlap, and fasted. ... The LORD said to Elijah: "See Ahab has HUMBLED himself before Me, because he has done this, I will NOT do what I promised DURING his lifetime."

1 Kings 22:13-16, 31, 34-35   The messenger said to Micaiah, "All the prophets are promising victory for the king. Be sure that you agree with them." Micaiah replied, "As surely as the LORD lives, I will SAY ONLY what the LORD TELLS me to say." When Micaiah arrived, Ahab asked him, "Micaiah, should we go to war against Ramoth-gilead?" Micaiah replied sarcastically, "Yes, go up and be victorious!" But the king replied sharply, "I demand that you SPEAK ONLY the TRUTH to me WHEN you SPEAK FOR the LORD!" ... The king of Aram said: "Attack only the king of Israel. Do not bother with anyone else!" An Aramean soldier randomly shot an arrow at the Israelite troops and hit Ahab between the joints of his armor. The blood ran down his chariot, and he died.

2 Kings 1:16
Elijah said to King Ahaziah, "This is what the LORD says: WHY did you send messengers to Baal, the god of Ekron, to ask whether you will recover? Is there NO God in Israel to answer your question? Because you have done this, you will surely DIE."

2 Kings 2:11, 23-24   As Elisha and Elijah were walking and talking, a chariot with horses of fire appeared. It drove between the 2 men, separating them, and Elijah was carried by a whirlwind into heaven. ... As Elisha was walking, a group of boys began mocking him, "Go away, baldy!" Elisha cursed them in the Name of the LORD. Two bears came out and mauled 42 of them.

2 Kings 6:15-20   When the servant of the man of God got up, there were troops, horses, and chariots everywhere. "What will we do now?" the young man cried to Elisha. "Do NOT be afraid!" Elisha told him. "There are MORE ON our side THAN ON theirs!" Then Elisha PRAYED, "LORD, open his eyes and let him see!" The LORD opened the young man's eyes, and he SAW the hillside was filled with horses and chariots of FIRE. As the Aramean army advanced, Elisha prayed, "LORD, please make them blind." The LORD struck them with blindness as Elisha had asked. ... The king's officer replied, "That could NOT happen even IF the LORD opened the windows of heaven!" The man of God said, "You will SEE it happen with your own eyes, BUT you will NOT eat any of it!" And so it was, for the people trampled him to death at the gate!

2 Kings 8:18 King Jehoram FOLLOWED the example of the kings of Israel and was as WICKED as King Ahab, for he had MARRIED one of Ahab's daughters. Jehoram did evil in the LORD's sight.

2 Kings 9:22, 30-36 King Joram demanded, "Do you come in peace, Jehu?" Jehu replied, "HOW can there be peace AS LONG AS the idolatry and witchcraft of your mother, Jezebel, are all around us?" ... Jezebel painted her eyelids and fixed her hair and shouted at Jehu, "Have you come in peace, you murderer?" Jehu shouted, "WHO is on my side?" Three eunuchs looked at him. "Throw her down!" Jehu yelled. So they threw her out the window, her blood spattered, and Jehu trampled her body under his horses' hooves. Then Jehu went into the palace, ate, and said, "Someone bury this cursed woman." But when they went out to bury her, they found only her skull, feet, and hands. Jehu said, "This FULFILLS the LORD's message through Elijah: 'Dogs will eat Jezebel's body.'"

2 Kings 10:10, 25, 27-29 You can be sure the message of the LORD spoken concerning Ahab's family will not fail. King Jehu commanded his officers, "Go in and kill all of them!" So they killed them all and dragged their bodies outside. Then Jehu's men WRECKED the temple of Baal, converting it into a public toilet. Jehu DESTROYED every trace of Baal worship from Israel. He did not, however, destroy the gold calves at Bethel and Dan, with which Jeroboam had caused Israel to sin.

2 Kings 12:2-3 King Joash did what was PLEASING in the LORD's sight, because Jehoiada the priest INSTRUCTED him. Yet, he did not destroy the pagan shrines, where people offered sacrifices.

2 Kings 17:6-18, 33-34, 38-41 Samaria fell, and the people of Israel were exiled to Assyria. This DISASTER CAME upon the people of Israel BECAUSE they worshiped OTHER gods. They FOLLOWED the practices of the pagan nations, as well as the practices the kings of Israel had introduced. They had also SECRETLY DONE many things that were NOT pleasing to the LORD. They BUILT pagan shrines in all their towns. They set up sacred pillars and Asherah poles at the top of every hill and under every green tree. Yes, they worshiped idols, DESPITE the LORD's specific and repeated warnings: "TURN FROM all your EVIL ways. OBEY My commands and decrees." But the Israelites would NOT listen. They were as STUBBORN as their ancestors who had REFUSED to believe in the LORD their God. They DESPISED all His warnings. They worshiped WORTHLESS idols, so they BECAME WORTHLESS themselves. They followed the example of the nations around them, DISOBEYING the LORD's command NOT to IMITATE them. They even sacrificed their own sons and daughters in the fire. They consulted fortune-tellers and practiced sorcery and sold themselves to evil. Because the LORD was very ANGRY with Israel, He SWEPT them away FROM His Presence. ONLY the tribe of Judah remained. ... Though they worshiped the LORD, they CONTINUED to FOLLOW their OWN gods according to the religious customs of the nations from which they came. They CONTINUE to follow their FORMER practices INSTEAD of TRULY worshiping the LORD and OBEYING His instructions. For the LORD said, "Do NOT forget My covenant, and do NOT worship OTHER gods. You must worship ONLY the LORD your God, who will rescue you from all your enemies." But the people would NOT listen and CONTINUED to FOLLOW their FORMER practices. And their descendants do the same.

2 Kings 18:3, 5-7, 19, 30, 32-33, 35   King Hezekiah did what was PLEASING in the LORD's sight, just as his ancestor David had done. He REMOVED the pagan shrines, smashed the sacred pillars, and cut down the Asherah poles. He broke up the bronze serpent that Moses had made, because the people were offering sacrifices to it. Hezekiah TRUSTED in the LORD, the God of Israel. There was no one like him among all the kings of Judah, either before or after his time. He remained FAITHFUL [trusting, loyal] to the LORD in everything, and he carefully OBEYED ALL the commands the LORD had given Moses. So the LORD was WITH him, and Hezekiah was successful in everything he did. ... The king of Assyria gave this message to Hezekiah: "What are you trusting in that makes you so confident? ... Do not listen to Hezekiah when he tries to mislead you by saying, 'The LORD will rescue us!' ... Have the gods of any other nations ever saved their people from the king of Assyria? ... So what makes you think that the LORD can RESCUE you from me?"

2 Kings 19:14-22, 28, 32, 34-37   After Hezekiah received the letter, he went up to the LORD's Temple and spread it out before the LORD. Hezekiah PRAYED: "O LORD, God of Israel, You ALONE are God of all the kingdoms of the earth. You ALONE created the heavens and the earth. O LORD, listen to Sennacherib's words of defiance against the living God. It is true, LORD, that the kings of Assyria have destroyed all these nations, throwing the gods of these nations into the fire and burned them. Of course the Assyrians could destroy them! They were NOT gods at all – ONLY idols of wood and stone shaped by human hands. Now, O LORD our God, RESCUE us from his power; then all the kingdoms of the earth will know that You ALONE are God." Isaiah sent this message to Hezekiah: "This is what the LORD says: I have heard your prayer. The LORD spoke this Word against King Sennacherib of Assyria: "WHO have you been defying and ridiculing? At WHO did you look with such haughty eyes? It was the Holy One of Israel! Because of your raging against Me and your arrogance, I will put My hook in your nose. I will make you return by the same road on which you came. His armies will NOT enter Jerusalem. They will NOT even shoot an arrow at it. For My own honor, I will DEFEND this city and protect it." That night the angel of the LORD KILLED 185,000 Assyrian soldiers. When the surviving Assyrians woke up the next morning, they found corpses everywhere. King Sennacherib of Assyria broke camp and RETURNED to Nineveh. While he was worshiping in the temple of his god Nisroch, his sons KILLED him with their swords.

2 Kings 20:16-17, 19   Isaiah said to Hezekiah, "The time is coming when everything in your palace – all the treasures stored up by your ancestors until now – will be carried off to Babylon. Nothing will be left, says the LORD." Hezekiah said, "This message you have given me from the LORD is good." For the king was thinking, "At least there will be peace and security during my lifetime."

2 Kings 21:2-13   King Manasseh DID what was EVIL in the LORD's sight, following the DETESTABLE practices of the pagan nations that the LORD had driven from the land ahead of the Israelites. … He REBUILT the pagan shrines his father, Hezekiah, had destroyed. He constructed altars for Baal and set up an Asherah pole, just as King Ahab of Israel had done. He BUILT pagan altars IN the Temple of the LORD. Manasseh also sacrificed his OWN son IN the FIRE. He PRACTICED sorcery and divination, and he consulted with mediums and psychics. Manasseh even MADE a carved image of Asherah and set it up IN the Temple, the very place where the LORD had told David: "My Name will be honored forever in this Temple. IF the Israelites will be careful to OBEY My commands – all the laws My servant Moses gave them – I will NOT send them into exile from this land." BUT the people REFUSED to listen, and Manasseh LED them to do EVEN MORE evil THAN the pagan nations that the LORD had destroyed. The LORD said through His prophets: "King Manasseh of Judah has done many detestable things. He is EVEN MORE wicked THAN the Amorites, who lived in this land before Israel. So this is what the LORD says: I will BRING such DISASTER on Jerusalem and Judah that the ears of those who hear about it will tingle with horror. I will JUDGE Jerusalem BY the SAME STANDARD I used FOR Samaria and the SAME MEASURE I used FOR the family of Ahab. I will WIPE AWAY the people of Jerusalem."

2 Kings 22:2, 8, 11, 13-14, 16-20 King Josiah DID what was PLEASING in the LORD's sight and FOLLOWED the example of his ancestor David. He did what was RIGHT. ... Hilkiah the high priest said, "I have FOUND the Book of the Law in the LORD's Temple!" ... When the king HEARD what was WRITTEN in the Book of the Law, he tore his clothes in despair and said, "Go to the Temple and speak to the LORD for me and for all Judah. For the LORD's great anger is burning against us because our ancestors have NOT obeyed the Words in this scroll. We have NOT been doing everything it says we must do." So they went to consult with the prophet Huldah. She was the wife of Shallum. She said to them, "This is what the LORD says: I am going to bring disaster on this city and its people. ALL the WORDS in the scroll will come TRUE. For My people have abandoned Me and offered sacrifices to pagan gods. My anger will burn against this place, and it will NOT be quenched. Go to the king of Judah and tell him: 'This is what the LORD, the God of Israel, says concerning the message you have just heard: You were SORRY and HUMBLED yourself BEFORE the LORD when you heard that I said this land will be cursed and become desolate. You tore your clothing in despair and wept before Me in REPENTANCE. I have indeed HEARD you, says the LORD. So I will NOT send the promised disaster UNTIL you have died and been buried in peace.'"

2 Kings 23:2-7, 10, 13, 20-22, 24-27 The king went up to the Temple of the LORD with all the people of Judah – all the people from the least to the greatest. The king READ the ENTIRE Book of the Covenant that was found in the LORD's Temple. The king RENEWED the covenant in the LORD's Presence. He pledged to OBEY the LORD by keeping ALL His commands, laws, and decrees with all his heart and soul, and all the people pledged themselves to the covenant. Then the king REMOVED from the LORD's Temple everything that were used to worship Baal, Asherah, and all the powers of the heavens. The king had all these things BURNED outside Jerusalem. He REMOVED the FALSE priests, who had been appointed by the previous kings of Judah, for they had offered sacrifices at the pagan shrines throughout Judah. They had also offered sacrifices to Baal, and to the sun, the moon, the constellations, and to all the powers of the heavens. He also TORE DOWN the living quarters of the male and female shrine prostitutes that were inside the Temple of the LORD. The king DESECRATED the altar of Topheth, so no one could ever again use it to sacrifice a son or daughter in the fire as an offering to Molech. The king also DESECRATED the pagan shrines King Solomon had built for Ashtoreth, the detestable goddess of the Sidonians; and for Chemosh, the detestable god of the Moabites; and for Molech, the vile god of the Ammonites. The king also TORE DOWN the pagan shrine that Jeroboam had made when he caused Israel to sin. He executed the priests of the pagan shrines on their own altars. Finally, he returned to Jerusalem. King Josiah said to all the people: "You must celebrate the Passover to the LORD your God, as required in this Book of the Covenant." There had not been a Passover celebration like that since the time when the judges ruled in Israel, nor throughout all the years of the kings of Israel and Judah. Josiah also got RID of the mediums and psychics, the household gods, the idols, and every other kind of detestable practice, both in Jerusalem and throughout the land of Judah. He did this in OBEDIENCE to the laws written in the scroll that the priest had found in the LORD's Temple. Never before had there been a king like Josiah, who TURNED to the LORD with ALL his heart and soul and strength, OBEYING ALL the laws of Moses. And there has NEVER been a king like him since. Even so, the LORD was very angry with Judah because of all the wicked things Manasseh had done. For the LORD said, "I will also banish Judah from My presence just as I have banished Israel. And I will reject My chosen city of Jerusalem and the Temple where My Name was to be honored."

2 Kings 24:3-4 These disasters happened to Judah because of the LORD's command. He had decided to BANISH Judah from His Presence BECAUSE of the many sins of Manasseh, who had filled Jerusalem with INNOCENT blood. The LORD would NOT forgive this.

2 Kings 25:8-11 Nebuzaradan, an official of Babylonian's King Nebuchadnezzar, arrived in Jerusalem and BURNED DOWN the Temple of the LORD, the royal palace, and all the houses of Jerusalem. He supervised the entire Babylonian army as they TORE DOWN the walls of Jerusalem. Nebuzaradan then TOOK as EXILES the rest of the population.

1 Chronicles 22:13   David said to Solomon, "You will be successful IF you carefully OBEY the decrees the LORD gave through Moses. BE strong and courageous. Do NOT be afraid or lose heart!"

1 Chronicles 28:8-10   David said, "With God as our witness, I give you this charge. Be careful to OBEY ALL the commands of the LORD your God, learn to KNOW God INTIMATELY. Worship and SERVE Him with your WHOLE heart and a WILLING mind. For the LORD SEES every heart and KNOWS every thought. IF you SEEK Him, you will FIND Him. IF you ABANDON [leave, neglect, shun] God, He will REJECT you FOREVER. So TAKE this SERIOUSLY."

1 Chronicles 29:10-15, 17-18   David praised the LORD: "LORD, may You be PRAISED forever and ever! Yours, O LORD, is the GREATNESS, the POWER, the GLORY, the VICTORY, and the MAJESTY. Everything in the heavens and on earth is Yours, O LORD, and this is Your Kingdom. We ADORE You as the One who is OVER ALL things. Wealth and honor come from You ALONE, for You RULE over everything. Power and might are in Your hand, and at Your discretion people are made great and given strength. O our God, we THANK You! Who am I, and who are my people, that we could give anything to You? Everything we have COMES FROM You, and we GIVE You ONLY what You first GAVE us! We are here for ONLY a MOMENT, visitors and strangers in the land. Our days on earth are like a passing SHADOW, gone so soon WITHOUT a trace. ... I know, my God, that You EXAMINE our hearts and are JOYFUL when You find DEPENDABLE HONESTY there. You know I have DONE ALL this with GOOD MOTIVES, and I have watched your people offer their gifts willingly and joyously. O LORD, the God of Abraham, Isaac, and Israel, MAKE Your people WANT to OBEY You. See to it that their love for You NEVER changes."

2 Chronicles 7:1-3, 13-14   When Solomon finished praying [at the dedication of the Temple], fire flashed down from heaven and burned up the burnt offerings and sacrifices, and the glorious Presence of the

LORD filled the Temple. The priests could not enter the Temple of the LORD because the glorious Presence of the LORD filled it. When all the people of Israel saw the fire coming down and the glorious Presence of the LORD filling the Temple, they fell face down on the ground and worshiped and praised the LORD, saying, "He is GOOD! His faithful LOVE endures FOREVER!" ... The LORD said to Solomon, "At times I might shut up the heavens so that no rain falls, or command grasshoppers to devour your crops, or send plagues among you. IF My people who are called by My Name will HUMBLE themselves, PRAY, SEEK My Face and TURN FROM their wicked ways, I will HEAR from heaven and will FORGIVE their sins and RESTORE their land."

2 Chronicles 15:1-8 The Spirit of God came upon Azariah the prophet and he shouted to King Asa, "Listen, the LORD will STAY WITH you as long AS you STAY WITH Him! Whenever you SEEK Him, you will FIND Him. But IF you ABANDON Him, He will ABANDON you. For a long time Israel was without the true God, without a priest to teach them, and without the Law to instruct them. But WHENEVER they were in trouble and TURNED TO the LORD, the God of Israel, and SOUGHT Him out, they FOUND Him. During those dark times, ... nation fought against nation, and city against city, for God was troubling them with every kind of problem. But as for you, BE strong and courageous, for your work will BE rewarded." When Asa heard this message from Azariah, he took courage and REMOVED ALL the DETESTABLE idols from the land.

2 Chronicles 16:7-10 Hanani the seer said to King Asa, "BECAUSE you have put your TRUST in the king of Aram INSTEAD of in the LORD, you MISSED your CHANCE. Do you not remember what happened to the Ethiopians and Libyans? At that time you relied on the LORD, and He handed them over to you. The LORD searches the earth to STRENGTHEN those who fully COMMIT to Him. WHAT a FOOL you have been! From now on you will be at war." Asa became so angry with Hanani for saying this that he threw him into prison and began to oppress some of his people.

2 Chronicles 19:2-3, 5-7, 10-11 Jehu said to King Jehoshaphat, "WHY should you help the wicked, who hate the LORD? Because of this, the LORD is very angry with you. There is some GOOD in you, for you REMOVED the Asherah poles from the land, and are COMMITTED to SEEKING God." ... King Jehoshaphat appointed judges saying to them, "Always THINK carefully before pronouncing judgment. Remember that you do NOT judge to please people BUT to please the LORD. He will be with you when you render the verdict in each case. FEAR [respect God's power and authority, because we desire to please] the LORD and JUDGE with DEPENDABLE HONESTY, for the LORD our God does NOT tolerate perverted justice, partiality, or the taking of bribes. When a case comes to you, WARN them NOT to sin against the LORD. Do this and you will not be guilty. Take COURAGE as you fulfill your duties, and may the LORD be WITH you who DO what is RIGHT."

2 Chronicles 20:3, 6-7, 9-12, 15-17, 20-24, 29, 32-33 [King] Jehoshaphat was terrified by this news and begged the LORD for guidance. … He prayed, "LORD, You ALONE are the God who is in heaven. You are Ruler of ALL the kingdoms of the earth. You are powerful and mighty; NONE can stand against You! O our God, You drove out those who lived in this land when your people Israel arrived! … Your people said, 'Whenever we are faced with any calamity such as war, plague, or famine, we can come to stand in Your Presence before this Temple where Your Name is honored. We can cry out to You to save us, and You will HEAR us and RESCUE us.' See what the armies of Ammon, Moab, and Mount Seir are doing. You would not let our ancestors invade those nations when Israel left Egypt, so they went around them and did not destroy them. See how they reward us! They come to throw us out of Your land. O our God, will You STOP them? We are POWERLESS against this mighty army. We do NOT know what to DO, but we are LOOKING to You for HELP." … Jahaziel said, "Listen, King Jehoshaphat! This is what the LORD says: Do NOT be afraid! Do NOT be discouraged by this mighty army, for the BATTLE is NOT yours, BUT God's. Tomorrow, march out against them. But you will NOT even need to fight. Take your positions; then STAND still and WATCH the LORD's VICTORY. The LORD is WITH you!" … On the way Jehoshaphat stopped and said, "Listen to me, all you people! BELIEVE in the LORD your God, AND you will be able to STAND FIRM." The king appointed singers to walk ahead of the army, PRAISING the LORD: "Give THANKS to the LORD; His faithful love endures forever!" AT the VERY MOMENT they BEGAN to SING and give praise, the LORD CAUSED the armies of Ammon, Moab, and Mount Seir to start fighting among themselves and killed each other. When the army of Judah arrived at the lookout point, all they saw were dead bodies lying on the ground as far as they could see. NOT a single one of the enemy had escaped. … When all the surrounding kingdoms heard that the LORD had FOUGHT against the enemies of Israel, the FEAR of God came over them. …

Jehoshaphat did what was PLEASING in the LORD's sight. However, he FAILED to remove all the pagan shrines, and the people NEVER fully committed themselves to follow the LORD.

2 Chronicles 24:17-22, 25 The leaders of Judah came to King Joash and PERSUADED him to LISTEN to their ADVICE. They ABANDONED the Temple of the LORD, and they worshiped Asherah poles and idols instead! The LORD sent prophets to bring them back to Him. The prophets WARNED them, but the people would NOT listen. The Spirit of God came upon Zechariah who said, "This is what God says: WHY do you DISOBEY the LORD's commands and KEEP yourselves FROM prospering? You have ABANDONED the LORD, and NOW He has ABANDONED you!" The leaders plotted to kill Zechariah, and stone him to death in the courtyard of the LORD's Temple. Zechariah's last words were, "May the LORD avenge my death!" ... The Arameans withdrew, leaving Joash severely wounded. His own officials plotted to kill him for murdering Zechariah, the son of Jehoiada the priest. They assassinated him as he lay in bed.

2 Chronicles 25:2, 14-16, 27 [King] Amaziah did what was pleasing in the LORD's sight, but NOT wholeheartedly. ... When King Amaziah returned from slaughtering the Edomites, he brought with him idols taken from the people of Seir. He SET them UP as his OWN gods, bowed down in front of them, and offered sacrifices to them! The LORD was very angry, and sent a prophet to ask, "WHY do you TURN to gods who could NOT even SAVE their own people from you?" But the king interrupted him and said, "Since when have I made you the king's counselor? Be quiet now before I have you killed!" The prophet stopped with this warning: "I know that God has determined to DESTROY you because you have done this and have REFUSED to accept my counsel." Amaziah REFUSED to listen. After Amaziah TURNED away FROM the LORD, there was a conspiracy and assassins killed him.

2 Chronicles 26:5, 16-21 AS LONG AS the king sought GUIDANCE from the LORD, God gave him success. When King Uzziah became powerful, he also became PROUD, which LED to his DOWNFALL. He sinned against the LORD by entering the sanctuary of the LORD's Temple and personally burning incense. Azariah the high priest went in to confront King Uzziah and said, "It is not for you, Uzziah, to burn incense to the LORD. That is the work of the priests alone. Get out of the sanctuary, for you have sinned. The LORD God will NOT honor you for this!" Uzziah became furious, BUT as he was standing there RAGING, leprosy suddenly broke out on his forehead. The king was eager to get out because the LORD had STRUCK him. King Uzziah had leprosy until he died. He lived in isolation in a separate house.

2 Chronicles 30:6-11, 18-20, 26   King Hezekiah said: "People of Israel, RETURN to the LORD, the God of Abraham, Isaac, and Israel, SO that He will RETURN to the few of us who have survived the conquest of the Assyrian kings. Do NOT be like your ancestors and relatives who abandoned the LORD, and became an object of derision. Do NOT be stubborn, as they were, but SUBMIT yourselves to the LORD. Worship the LORD your God so that His fierce anger will turn away from you. ... If you return to the LORD, your relatives and your children will be treated mercifully by their captors, and they will be able to return to this land. The LORD your God is gracious and merciful. IF you RETURN to Him, He will NOT continue to turn His face from you." ... MOST of the people from Israel just LAUGHED at the message. ... SOME people HUMBLED themselves and went to Jerusalem. ... The LORD listened to Hezekiah's prayer and healed the people. ... There was great JOY in the city, for Jerusalem had not seen a celebration like this one since the days of King Solomon.

2 Chronicles 32:6-8, 24-26   Hezekiah said: "BE strong and courageous! Do NOT be afraid or discouraged because of the king of Assyria, for there is a Power FAR GREATER on our side! He may have a great army, but they are merely men. We have the LORD our God to HELP us and to FIGHT our battles for us!" Hezekiah's words greatly ENCOURAGED the people. ... Hezekiah became deathly ill. He prayed to the LORD, who healed him. But Hezekiah did NOT respond APPROPRIATELY to the KINDNESS, and he BECAME PROUD. So the LORD's anger came against him and against Judah and Jerusalem. Then Hezekiah HUMBLED himself and REPENTED of his pride, as did the people. The LORD's anger did not fall on them during Hezekiah's lifetime.

2 Chronicles 33:6, 9-13, 15-16, 22-24   Manasseh also sacrificed his OWN sons in the FIRE in the valley of Ben-Hinnom. He PRACTICED sorcery, divination, and witchcraft, and he consulted with mediums and psychics. He DID MUCH that was EVIL in the LORD's sight, arousing His anger. Manasseh LED the people of Judah and Jerusalem to do EVEN MORE evil THAN the pagan nations that the LORD had destroyed when the people of Israel entered the land. The LORD spoke to Manasseh and his people, but they IGNORED all His warnings. So the LORD sent the commanders of the Assyrian armies, and they took Manasseh prisoner.

They put a ring through his nose, bound him in bronze chains, and led him away to Babylon. But while in DEEP DISTRESS, Manasseh SOUGHT the LORD his God and sincerely HUMBLED himself before the God of his ancestors. And when he PRAYED, the LORD listened to him and was moved by his request. So the LORD brought Manasseh back to Jerusalem and to his kingdom. Then Manasseh finally REALIZED that the LORD ALONE is God! After this Manasseh REMOVED the foreign gods and the idol FROM the LORD's Temple. He TORE DOWN all the altars he had built on the hill where the Temple stood and all the altars that were in Jerusalem, and he dumped them outside the city. Then he RESTORED the ALTAR of the LORD and sacrificed peace offerings and thanksgiving offerings on it. He also ENCOURAGED the people of Judah to WORSHIP the LORD, the God of Israel. ... Amon did what was EVIL in the LORD's sight, just as his father, Manasseh, had done. He worshiped and sacrificed to all the idols. Unlike his father, he did NOT humble himself before the LORD. Amon sinned EVEN MORE. Amon's own officials ASSASINATED him.

2 Chronicles 34:33 Josiah REMOVED all detestable idols from the entire land of Israel, requiring everyone to worship the LORD. Throughout his lifetime, they did NOT turn from the LORD.

2 Chronicles 36:13-23 Zedekiah rebelled against King Nebuchadnezzar, EVEN THOUGH he had taken an oath of loyalty in God's Name. Zedekiah was a hard and stubborn man, REFUSING to turn to the LORD. All the leaders of the priests and the people became MORE UNFAITHFUL [disloyal]. They FOLLOWED all the pagan practices of the surrounding nations, DESECRATING the Temple of the LORD. The LORD repeatedly sent His prophets to warn them, for He had compassion on His people. But the people MOCKED these messengers of God and DESPISED their words. They SCOFFED at the prophets UNTIL the LORD's anger could no longer be restrained and nothing could be done. The LORD handed all of them over to the Babylonians, who had NO PITY on the people, to kill both young men and young women, the old and the infirm. King Nebuchadnezzar took home to Babylon all the articles used in the Temple of God, and the treasures from both the LORD's Temple and from the palace of the king and his officials. Then his army burned the Temple of God, tore down the walls of Jerusalem, burned all the palaces, and completely destroyed everything of value. The few who survived were taken as exiles to Babylon, and they became servants until the kingdom of Persia came to power. So the message of the LORD spoken through Jeremiah was FULFILLED. The land finally enjoyed its Sabbath rest, lying desolate until the 70 years were fulfilled, just as the prophet had said. In the first year of King Cyrus of Persia, the LORD fulfilled the prophecy he had given through Jeremiah. This is what King Cyrus says: "The LORD, the God of heaven, has given me all the kingdoms of the earth. He has appointed me to build Him a Temple at Jerusalem, in Judah. Any of you who are the LORD's people may go there for this task. And may the LORD your God be with you!"

Ezra 7:9-10 The gracious hand of God was on him, BECAUSE Ezra had determined to STUDY and OBEY the Law of the LORD and to TEACH those decrees and regulations to the people of Israel.

Ezra 8:31-32 God PROTECTED and saved us from enemies and bandits. So we arrived SAFELY.

Ezra 9:10-12, 14-15 God, your prophets warned us, "The land you are entering is totally defiled by the DETESTABLE practices of the people living there. The land is filled with CORRUPTION. Do NOT let your daughters marry their sons! Do NOT let your sons marry their daughters! Do not ever promote the peace and prosperity of those nations. IF you FOLLOW these instructions, you will be strong and enjoy the good things the land produces, and you will leave prosperity to your children." BUT even so, we are AGAIN breaking your commands and intermarrying with people who do these detestable things. O LORD, God of Israel, You are JUST. We come before You in our guilt as nothing, NONE of us can stand in Your Presence.

Nehemiah 6:14-16 Remember, O my God, all the EVIL things that Tobiah and Sanballat have done. Remember Noadiah and all the prophets like her who have TRIED to INTIMIDATE me. The entire WALL around Jerusalem was FINISHED – in just 52 days. When our enemies heard about it, they were frightened and humiliated. They REALIZED this work was done WITH our God's HELP.

Nehemiah 8:3, 7-8, 10, 12 Ezra from early morning until noon, READ aloud to everyone who could understand. All the people LISTENED closely to the Book of the Law. … The Levites then read from the Book of the Law of God and clearly EXPLAINED the MEANING of what was being read, helping the people understand each passage. … Nehemiah continued, "Go and celebrate, SHARE gifts of food with people who have nothing prepared. Do NOT be dejected and sad, for the JOY of the LORD is your strength!" ... So the people celebrated with great JOY because they had HEARD God's Words and UNDERSTOOD them.

Nehemiah 9:2-3, 32-36 Those of Israelite descent separated themselves from foreigners as they confessed their own sins and the sins of their ancestors. They stood for 3 hours while the Book of the Law of the LORD was read to them. For 3 more hours they confessed their sins and worshiped the LORD. ... God, the great, mighty, awesome God, keeps His covenant of unfailing love. Great trouble has come upon us and our leaders and priests. EVERY TIME You punished us You were BEING JUST. We have sinned greatly, and You GAVE us only WHAT we DESERVED. Our kings, leaders, priests, and ancestors did NOT obey Your Law OR listen to the warnings in Your commands and laws. They did NOT serve You, though You showered Your goodness on them. They REFUSED to TURN FROM their wickedness. So NOW TODAY we are slaves in the land of plenty that You GAVE our ancestors for their enjoyment!

Esther 4:14-16
Mordecai said, "IF you KEEP QUIET at a time like this, deliverance for the Jews will come from ANOTHER place, BUT you will die. PERHAPS you were MADE queen FOR just such a TIME as THIS?" Esther replied to Mordecai, "Go, hold a fast on my behalf. I and my maids will also fast. After that I will go to the king, though it is against the law; and if I perish, I perish."

Job 1:21-22
Job said, "I came naked from my mother's womb, and I will be naked when I leave. The LORD GAVE me what I had, and the LORD has TAKEN it away. PRAISE the Name of the LORD!" In all of this, Job did NOT sin BY blaming God.

Job 3:20, 23, 25-26 Job said, "WHY give life to those who are BITTER? ... WHY is life given to those with no future? ... What I always FEARED has happened to me. ... I have no peace, no quietness, no rest; ONLY trouble."

Job 4:17 ERV A person CANNOT be MORE right THAN God. People CANNOT be MORE pure THAN their Maker.

Job 5:8-9 ERV If I were you, I would TURN to God and TELL Him about my problems. People cannot understand the WONDERFUL things God does. His MIRACLES are too many to count.

Job 6:25-26 ERV   Honest words are POWERFUL, but your arguments prove NOTHING. Do you think your words are convincing when you DISREGARD my cry of desperation?

Job 7:7, 17 ERV   God, remember, my life is like a breath. I will NOT GET a SECOND CHANCE to enjoy it. What are people, that You make so much of us, that You think of us so often?

Job 8:13-14   All who FORGET God: their HOPE evaporates. They are leaning on a spider's web.

Job 11:7 ERV   Do you think you really completely UNDERSTAND God All-Powerful?

Job 12:2-3, 13, 16-17, 19, 21-22   You people really KNOW everything, don't you? And when you die, wisdom will die with you! Well, I know a few things myself – and you are NO better than I am. ... TRUE WISDOM and POWER are found in God; counsel and understanding are His. ... God is strong and ALWAYS WINS. He controls those who FOOL others and those who are FOOLED. He strips advisors of their wisdom and makes leaders act like fools. ... He strips priests of their power and removes those who feel so secure in their position. ... He brings disgrace to important people. He takes power away from rulers. He EXPOSES the darkest SECRETS.

Job 13:4-5, 7   You SMEAR me with LIES. As physicians, you are WORTHLESS quacks. Be SILENT! That's the WISEST thing you could do. Are you defending God with lies for His sake?

Job 14:5   God DECIDES the LENGTH of our LIVES, and we are NOT given a minute longer.

Job 15:2-6   A WISE man would NOT answer with such EMPTY talk! Have you NO fear of God, NO reverence for Him? Your SINS are telling your mouth WHAT to SAY. Your words are based on clever DECEPTION. Your own mouth condemns you, not I. Your own lips testify against you.

Job 16:4-5   I could spout criticism. But I will ENCOURAGE you and try to take away your grief.

Job 17:3-4 ERV   God, give me some SUPPORT. No one else will! My friends' MINDS are CLOSED. They do NOT understand. Please do NOT let them win.

Job 18:3 ERV   Why do you THINK we are STUPID, like dumb cows?

Job 19:3-5 You have INSULTED me 10 times. You should be ashamed. Even if I have sinned, that is MY concern, NOT yours. You think you are better, using my humiliation as evidence of my sin.

Job 19:25-27, 29 I KNOW that my Redeemer LIVES, and He will stand upon the earth at last. After my body has decayed, yet in my body I will SEE God! I am overwhelmed at the thought! ... You should FEAR punishment yourselves, for your attitude DESERVES punishment.

Job 21:2-3, 22, 34 LISTEN closely to what I am saying. Let this be your way of COMFORTING me. Be PATIENT while I speak. After I have spoken, you may resume mocking me. ... WHO can TEACH a lesson TO God, since He judges even the most powerful? ... How can your empty clichés comfort me? All your EXPLANATIONS are LIES!

Job 24:23-24 The wicked may be allowed to live, but God is always WATCHING them. And though they are great now, in a moment they will be gone like all others, cut off like heads of grain.

Job 27:4-5 My lips will speak NO lies. I will NEVER concede that you are right.

Job 28:28 ERV God said, "To FEAR [honor God's power and authority because we desire to please Him] and RESPECT the Lord is WISDOM. To TURN from evil is UNDERSTANDING."

Job 29:12-13, 16 I assisted the poor in their need and orphans who required help. I helped those without hope. I caused the widows' hearts to sing for joy. I assisted strangers who needed help.

Job 30:1 I am mocked by people younger than I, whose fathers are not worthy to run with my dogs.

Job 33:14-18 God SPEAKS again and again, though people do NOT recognize it. He speaks in DREAMS, ... when deep sleep falls on people as they lie in their beds. He whispers in their ears and terrifies them with warnings. He TURNS them FROM doing wrong. He keeps them FROM pride. He protects them FROM death.

Job 38:1-4, 12, 33 The LORD answered Job: "WHO is this that questions My wisdom with such IGNORANT words? I have some questions for you. Where were you when I laid the foundations of the earth? Tell me, IF you KNOW so MUCH. Have you ever commanded the morning to appear? Do you know the laws of the universe? Can you use them to regulate the earth?"

Job 41:10-11   The LORD said: "Since no one DARES to disturb Leviathan, WHO can stand up to Me? WHO has given Me anything that I need to pay back? Everything under heaven IS Mine."

Job 42:1-2, 5-6, 7-8, 10   Job replied to the LORD: "I know that You can do anything, and no one can stop You. I had only heard about You before, but now I have seen You with my own eyes. I take back everything I said, and I sit in dust and ashes to show my REPENTANCE." After the LORD had finished speaking to Job, he said to Eliphaz the Temanite: "I am angry with you and your 2 friends, for you have NOT spoken accurately about Me, AS my servant Job has. My servant Job will pray for you, and I will accept his prayer on your behalf. I will NOT TREAT you AS you DESERVE." When Job PRAYED for his friends, the LORD RESTORED Job and gave him TWICE as much as before!

Psalms 1:1-3
The JOYS of those who do NOT follow the ADVICE of the wicked, or stand WITH sinners, or join WITH mockers. They DELIGHT in the Law of the LORD, meditating day and night.

Psalms 2:1-5   WHY are the nations so ANGRY? WHY do they WASTE their TIME with FUTILE plans? The rulers plot together AGAINST the LORD and AGAINST His Anointed One [Jesus]. "Let us," they cry, "FREE ourselves FROM slavery to GOD." But GOD who rules in heaven LAUGHS. Then in anger He REBUKES them.

Psalm 5:1-2, 4-12   LORD, HEAR me as I pray, pay attention to my groaning. Listen to my cry for HELP, my King and my God, for I PRAY to no one but You. ... God, You take NO pleasure in wickedness, You can NOT tolerate the sins of the wicked. Therefore, the proud may NOT stand in Your Presence, for You HATE all who do EVIL. You will destroy those who tell LIES. The LORD DETESTS murderers and deceivers. Because of Your unfailing love, I can enter Your house; I will worship You with deepest AWE. LEAD me in the RIGHT path, LORD, or my enemies will conquer me. Make Your Way plain for me to FOLLOW. My enemies cannot speak a truthful word. Their deepest desire is to destroy others. Their talk is FOUL. Their tongues are filled with FLATTERY. God, declare them guilty. Let them be caught in their own TRAPS, for they have rebelled against You. Let all who take REFUGE in You be FULL of JOY. Spread Your protection over them, that all who love You may be filled with JOY. LORD, You surround them with Your Shield of Love.

Psalms 7:1, 3-5, 10, 14 AMP ERV, 16-17 LORD, I come to you for protection. Save me from my persecutors! ... Lord, IF I have done wrong or IF I have betrayed a friend, THEN let my enemies trample me. ... God is my SHIELD, saving those whose hearts are TRUE and RIGHT. ... The minds of wicked men are full of evil, they are pregnant with wicked plans, which give birth to lies. ... The trouble they make for others backfires on them. I will THANK the Lord because He is just.

Psalm 9:1-2 I will give THANKS to the Lord with my whole heart. I will tell of all the WONDERFUL things You have done. I will be filled with JOY because of You.

Psalm 10:16 The LORD is King FOREVER and ever! The GODLESS nations will VANISH.

Psalms 11:1, 3-5, 7 I TRUST the Lord for protection. ... The foundations of law and order have collapsed. WHAT can the righteous DO? But the LORD ... still RULES from heaven. He WATCHES everyone closely, EXAMINING every person. ... The Lord HATES those who love VIOLENCE. ... The people who DO RIGHT will SEE the Lord who loves JUSTICE.

Psalm 16:8-11 I know the LORD is ALWAYS with me. I will NOT be shaken, for He is right beside me. ... My heart is glad, and I am FULL of JOY. My body rests in safety. For You will NOT leave my soul among the dead or allow your Holy One [Jesus] to rot in the grave. You show me the WAY of life, granting me the JOY of Your Presence, and the pleasure of living WITH You forever!

Psalm 18:30 God's way is perfect. All the LORD's promises prove TRUE. He is a shield for all who TRUST Him.

Psalm 19:1, 7-8, 12-14 The heavens PROCLAIM the glory of God. The skies DISPLAY His craftsmanship. ... The instructions of the LORD are perfect, REVIVING the soul. The decrees of the LORD are trustworthy, making WISE the simple. The commandments of the LORD are RIGHT. ... LORD, how can I know all the sins lurking in my heart? Cleanse me from these hidden faults. KEEP your servant from DELIBERATE sins! Do NOT let them CONTROL me. THEN I will be free of guilt and innocent of great sin. May the words of my mouth and the meditation of my heart be PLEASING to You, O LORD, my Rock and my Redeemer.

Psalm 20:1, 7 In times of trouble, may the LORD answer your cry. ... Some nations boast of their chariots and horses, but we BOAST in the Name of the LORD our God.

Psalm 21:6 You have given him the JOY of Your Presence.

Psalm 23:1-6 The LORD is my shepherd; I have all that I need. He lets me REST beside peaceful streams. He RENEWS my strength. He GUIDES me along RIGHT paths, bringing honor to His Name. Even WHEN I walk through the valley of the shadow of death, I will NOT be afraid, for You are CLOSE BESIDE me. You PROTECT and COMFORT me. You prepare a feast for me in the presence of my enemies. My cup overflows with blessings. Your goodness and unfailing love pursue me all my life. I will LIVE in the house of the LORD FOREVER.

Psalms 24:1, 3-5 The earth is the LORD's, and everything in it. All people BELONG to Him. WHO may stand in the Lord's holy place? ONLY those whose hands and hearts are pure, who do NOT worship idols and NEVER tell lies. They will have a RIGHT RELATIONSHIP with God their Savior.

Psalm 25:4-5 LORD, SHOW me the RIGHT path to follow. LEAD me by Your TRUTH, for You are the God who SAVES me. All day long I put my HOPE in You.

Psalms 27:1 The LORD is my LIGHT and my SALVATION – so WHY should I be afraid? The Lord is my fortress, protecting me from danger, so WHY should I tremble?

Psalm 31:15 My FUTURE is in Your hands. Rescue me from those who hunt me down relentlessly.

Psalm 32:1-6 What JOY for those whose disobedience is FORGIVEN! What JOY for those who live in HONESTY! When I REFUSED to confess my sin, I groaned all day long. Your hand of discipline was heavy on me. Finally, I CONFESSED all my sins to You and STOPPED trying to hide my guilt. And You FORGAVE me! All my guilt is gone. Therefore, let all the godly PRAY to You WHILE there is STILL TIME, that they may NOT die in judgment.

Psalm 33:8, 12 Let the whole world FEAR [respect and honor God's power and authority, because we desire to please] the LORD, and let everyone stand in AWE of Him. What JOY for the nation whose God is the LORD.

Psalms 34:1-2, 4, 17-19 I will PRAISE the LORD CONTINUALLY. I will boast ONLY in the LORD, let the helpless be encouraged. I prayed to the LORD, and He answered me. He FREED me FROM all my fears. The LORD hears His people when they call for help. He rescues them from all their troubles. The LORD is CLOSE TO the brokenhearted. He RESCUES those whose spirits are crushed. The righteous person faces many troubles, but the Lord comes to the rescue each time.

Psalms 36:1-4 Sin whispers to the wicked, deep within their hearts. They have NO fear of God at all. In their BLIND conceit, they CANNOT see how wicked they really are. Everything they SAY is crooked and deceitful. They REFUSE to act wisely or do good. Their actions are never good. They make NO attempt to TURN FROM evil.

Psalm 37:1-2, 4-5, 8, 23-24 Do NOT worry about OR envy those who DO wrong. Like spring flowers, they soon wither. Take DELIGHT in the LORD, and He will GIVE you your heart's desires. The LORD directs the steps of the godly. Commit everything you do to the LORD. Trust Him, and He will help you. STOP being angry! TURN FROM your rage! Do NOT lose your temper – it leads to harm. Though the godly stumble, they will never fall, for the Lord holds them by the hand.

Psalms 40:1-3 I WAITED patiently for the LORD to HELP me. He heard my cry. He drew me up FROM the pit of despair, OUT of the miry clay, and set my feet upon SOLID ground, giving me a new PRAISE song to sing to God. Many who SEE with fear and awe put their TRUST in the LORD.

Psalm 45:6 ERV God, Your kingdom will last FOREVER. You use Your authority for JUSTICE.

Psalms 46:1-3, 6-8, 10 God is our REFUGE and strength, always READY to help in times of trouble. So we will NOT fear when earthquakes come and the mountains crumble into the sea. Let the oceans roar and foam. … The nations are in chaos, and their kingdoms crumble! God's voice thunders, and the earth melts! The LORD is here AMONG us and is our fortress. Come, SEE the glorious works of the Lord. … The LORD says, "Be STILL, and KNOW that I AM God!"

Psalm 51:1-4, 10-13, 17 Have MERCY on me, O God, because of Your unfailing love. PURIFY me from my sin. For I recognize my rebellion. Against You alone, have I sinned. I did what is evil in Your sight. Your judgment against me is JUST. … Create in me a CLEAN heart, O God. Renew a LOYAL spirit within me. Do NOT banish me from Your

Presence, and do NOT take Your Holy Spirit from me. RESTORE to me the JOY of Your salvation, and MAKE me WILLING to OBEY You. THEN I will teach Your Ways to rebels, and they will return to You. ... The sacrifice You desire is a BROKEN spirit. You will NOT reject a broken, REPENTANT heart.

Psalms 55:22   GIVE your burdens TO the LORD, and He will take CARE of you.

Psalms 56:1-2, 4-5, 7, 12-13   God, have MERCY on me. I am hounded by those who slander me, and many are attacking me. ... I TRUST in God, so WHY should I be afraid? WHAT can MERE mortals DO to me? They are always twisting what I say; they are plotting to harm me. ... God, bring them down. ... I will offer a sacrifice of THANKS for Your help. For you have RESCUED me from death; you have KEPT my feet FROM slipping. So NOW I can WALK in Your Presence.

Psalms 57:7, 10-11   My heart is CONFIDENT in You, O God. I can sing Your PRAISES, for Your unfailing love and faithfulness are as high as the heavens. May Your glory SHINE over all the earth.

Psalm 62:1-2, 5   I WAIT quietly before God, for my VICTORY comes from Him. The LORD ALONE is my salvation, and my fortress where I will never be shaken, ... for my HOPE is in Him.

Psalm 63:1-8, 11 ERV   God, You ARE my God. I am SEARCHING hard to FIND You. I thirst for You in this dry and weary land. I have seen Your strength and glory. Your faithful love is BETTER than life, so with my lips and by my life, I will PRAISE You. I pray ONLY in Your Name. When I sit down to satisfy my hunger, my JOYFUL lips hunger to praise You! I think about You in the middle of the night, because You help me. I STAY CLOSE to You, and JOYFULLY sing under Your protection! ... All who TRUST in You will PRAISE You, while LIARS will be SILENCED.

Psalm 67:1-3   May God be gracious to us and bless us, that Your Ways and Your Salvation may be KNOWN among all nations. May all the peoples PRAISE You, O God.

Psalm 68:3   The GODLY [committed to obeying God] have JOY and DELIGHT in God's Presence.

Psalm 69:4, 28   Those who HATE me WITHOUT cause outnumber the hairs on my head. Many enemies try to DESTROY me with LIES, demanding that I give back what I didn't steal. ... ERASE their names from the Book of Life, do NOT let them be among the RIGHTEOUS [being right, based on God's standard, includes thoughts, words and actions].

Psalm 84:10 A single day in Your courts is BETTER than a thousand anywhere else! I would rather be a gatekeeper in the house of my God THAN live the "good" life in the homes of the wicked.

Psalm 89:14 ERV Your Kingdom is built on TRUTH and JUSTICE. LOVE and FAITHFULNESS are your servants before Your Throne.

Psalms 91:1-2, 5-7, 9 ERV, 14-16 Those who LIVE in the shelter of the Most High will find REST in the shadow of the Almighty. The LORD ALONE is my refuge, my place of safety. He is my God, and I TRUST Him. … Do NOT be afraid of the terrors of the night, NOR the arrow that flies in the day. Do NOT dread the disease that stalks in darkness, NOR the disaster that strikes at midday. Though a thousand fall at your side, these evils will NOT touch you. … IF you TRUST in the Lord for protection. … The Lord says, "I will RESCUE those who love Me. I will PROTECT those who trust in My Name. I will ANSWER when they call on Me. I will be WITH them in trouble."

Psalm 95:7-8, 10-11 LISTEN to His Voice TODAY! The LORD says, "Do NOT harden your hearts as Israel did, who refused to do what I said. They NEVER entered My place of rest."

Psalm 100:2-5 Worship the LORD with GLADNESS, singing with JOY. The LORD is God! He made us, and we are His. Enter His gates with THANKSGIVING to Him, for the LORD is GOOD.

Psalms 103:1-4 Let all that I am PRAISE the LORD with my whole heart. May I NEVER forget the GOOD things He DOES for me. He FORGIVES all my sins and HEALS all my diseases. He REDEEMS me from death and crowns me with LOVE and tender MERCIES.

Psalm 109:1-5, 20-22, 25-31 O God, whom I praise, do NOT stand silent while the wicked slander me and tell lies about me. They surround me with hateful words and fight against me for no reason. I love them, but they try to destroy me with accusations even as I am praying for them! They repay evil for good, and hatred for my love. … May their curses become the LORD's punishment for my accusers who speak evil of me. Rescue me because You are so faithful and good. For I am poor and needy, and my heart is full of pain. … I am a joke to people everywhere; when they see me. Help me, O LORD my God! Save me because of

Your unfailing love. Let them see that You have done it, LORD. Let them curse me if they like, but You will bless me! When they attack me, they will be disgraced and humiliated! But I, Your servant, will be FULL of JOY! I will GIVE repeated THANKS to the LORD, praising Him to everyone. For He stands with the needy, ready to save them.

Psalm 116:15 PRECIOUS in the sight of the LORD is the death of His FAITHFUL ones.

Psalms 118:4-8 Let all who fear [reverential awe, honor, respect] the LORD repeat: "His faithful love endures forever." In my distress I prayed to the Lord, and the Lord answered me and set me free. The LORD is FOR me, so I will have NO fear. WHAT can MERE people DO to me? Yes, the LORD will HELP me. ... It is BETTER to take refuge in the LORD THAN to trust people.

Psalms 119:9, 11, 28-29, 89, 105, 130 How can a young person stay PURE? By OBEYING Your Word. ... I have hidden Your Word in my heart, that I might not sin against You. ... I weep with sorrow; ENCOURAGE me by Your Word. ... KEEP me from LYING to MYSELF; give me the privilege of knowing Your Instructions. ... Your eternal Word, O LORD, stands firm. Your Word GUIDES me and is a LIGHT for my path ... so even the simple can understand.

Psalms 122:1, 6 I was GLAD when they said to me, "Let us go to the house of the LORD!" ... Pray for PEACE in Jerusalem. May all who love this city prosper.

Psalm 126:5 Those who plant in TEARS will harvest with shouts of JOY.

Psalm 127:1 UNLESS the LORD builds a house, the work of the builders is wasted. UNLESS the LORD protects a city, guarding it with sentries will do no good.

Psalms 128:1-6 How JOYFUL are those who RESPECTFULLY fear [reverential awe, honor] the LORD – all who FOLLOW His ways! You will enjoy the fruit of your labor. How JOYFUL ... you will be! Your wife will be ... flourishing within your home. Your children will be ... vigorous as they sit around your table. ... May you see Jerusalem prosper as long as you live. May you live to enjoy your grandchildren. May Israel have peace!

Psalms 135:18 Those who MAKE idols BECOME like THEM, as do ALL who trust in idols!

Psalm 139:1, 4-5, 7, 12-16 LORD, You have EXAMINED my heart and KNOW everything about me. ... You know what I am going to say even before I say it, LORD. You go before me and follow me. ... I can NEVER get away from Your Presence! ... To You the night shines as bright as day. Darkness and light are the same to You. You made all the delicate, inner parts of my body in my mother's womb. Thank you for making me so wonderfully complex! You watched me as I was woven together in the dark of the womb. Every day of my life was RECORDED in Your Book.

Psalm 143:8 Let me HEAR of Your unfailing love each morning, for I am trusting You. SHOW me where to walk, for I give myself to You.

Psalms 145:18-19, 21 The LORD is CLOSE to all who CALL on Him in TRUTH. He grants the desires of those who fear [reverential awe, respect] Him. He hears their cries for help and rescues them. I will praise the LORD, and may everyone on earth bless His Holy Name forever and ever.

Psalm 146:8-9 The LORD opens the eyes of the blind. The LORD lifts up those who are down. The LORD cares for the foreigners, orphans and widows. The LORD frustrates the plans of the wicked.

Psalms 150:1-2, 6 PRAISE the LORD! Praise Him for His mighty works! Praise His unequaled greatness! ... Let everything that breathes sing praises to the LORD! PRAISE the LORD!

Proverbs 1:7, 10

FEAR [reverential awe, honor, respect] of the LORD is the BEGINNING of TRUE knowledge, but FOOLS DESPISE wisdom and discipline. ... IF sinners ENTICE you, TURN FROM them!

Proverbs 3:5-7, 25-29, 31-32 TRUST in the LORD with all your heart; do NOT DEPEND on your own understanding. SEEK His will in ALL you DO, and He will SHOW you WHICH path to take. Do NOT be impressed with your own wisdom. Instead, fear [reverential awe, honor, respect] the Lord and TURN FROM evil. ... You need NOT be afraid of sudden disaster or the destruction that comes on the wicked, for the LORD is your security. He will KEEP you FROM being caught in a TRAP. ...Do NOT withhold good WHEN it is in your power to HELP. If you can help your neighbor NOW, do NOT say, "Come back tomorrow." ... Do NOT envy violent people or copy their ways. Such wicked people are DETESTABLE to the LORD, but He offers FRIENDSHIP to the godly.

Proverbs 4:19, 23-25, 27   The way of the WICKED is like total DARKNESS. They have NO idea what they are stumbling over.   ... GUARD your HEART above all else, for it DETERMINES the course of your life. AVOID perverse talk. STAY FROM corrupt speech. Look STRAIGHT ahead [not to the left or the right]. Do NOT get sidetracked. ... KEEP FROM following evil.

Proverbs 6:16-19, 32   The LORD HATES 7 things: haughty [proud, arrogant] eyes, a lying tongue, hands that kill the innocent, a heart that plots evil, feet that race to do wrong, a false witness who pours out lies, and a person who sows discord [division] in a family. ... The man who commits adultery is an UTTER FOOL, for he DESTROYS himself.

Proverbs 8:13   All who FEAR [reverential awe, honor, respect] the LORD will HATE evil.   Therefore, I HATE pride and arrogance, corruption and perverse speech.

Proverbs 9:10   FEAR [respect God's power and authority, not because He is angry with us, but because we desire to please Him] of the LORD is the FOUNDATION of WISDOM. Knowledge of the Holy One results in GOOD judgment.

Proverbs 12:5, 8, 11   The thoughts of the godly [committed to obeying God] are JUST. The advice of the WICKED is DECEITFUL. A sensible person wins admiration, but a WARPED mind is DESPISED. ... A person who CHASES FANTASIES has NO sense.

Proverbs 13:13 NKJV   He who DESPISES God's Word will be DESTROYED.

Proverbs 14:33 ESV   Wisdom rests in people of understanding, but it makes itself known even in the midst of fools.

Proverbs 15:1   A GENTLE answer DEFLECTS anger, but harsh words make tempers flare.

Proverbs 16:24-25   KIND words are like honey – sweet to the soul and HEALTHY for the body.   There is a PATH before each person that SEEMS right, but it ENDS IN death.

Proverbs 17:22   A JOYFUL [thankful, laughing] heart is good medicine.

Proverbs 18:2, 12-13, 15, 21, 24   FOOLS have NO interest in UNDERSTANDING, but ONLY in expressing their OPINIONS. ... Haughtiness [contempt, pride] goes BEFORE destruction.   Humility precedes honor. Answering BEFORE listening to the facts is FOOLISH.

... Intelligent people are always READY to LEARN. Their ears are open for knowledge. ... The tongue BRINGS death OR life, those who love to TALK will reap the CONSEQUENCES. ... The man with too many "friends" of the world will be RUINED, but there is a Friend who is more reliable than a brother.

Proverbs 19:21-23   You can make plans, BUT the LORD's purpose will prevail. LOYALTY makes a person attractive. It is BETTER to be poor THAN dishonest. FEAR [respect God's power and authority because we desire to please Him] of the LORD LEADS to life.

Proverbs 21:23   Watch your tongue and KEEP your mouth SHUT, and you will stay out of trouble.

Proverbs 22:6, 24-25   DIRECT your CHILDREN onto the RIGHT path, and when they are older, they will NOT leave it. ... Do NOT be friends with ANGRY people, or you will learn to be like them and be a DANGER to your soul.

Proverbs 23:7 NKJV   For AS he THINKS in his heart, so IS he.

Proverbs 24:11-12   RESCUE those who are unjustly sentenced to die. Do NOT excuse yourself by saying, "We did not know." God KNOWS you KNEW. God REPAYS people AS their ACTIONS DESERVE.

Proverbs 26:4-5, 11-12   Do NOT answer the FOOLISH arguments of fools, or YOU will BECOME as foolish as they are. Be sure to ANSWER the FOOLISH arguments of fools, or THEY will BECOME "wise" in their own eyes. ... As a dog returns to its vomit, so a FOOL REPEATS his FOOLISHNESS. There is more hope for FOOLS than for people who THINK they are WISE.

Proverbs 28:13   People who CONCEAL their sins will NOT prosper, but IF they CONFESS and TURN FROM sin, they will receive MERCY.

Proverbs 29:11, 25   FOOLS vent their ANGER, but the wise quietly holds it back. FEARING people is a dangerous TRAP, but TRUSTING the Lord means SAFETY.

Proverbs 30:5-6, 8-9,11-13   EVERY Word of God proves TRUE. He is a shield to all who come to Him for protection. Do NOT ADD to His Words, OR He may rebuke you and expose you as a LIAR. ... First, help me NEVER to tell a LIE. Second, give me neither poverty nor riches! GIVE me just enough. IF I grow rich, I may deny You. IF I am poor, I may steal and insult God's Holy Name. ... Some people curse their father and do not thank their mother. They are PURE in their OWN eyes, BUT they are filthy and unwashed. They look WITH proud, disdainful glances.

Proverbs 31:8-9 SPEAK up for those who cannot speak for themselves; ensure JUSTICE for those being crushed. Yes, SPEAK up for the poor and helpless, and see that they get JUSTICE.

Ecclesiastes 1:9, 11, 14
History REPEATS itself. NOTHING in this world is truly NEW. … We do NOT remember what happened in the past, and in the future, no one will remember what we are doing now. … I observed everything IN THIS world, and it is all MEANINGLESS.

Ecclesiastes 2:1-3, 11, 13, 16-17, 20, 22-25 I said to myself, "Let's try pleasure, with having the 'good things' in life." But I found that this, too, was MEANINGLESS. I said, "What good does it do to seek pleasure?" I decided to cheer myself with wine. And while still seeking wisdom, I clutched at FOOLISHNESS. In this way, I tried to experience the only happiness most people find during their brief life IN THIS world. … As I looked at everything I had worked so hard to accomplish, it was all so MEANINGLESS. There was NOTHING worthwhile anywhere. … Wisdom is BETTER than foolishness, just as light is BETTER than darkness. For the wise can see where they are going, but fools walk in the dark. … Yet the wise and the foolish BOTH die. The wise will not be remembered any longer than the fool. In the days to come, BOTH will be forgotten. I came to hate life because everything done here is so troubling. Everything is MEANINGLESS in this world. … I gave up in despair, questioning the value of all my hard work in this world. … What do people get in this life for all their hard work and anxiety? Their days of labor are filled with pain and grief; even at night their minds cannot rest. It is all MEANINGLESS. I decided there is nothing better than to enjoy food and drink and to find satisfaction in work. Then I REALIZED that these PLEASURES are FROM God. Who can enjoy anything apart from Him?

Ecclesiastes 3:1, 11-14, 16-18 For everything there is a SEASON, a time for every activity. ... God has planted ETERNITY in humans, but people CANNOT see God's work from beginning to end. There is nothing better than to be happy and enjoy ourselves as long as we can. People should eat, drink and enjoy the fruits of their labor, for these are GIFTS from God. Whatever God DOES is FINAL. Nothing can be added to it or taken from it. God did this so that people would RESPECT Him. ... In this world there is evil in the courts, which are corrupt! In due season God will JUDGE everyone, both good and bad, for ALL their DEEDS. God proves to people that they are like animals.

Ecclesiastes 4:1, 4-6 ERV   I observed all the OPPRESSION in this world. I saw the tears of the oppressed, with no one to comfort them. The oppressors have great power, and their victims are helpless. Most people are motivated to success because they envy their neighbors. Some people say, "It is foolish to not work, you will starve to death." Maybe that is true. But I say it is BETTER to be SATISFIED with the few things you have THAN to always be STRUGGLING to get more.

Ecclesiastes 5:1-3, 5, 7, 10-11, 15-17, 19-20   In the house of God, keep your ears OPEN and your mouth SHUT. It is evil to make MINDLESS offerings to God. Do NOT make rash promises to God. TOO MANY WORDS make you a FOOL. It is better to say NOTHING than NOT keep a promise. Talk is cheap, like daydreams. RESPECT God instead. Those who love money will NEVER have enough. How MEANINGLESS to THINK that WEALTH brings TRUE happiness! The more you have, the more people come to help you spend it! We all come to the end of our lives as naked and empty-handed as on the day we were born. We cannot take our riches with us. All their hard work is for nothing. Throughout their lives, they live under a cloud – frustrated, discouraged, and angry. To ENJOY your work and ACCEPT your lot in life – this is indeed a GIFT from God. God keeps such people so BUSY ENJOYING life that they take NO time to brood over the past.

Ecclesiastes 6:9   ENJOY what you have RATHER THAN desiring what you do NOT have.

Ecclesiastes 7:2, 4-5, 8-10, 18   Better to spend your time at funerals than at parties. EVERYONE DIES – the living should take this to heart. ... A WISE person thinks a lot about death, while a FOOL thinks only about having a good time. BETTER to be criticized by a wise person THAN to be praised by a fool. ... Finishing is BETTER than starting. BETTER to be gentle and patient THAN proud and impatient. CONTROL your temper, for ANGER labels you a FOOL. Do NOT long for "the good old days." This is NOT wise. ... Pay attention to these instructions, for anyone who FEARS [respects, honors] God will AVOID both EXTREMES.

Ecclesiastes 8:17   NO ONE can DISCOVER everything God is DOING in this world, no matter what they claim.

Ecclesiastes 9:9   Live HAPPILY with your WIFE through all the days that God has given you.

Ecclesiastes 10:2, 4, 14 NKJV   The heart of the WISE inclines to the RIGHT, but the heart of the FOOL to the LEFT. ... A QUIET spirit can overcome even great mistakes. ... FOOLS CHATTER on and on. NO ONE really KNOWS what is going to happen.

Ecclesiastes 11:1, 4, 9 ERV, 10   DO GOOD WHEREVER you go. After a while, the good you do will come back to you. ... There are some things that you CANNOT be sure of. You must TAKE a CHANCE. IF you wait for perfect weather, you will NEVER plant your seeds. IF you are afraid that every cloud will bring rain, you will NEVER harvest your crops. ... It is wonderful to be young! Enjoy every minute of it. ... REMEMBER that you must GIVE an ACCOUNT to God for EVERYTHING you DO. ... REFUSE to WORRY, and keep your body healthy.

Ecclesiastes 12:1, 12-14 AMP   Do NOT let the excitement of youth cause you to FORGET your Creator. Honor Him in your youth before you grow old and say, "Life is not pleasant anymore." ... Be careful, for reading books is endless, and wears you out. My final CONCLUSION: FEAR [respect God's power and authority, because we desire to please] God and OBEY His commands, for this is everyone's DUTY [original purpose, foundation for true joy]. God will JUDGE us for EVERYTHING we DO, including every SECRET thing, whether good or bad.

Song of Songs 2:4, 15-16   It is obvious how much He loves me. ... Catch ALL the foxes, those LITTLE foxes, before they RUIN the vineyard of love! ... My lover is mine, and I am His.

Isaiah 1:2-3, 15-20, 23-28, 31   The LORD says: "The children I raised and cared for have rebelled against Me. Even a DONKEY recognizes its master's care – but Israel does NOT know its Master. My people do NOT recognize My care for them. ... Though you offer many prayers, I will NOT listen, for your hands are covered with the blood of innocent victims. ... TURN FROM your evil ways. Learn to DO good. SEEK justice. HELP the oppressed. DEFEND the cause of orphans. FIGHT FOR the rights of widows." ... The LORD says, "Though your sins are like scarlet, I will make them as white as snow. IF you will only OBEY Me, you will have plenty to eat. But IF you turn away and refuse

to listen, you will be devoured by your enemies. I, the LORD, have spoken!" ... Your LEADERS are rebels, the companions of THIEVES. All of them love BRIBES and demand payoffs, but they REFUSE to defend orphans or widows. The LORD of Heaven's Armies, says, "I will take revenge on My enemies! I will melt you down and remove all your impurities. I will give you good judges and wise counselors like you used to have. Then Jerusalem will again be called 'Home of Justice, Faithful City.' Those who REPENT will be revived by righteousness. BUT rebels, sinners, and those who desert the LORD will be DESTROYED. ... They and their evil works will BURN UP together."

Isaiah 2:2-3, 22 In the LAST DAYS, the mountain of the LORD's house will be the most important place on earth. People from many nations will say, "Come, let us go up to the mountain of the LORD. He will TEACH us His ways, and we will WALK in His paths." ... Do NOT put your trust in humans. They are as frail as breath. What good are they?

Isaiah 3:9-11 ERV, 12 They are LIKE the people of Sodom; they do NOT care who SEES their sin. It will be very BAD for wicked people, BECAUSE they will GET WHAT they DESERVE. They will GET WHAT they DID to others. Childish leaders OPPRESS My people, and women rule over them. O My people, your leaders MISLEAD you; they send you down the WRONG road.

Isaiah 5:11-12, 18, 20-21, 23, 25 What SORROW for those who get up looking for an alcoholic drink and spend evenings drinking wine to become flaming drunk. They furnish wine and lovely music at their grand parties, BUT they NEVER think about the LORD. ... What SORROW for those who drag wickedness behind them like a cart, with ropes made of LIES! ... What SORROW for those who say that EVIL is GOOD and GOOD is EVIL. ... What SORROW for those who are "wise" in their OWN eyes and think themselves so clever. ... They take BRIBES to let the wicked go FREE, and they PUNISH the innocent. ... That is WHY the LORD's anger burns ... to crush them!

Isaiah 6:1, 5, 7-8 It was in the year King Uzziah died that I saw the LORD. He was sitting on a lofty throne, and the train of His robe filled the Temple. ... I said, "I am doomed, for I am a sinful man. I have filthy lips, and I live among a people with filthy lips. Yet I have seen the King, the LORD of Heaven's Armies." ... The seraphim touched my lips with a burning coal from the altar and said, "See, this coal has touched your lips. Now your guilt is removed, and your sins are forgiven." The Lord asked,

"WHO should I SEND as a messenger to this people for Us?" I said, "Here I am. SEND me."

Isaiah 7:4-5, 7, 9, 14   Tell King Ahaz to STOP worrying, to NOT fear the anger of those 2 burned-out embers, King Rezin of Syria and King Pekah of Israel. ... The LORD says: "This invasion will never happen. ... UNLESS your FAITH [trust, loyalty] is FIRM, I CANNOT make you STAND FIRM." ... The LORD will give you the sign. Look! The virgin will conceive a child! She will give birth to a son and will call Him IMMANUEL (which means "God is WITH us").

Isaiah 8:11-15, 19-20   The LORD gave me a strong warning: NOT to think LIKE everyone else does. He said, "Do NOT call everything a CONSPIRACY, and do NOT live in DREAD of what frightens them. Make the LORD of Heaven's Armies HOLY in your life. He is the One you should FEAR [reverential awe, honor, respect] and tremble. He will keep you safe. But to Israel and Judah He will be a rock that makes them fall. Many will stumble and fall, never to rise again." ... Someone may say to you, "Let's ask the mediums and those who consult the spirits of the dead. They will tell us what to do." BUT people should ASK God for GUIDANCE! Should the living seek guidance from the dead? LOOK to God's instructions! People who CONTRADICT His Word are in the DARK.

Isaiah 9:1-2, 6-7, 13-17   The time of darkness and despair will NOT go on forever. The land of Zebulun and Naphtali will be humbled, but there will be a time in the FUTURE when Galilee of the Gentiles, will be filled with glory. The people who walk in darkness will SEE a great LIGHT. ... For a child is born to us, a SON is given to us. He will be CALLED: Wonderful Counselor, Mighty God, Everlasting Father, Prince of Peace. His government and its peace will NEVER END. He will rule with fairness and justice from the throne of his ancestor David for all eternity. ... After all this punishment, the people will STILL NOT repent. They will NOT seek the LORD of Heaven's Armies. Therefore, in a single day the LORD will DESTROY BOTH the LEADERS of Israel and the LYING prophets. For the leaders have MISLED the people down the path of destruction. For they are all wicked HYPOCRITES, and they all speak FOOLISHNESS.

Isaiah 10:1-3, 12-13, 15-16, 20-23   What sorrow awaits the UNJUST judges and those who issue UNFAIR laws. They DEPRIVE the poor of justice and DENY the rights of the needy among My people. They PREY on widows and orphans. What will you do WHEN I send disaster? To

WHO will you turn for help? ... After the Lord has used the king of Assyria to accomplish His purposes, He will PUNISH him – for he is PROUD and ARROGANT. He boasts, "By my own power I have done this. With my own shrewd wisdom I planned it. I have broken down the defenses of nations and carried off their treasures. I have knocked down their kings like a bull." ... IS the saw GREATER than the person who saws? Can a wooden cane walk by itself? ... Therefore, the LORD of Heaven's Armies, will send a plague among Assyria's proud troops. The LORD will burn up the enemy in a single night. ... In that day the REMNANT left in Israel, the survivors, will faithfully TRUST the LORD. Though the people of Israel are as numerous as the sand of the seashore, ONLY a REMNANT of them will RETURN. The LORD has rightly decided to destroy His people. The LORD of Heaven's Armies, has decided to destroy the entire land.

Isaiah 11:2-5 The Spirit of the LORD will rest on Him – the Spirit of wisdom and understanding, the Spirit of counsel and strength, the Spirit of knowledge and the fear of the LORD. He will DELIGHT in OBEYING the LORD. He will NOT judge by appearance NOR make a decision based on hearsay. He will give JUSTICE and make FAIR decisions for the exploited. One breath from His mouth will destroy the wicked. He will be RIGHTEOUS and TRUE.

Isaiah 13:6-9 Scream in terror, for the Day of the LORD has arrived – the time the Almighty will destroy. Everyone is paralyzed with fear. Every heart melts. Pangs of anguish grip them. They look helplessly at one another, their faces aflame with fear. ALL the sinners will be DESTROYED.

Isaiah 14:12-16, 27 How you [Satan, Lucifer] are FALLEN from heaven, O shining star! You have been thrown down to the earth, you who destroyed the nations of the world. You said, "I will ascend to heaven and set my throne above God's stars. I will climb to the highest heavens and BE LIKE the Most High." INSTEAD, you will be BROUGHT DOWN to the place of the dead. Everyone there will stare at you and ask, "Can this be the one who made the kingdoms of the world tremble?" ... The LORD of Heaven's Armies speaks – WHO can STOP His plans?

Isaiah 17:7-8 Then at last the people will LOOK to their Creator, the Holy One of Israel. They will NO LONGER LOOK to their idols for help or worship what their own hands have made.

Isaiah 25:1, 8-9 LORD, I will HONOR and PRAISE Your Name, for You ARE my God. You do such wonderful things! You planned them long ago, and now You have accomplished them. … He will SWALLOW up death forever! The Sovereign LORD will WIPE AWAY all tears. He will REMOVE forever all insults and mockery against His people. The LORD has spoken! In that day the people will proclaim, "This is our God! We TRUSTED in Him, and He SAVED us! This is the LORD, in whom we trusted. Let us be JOYFUL in the SALVATION He BRINGS!"

Isaiah 26:3-5, 19 You will KEEP in perfect PEACE all who TRUST in You, all whose thoughts are fixed on You! He HUMBLES the proud and BRINGS DOWN the arrogant to the dust. … But those who DIE in the LORD will LIVE; their bodies will RISE again and sing for JOY!

Isaiah 28:16, 24 The LORD says: "I am placing a foundation stone [Jesus] in Jerusalem. It is a precious cornerstone that is safe to build on. Whoever BELIEVES will NEVER be shaken. … Does a farmer ALWAYS plow and NEVER plant?" [Does good deeds, never tells the Way of Salvation?]

Isaiah 29:13-16, 19-21 The LORD says: "They honor Me with their lips, BUT their hearts are FAR FROM Me. Their worship of Me is nothing but MAN-MADE RULES learned by ROTE. I will again astound these HYPOCRITES with amazing wonders. The wisdom of the wise will pass away, and the intelligence of the intelligent will disappear. What SORROW awaits those who try to hide their plans from the LORD, who do their evil deeds in the dark! 'The LORD does not know what's going on!' they say. HOW FOOLISH can you be? He is the Potter, and He is certainly GREATER than you, the clay! Should the CREATED thing say of the One who MADE it, 'He did NOT make me?' [believe evolution?] Does a jar ever say, 'The potter who made me is stupid?' … The HUMBLE [gentle, teachable, trusting God] will be filled with JOY from the LORD. … The scoffer will be GONE, the arrogant will DISAPPEAR, and those who plot evil will be KILLED. Those who convict the innocent with false testimony, use trickery to pervert justice, and tell lies will DISAPPEAR."

Isaiah 30:9-13, 15, 18 These people are STUBBORN rebels who REFUSE to pay attention to the LORD's instructions. They tell the prophets, "Do NOT tell us what is right. Tell us nice things. Tell us LIES. Get off your NARROW path. Stop telling us about your Holy One of Israel." The Holy One of Israel replies: "Because you DESPISE what I tell you and TRUST in oppression and lies, DISASTER will come upon you suddenly." ... The LORD says: "ONLY in RETURNING to Me will you be SAVED." ... The LORD must WAIT for you to COME to Him so He can SHOW you His Love and Compassion. ... Blessed are those who WAIT for His help.

Isaiah 34:2, 4, 10   The LORD is enraged against the nations. ... He will completely destroy them. The heavens above will MELT AWAY and disappear like a rolled-up scroll. ... This JUDGMENT will NEVER END, the smoke of its BURNING will rise FOREVER.

Isaiah 35:3-4, 8-10   STRENGTHEN those who have tired hands, and ENCOURAGE those who have weak knees. Say to those with fearful hearts, "Be strong, and do NOT fear, for your God is coming to SAVE you." ... A great road will be named the Highway of Holiness. Evil-minded people will NEVER travel on it. It will be ONLY for those who WALK in God's Ways. Fools will NEVER walk there. There will be NO dangers. ONLY the REDEEMED will walk on it. Sorrow and mourning will disappear, and they will be FILLED with JOY and GLADNESS.

Isaiah 40:3, 5-6, 8-10, 12-15, 17-19, 21-29, 31   The voice is shouting, "Clear the way through the wilderness for the LORD!" ... Then the glory of the LORD will be revealed. ... People are like the grass. Their beauty fades as quickly as flowers in a field. ... The grass withers and the flowers fade, but the Word of our God stands FOREVER. Shout, and do NOT be afraid. Tell the towns of Judah, "Your God is coming!" The Sovereign LORD is coming in power. He brings His reward with Him as He comes. ... WHO else has held the oceans in His hand? WHO else has measured the heavens? WHO else knows the weight of the earth or has weighed the mountains? WHO is able to ADVISE the Spirit of the LORD? WHO knows enough to TEACH Him? Did someone show Him the path of justice? No! All the NATIONS are NOTHING more than dust. ... He picks up the whole earth as if it is a grain of sand. The nations of the world are worth NOTHING to Him. They count for less than nothing – mere emptiness. To WHO can you COMPARE God? ... Can He be compared to an idol? ... Have you NOT heard? Do you NOT understand? Are you DEAF to the Words of God – the Words He gave BEFORE the world began? Are you so ignorant? God sits above the CIRCLE of the earth. The people below seem like grasshoppers to Him! He spreads out the heavens like a curtain and makes His tent from them. He JUDGES the great people of the world and brings them all to nothing. They hardly get started, barely taking root, when He blows on them and they wither like chaff. "To WHO will you compare Me? WHO is My equal?" asks the Holy One. Look up into the heavens. WHO created all the stars? He brings them out, calling each by its name. Because of His great power and incomparable strength, not a single one is missing. HOW can you say the LORD does NOT see your troubles? How can you say God ignores your rights? Have you NEVER heard? Have you NEVER understood? The LORD is the everlasting God, the Creator of all the earth. He NEVER grows weak or weary. No one can measure the depths of His understanding. He gives power to the weak and strength to the powerless. ... Those who TRUST in the LORD will FIND new STRENGTH. ... They will run and NOT grow weary. They will walk and NOT faint.

Isaiah 41:10, 12-13, 21-24 "Do NOT be afraid, for I am WITH you. Do NOT be discouraged, for I AM your God. I will strengthen you and help you. I will hold you up with My victorious right hand. Those who attack you will come to nothing. ... Present the case for your idols. Let your idols show what they can do. Let them try to tell us what happened long ago so that we may CONSIDER the EVIDENCE. Or let them tell us what the future holds, then we will know you are gods. Do anything – good or bad! Do something that will amaze and frighten us. But no! You are less than NOTHING and can do nothing at all. Those who CHOOSE IDOLS are FOOLS!" says the LORD.

Isaiah 42:8-9, 23 "I AM the LORD! I will NOT give My glory to idols. Everything I PROPHESY comes TRUE. I will TELL you the FUTURE before it happens." says the LORD. "Will you pay attention to this warning? Will you ever learn to LISTEN?"

Isaiah 43:1-3, 10-13, 18-19 The LORD who CREATED you says, "Do NOT be afraid, for I have RANSOMED you. I have called you by name; you are Mine. When you go through deep waters, I will be WITH you. When you go through rivers of difficulty, you will NOT drown. When you walk through the fire of oppression, you will NOT be burned up. ... I AM the LORD and YOUR Savior. You have been chosen to know Me, BELIEVE in Me, and understand that I ALONE am God. There is NO OTHER God – there NEVER has been, and there NEVER will be. I AM the LORD, and there is NO OTHER Savior. You are My WITNESSES that I AM the ONLY God. From eternity to eternity I AM God. No one can snatch anyone out of My hand. No one can undo what I did. ... FORGET the former things. Do NOT dwell on the past. I AM doing a NEW thing!"

Isaiah 44:6-7, 9-10, 18-20, 22, 24-26   The LORD says: "I AM the First and the Last; there is NO OTHER God. WHO is like Me? Let him do as I have done since ancient times when I established a people and explained its future. … How FOOLISH are those who manufacture idols, that are really WORTHLESS. Who but a FOOL would make his own god – an idol that cannot help him one bit? … Such STUPIDITY and IGNORANCE! They cannot see. Their minds are shut, and they CANNOT THINK. The person who made the idol NEVER stops to CONSIDER, 'Why, it's just a block of wood! I burned half of it for heat and used it to bake my bread and roast my meat. How can the rest of it be a god? Should I bow down to worship a piece of wood?' The poor, DELUDED FOOL trusts something that CANNOT help him at all. Yet he cannot ASK, 'Is this idol a LIE?' … RETURN to Me, for I have PAID the price to SET you FREE." … The LORD – your REDEEMER and CREATOR – says: "I AM the LORD, who made all things. Who was with Me when I made the earth? I EXPOSE the FALSE prophets as LIARS and make fools of fortune-tellers. The wise give bad advice, thus proving them to be fools. But I carry out the PREDICTIONS of My prophets!"

Isaiah 45:9, 11-12, 21-22   The LORD says: "SORROW awaits those who ARGUE with their CREATOR. Does the clay argue with the potter saying, 'Stop, you are doing it wrong!' Does the pot exclaim, 'How clumsy can you be?'" … This is what the LORD, your Creator, says: "Do you QUESTION what I do for My children? I made the heavens and the earth and created people to live on it." … What idol ever told you what would happen? Was it not I, the LORD? For there is NO OTHER God but Me, a righteous God and Savior. Let all the world LOOK to Me for salvation!"

Isaiah 46:4-12   The LORD says: "I will be your God throughout your lifetime. I made you, I care for you, I carry you along and save you. To WHO will you COMPARE Me? WHO is My equal? Some people pour out their silver and gold and make a false god [idol]. They bow down and worship it! They carry it around. It CANNOT even move! When someone prays to it, there is NO answer. It CANNOT rescue anyone from trouble. Do not forget this! REMEMBER the THINGS I have DONE in the past. I ALONE am God, and there is NONE LIKE Me! ONLY I can tell you the FUTURE before it happens. Everything I plan will come to pass, for I DO WHATEVER I wish. LISTEN to Me, you stubborn people who are so far from doing right."

Isaiah 47:7-8, 10-11, 14 The LORD says: "You [Babylon] said, 'I will reign forever!' You did not reflect on your ACTIONS, nor THINK about their CONSEQUENCES. Listen, you pleasure-loving kingdom, living at ease and feeling secure. You felt secure in your wickedness. 'No one sees me,' you said. But your 'wisdom' and 'knowledge' have LED you ASTRAY. So disaster will overtake you. You will NOT be able to BUY your WAY OUT. A catastrophe will strike you suddenly, one for which you are not prepared. WHERE are all your astrologers, who make predictions? They CANNOT SAVE themselves from the FLAME. You will get NO help from them."

Isaiah 48:5-11, 22 "I told you beforehand what I was going to do. Then you can never say, 'My idols did it!' You hear My PREDICTIONS and see them FULFILLED, but you REFUSE to admit it. I will refine you, in the furnace of suffering. I will rescue you! I will NOT share My glory with idols! There is NO peace for the wicked," says the LORD.

Isaiah 49:5-6, 15-16 The LORD speaks – the One who FORMED me IN my mother's WOMB to be His servant. The LORD has given me strength. He says, "You will do more than restore the people of Israel to Me. I will make you a light to the Gentiles, and you will bring My salvation to the ends of the earth. Can a mother forget her nursing child? But even if that were possible, I would NOT forget you! See, I have WRITTEN your name ON the palms of My hands."

Isaiah 50:5-7, 9-11 The Sovereign LORD has spoken to me, and I have listened. I have not rebelled or turned away. I offered my back to those who beat me and my cheeks to those who pulled out my beard. I did not hide my face from mockery and spitting. Because the Sovereign LORD helps me, I will not be disgraced. Therefore, I have set my face like a stone, DETERMINED to DO His will. I know that I will not be put to shame. ... The Sovereign LORD is on my side! Who will declare me guilty? All my enemies will be destroyed like old clothes that have been eaten by moths! "Who among you FEARS [respects, honors] the LORD and OBEYS His instructions? IF you are walking in darkness, TRUST in the LORD and RELY on your God. Watch out! You who LIVE in your OWN light. The reward you will receive from Me: you will GO DOWN in great torment!" says the LORD.

Isaiah 52:13-14 My servant will be highly exalted. His face was so disfigured He seemed hardly human, and from His appearance, one would scarcely know He was a man.

Isaiah 53:3-6, 10-11   [This prophecy about Jesus was written 700 years before Jesus came to die to pay the penalty for our sins, so we may be reconciled back to God.]   He was despised and rejected, a man of sorrows, acquainted with deepest grief. We turned our backs on Him, looked the other way, and we did NOT care. Yet it was OUR weaknesses He carried. It was OUR sorrows that weighed Him down. And we thought His troubles were a punishment from God, a punishment for His own sins! But He was pierced for OUR rebellion, crushed for OUR sins. He was beaten so we could be whole. He was whipped so we could be healed. All of us, like sheep, have strayed away. We have LEFT God's paths to follow OUR own path. Yet the LORD LAID on Him the sins of us all. … It was the LORD's good plan to crush Him. … My Righteous Servant will make it possible for MANY to be counted righteous, for He will bear ALL their sins.

Isaiah 53:3-6   [*Speak out loud YOUR name in the blanks*]   He was despised and rejected, a man of sorrows, acquainted with deepest grief. I turned my back on Him, looked the other way, and did not care. Yet He was pierced for _____ rebellion. He was crushed for _____ sins. He was beaten so _____ could be made whole. He was whipped so _____ could be healed. _____, like sheep, have strayed away. _____ has left God's paths to follow _____ own path. Yet the LORD laid on Him all of _____ sins.

Isaiah 54:17   The LORD says: "In that coming day NO weapon turned against you will succeed. You will silence every voice raised to accuse you. These benefits are enjoyed by the servants of the LORD, their VINDICATION [free from blame or guilt] will come FROM Me. I, the LORD, have spoken!"

Isaiah 55:1-3, 6-9, 12   The LORD says, "Is anyone thirsty? Come and drink – it's all free! Why pay for food that does you no good? LISTEN to Me, and eat what is good. Listen, and you will find life. SEEK the Lord WHILE you can FIND Him. Call Him NOW while He is NEAR. Let the wicked CHANGE their ways and BANISH every evil thought. Let them TURN to the LORD, for He FORGIVES. … My Thoughts are NOTHING LIKE your thoughts. My ways are FAR BEYOND anything you can imagine. As the heavens are higher than the earth, so My Ways are HIGHER than your ways and My Thoughts HIGHER than your thoughts. … You will live in JOY and PEACE!"

Isaiah 56:1-2, 6-7, 11   The LORD says: "Be JUST and FAIR to all. Do what is right and good, for I am coming SOON to rescue you. Blessed are all those who are careful to do this. Blessed are those who HONOR My Sabbath days of rest and keep themselves from doing wrong. ... I will also bless the foreigners who commit themselves to the LORD, who serve Him and love His Name, and do not desecrate the Sabbath day of rest. I will fill them with JOY in My Temple which will be called a House of Prayer for all nations. ... Like GREEDY dogs, they are NEVER satisfied. They are ignorant shepherds, all following their OWN path and intent on personal gain."

Isaiah 57:1-2, 4-6, 11-13, 15, 20-21   The godly often die BEFORE their time. ... God is protecting them FROM the evil to come. Those who follow GODLY paths [committed to obeying God] will REST in PEACE when they die. ... The LORD says, "You children of sinners and liars! You WORSHIP your idols with great passion. You SACRIFICE your children. Do you THINK all this MAKES Me HAPPY? ... Are you afraid of these idols? Is that why you have lied to Me and forgotten Me and My Words? I will EXPOSE your 'good' deeds. NONE of them will HELP you. See if your idols can save you. ... I LIVE in the Holy Place WITH those who are HUMBLE [gentle, teachable, trusting God, not pride in self]. I RESTORE the crushed spirit of the HUMBLE. I REVIVE the courage of those who REPENT. ... Those who REJECT Me are like the restless sea, which continually churns up mud and dirt. There is NO peace FOR the wicked."

Isaiah 58:2-8, 13-14   The LORD says, "They ACT so pious! They SEEM delighted to learn about Me. They ask Me to take action on their behalf, PRETENDING they want to be near Me. 'We have fasted before you!' they say. 'Why aren't You impressed? We have been very hard on ourselves, and You don't even notice it!' I will tell you WHY! It's BECAUSE you are fasting to PLEASE yourselves. Even while you fast, you KEEP oppressing your workers. What good is fasting when you KEEP on fighting and quarreling? This kind of fasting will NEVER get you anywhere with Me. You 'humble' yourselves BY going through the motions of penance, bowing your heads like reeds in the wind. You dress in burlap and are covered in ashes. Is this what you call fasting? Do you really THINK this will please the LORD? NO, this is the kind of FASTING I want: FREE those who are wrongly imprisoned; LIGHTEN the burden of those who work for you. Let the oppressed go FREE, and REMOVE the chains that bind people. SHARE your food with the hungry, and GIVE shelter to the homeless. GIVE clothes to those who need them, and do NOT hide from relatives who need your help. THEN your salvation will come. ... Keep the Sabbath day holy. Do NOT pursue your own interests, but ENJOY the Sabbath and DELIGHT in the LORD's holy day. HONOR the Sabbath in everything you do on that day. ... THEN the LORD will BE your DELIGHT."

Isaiah 59:1-4, 7-8, 13-15, 17-18, 20 Listen! The LORD is NOT too weak to save you, NOR is He too deaf to hear you call. It is your sins that have CUT you OFF from God. Because of your sins, He will not listen to you anymore. Your lips are full of LIES and CORRUPTION. No one cares about being fair and honest. The people's lawsuits are based on LIES. They conceive EVIL deeds. ... Their feet run to do evil, and they rush to commit murder. They THINK ONLY about sinning. Misery and destruction always FOLLOW them. They do NOT know where to find peace OR what it means to be just and good. Our sins are piled up before God and testify against us. ... We know how UNFAIR and oppressive we have been, carefully planning our deceitful LIES. Our courts OPPOSE the righteous, and justice is nowhere to be found. TRUTH and HONESTY has been OUTLAWED. Anyone who renounces evil is ATTACKED. The LORD was DISPLEASED to find there was NO justice. He will REPAY His enemies for their evil deeds. ... "The Redeemer will come to BUY BACK those who have TURNED from their sins," says the LORD.

Isaiah 61:1-2 [Luke 4:18] The Spirit of the LORD is upon Me, for the LORD has anointed Me to bring good news to the poor. He has sent Me to comfort the brokenhearted and to proclaim that captives will be released and prisoners will be freed. He has sent Me to tell those who mourn that the time of the LORD's favor has come, and with it, the day of God's anger against their enemies.

Isaiah 64:6-7 We are all INFECTED and IMPURE with sin. OUR "righteous" deeds, are nothing but FILTHY rags. NO one calls on Your Name OR pleads with You for MERCY. Therefore, You have TURNED us OVER TO our sins.

Isaiah 65:1, 11-12, 17 The LORD says, "I was READY to RESPOND, but NO one ASKED for help. I was READY to be FOUND, but NO one was LOOKING for Me. The nation did NOT call on My Name. Because you have FORSAKEN the LORD ... and because you prepared feasts to HONOR the god of LUCK and ... the god of FATE [destiny] now I will "DESTINE" you for the sword, bowing down before the executioner. For when I called, you did NOT answer. When I spoke, you did NOT listen. You DELIBERATELY sinned ... and CHOSE to DO what you KNOW I

DESPISED. ... I AM creating NEW heavens and a NEW earth, and NO one will THINK about the OLD ones anymore."

Isaiah 66:1-3 ERV, 22, 24   This is what the LORD says: "Heaven is My throne, and the earth is My footstool. Could you build me a temple as good as that? ... I have made both heaven and earth; they and everything in them are Mine. ... I will CARE FOR those who are HUMBLE [gentle, teachable, trusting God, not pride in self] and OBEY My commands. BUT those who choose their OWN ways – delighting in their detestable sins – will NOT have their offerings accepted. When such people sacrifice a bull, it is no more acceptable than a human sacrifice. When they sacrifice a lamb, it is as though they had sacrificed a dog! ... As surely as My NEW heavens and earth will remain, so will you always BE My people. ... As they go out, they will see the dead bodies of those who have rebelled against Me. The worms that devour them will NEVER die. The fire that burns them will NEVER go out."

Jeremiah 1:5-7, 17, 19
The LORD says, "I KNEW you BEFORE I FORMED you in your mother's WOMB. BEFORE you were BORN I set you apart and appointed you as my prophet to the nations." I said, "O Sovereign LORD, I cannot speak for you! I am too young!" The LORD replied, "Do NOT say, 'I am too young,' for you must go wherever I send you and say whatever I tell you. Get up and prepare for action. Go out and tell them everything I tell you to say. Do not be afraid of them, or I will make you look foolish in front of them. They will fight you, but they will fail. For I am WITH you, and I will take CARE of you. I, the LORD, have spoken!"

Jeremiah 2:5, 11, 13, 17, 19, 28, 31, 35   The LORD says: "What did your ancestors find wrong with Me that led them to stray so far from Me? They worshiped WORTHLESS idols, only to become WORTHLESS themselves. ... Has any nation ever TRADED its gods for new ones, even though they are NOT gods at all? Yet My people have EXCHANGED their glorious God FOR worthless idols! ... My people have done two EVIL things: They have abandoned Me – the fountain of living water. And they have dug for themselves cracked cisterns that can hold no water at all! ... You have brought this upon yourselves by rebelling against the LORD your God, even though He was leading you on the way! Your WICKEDNESS will BRING its OWN PUNISHMENT. You will see what an evil, bitter thing it is to ABANDON the LORD your God and NOT to fear [reverential awe, honor, respect] the LORD of Heaven's

Armies! ... Why not call on these gods you have made? When trouble comes, LET them SAVE you IF they can! LISTEN to the Words of the LORD! ... WHY do My people SAY, 'At last we are free from God! We do NOT need Him anymore!' ... You say, 'I have done NOTHING wrong. Surely God is not angry with me!' Now I will PUNISH you severely BECAUSE you CLAIM you have NOT sinned."

Jeremiah 3:13 The LORD says, "ADMIT your guilt. ADMIT you rebelled against the LORD and committed adultery against Me by worshiping idols. CONFESS you refused to LISTEN to ME."

Jeremiah 4:1, 4, 18, 22 The LORD says, "IF you WANT to RETURN to Me, you CAN. You can THROW AWAY your detestable idols and stray away NO MORE. People of Judah and Jerusalem, SURRENDER your pride and power. CHANGE your hearts before the LORD, OR My anger will burn like an unquenchable fire because of all your sins. Your OWN actions have BROUGHT this upon you. This punishment is BITTER! My people are FOOLISH and do NOT know Me. They are STUPID children who have NO understanding. They are CLEVER enough at doing WRONG, but they have NO idea how to do RIGHT!"

Jeremiah 5:12-14, 27-31 The LORD God of Heaven's Armies says: "They have LIED about the LORD saying, 'He will NOT bother us! God's prophets are all windbags who do NOT really speak for Him. Let their predictions of disaster fall on themselves!' ... Because the people are talking like this, My messages will flame out and burn the people like kindling wood. ... Their homes are filled with evil plots. And now they are great and rich. There is NO limit to their wicked deeds. They REFUSE to provide justice to orphans and DENY the rights of the poor. Should I not PUNISH them for this? ... The prophets give FALSE prophecies, and the priests RULE with an iron hand. Worse yet, My people LIKE it that way! But WHAT WILL you do WHEN the END COMES?"

Jeremiah 6:13, 15 "From the least to the greatest, their lives are ruled by GREED. From prophets to priests, they are all FRAUDS. ... Are they ashamed of their DISGUSTING actions? NOT AT ALL – they do NOT even know how to blush! Therefore, they will lie among the slaughtered when I PUNISH them," says the LORD.

Jeremiah 7:16, 19 "Pray NO more for these people, Jeremiah, for I will NOT listen to you. ... Am I the one they are hurting?" asks the LORD. "They HURT themselves, to their OWN shame."

Jeremiah 8:5-6, 9   The LORD asks, "WHY do these people stay on their SELF-DESTRUCTIVE path? WHY do the people REFUSE to turn back to the LORD? They CLING to their LIES. I listen and do NOT hear a word of truth. Is anyone SORRY for doing wrong? Does anyone say, 'What a TERRIBLE thing I have done'? NO! ... These 'wise' teachers will fall into the TRAP of their own FOOLISHNESS, for they have REJECTED the Word of the LORD. Are they so 'wise' after all?"

Jeremiah 9:23-24   The LORD says: "Do NOT let the wise boast in their wisdom, or the powerful boast in their power, or the rich boast in their riches. BUT those who wish to boast should boast in this ALONE: that they truly KNOW Me and understand that I AM the LORD who demonstrates unfailing love and who brings justice and righteousness to the earth, and that I DELIGHT in these things."

Jeremiah 10:2-3, 5, 8, 10-12, 14-18, 21, 23-24   The LORD says: "Do NOT act like the other nations, who try to read their future in the stars. Do NOT be afraid of their predictions, even though other nations are terrified by them. Their WAYS are FUTILE and FOOLISH. ... Do NOT be afraid of such gods, for they can neither harm you nor do you any good." ... People who worship idols are STUPID and FOOLISH. ... The LORD is the ONLY TRUE God. He is the LIVING God and the everlasting King! ... The nations cannot stand up to His wrath. Say this to those who worship other gods: "Your so-called gods, who did NOT make the heavens and earth, will VANISH from the earth and from under the heavens." ... God MADE the earth by His power, and He PRESERVES it by His wisdom. ... The whole human race is FOOLISH and has NO knowledge! ... The idols they make are a FRAUD. These idols have NO breath or power. Idols are WORTHLESS; they are ridiculous LIES! On the Day of Reckoning they will all be DESTROYED. But the God of Israel is NO idol! He is the CREATOR of EVERYTHING that exists. ... The LORD of Heaven's Armies is His Name! Pack your bags and prepare to leave. ... The LORD says: "I will fling out all you who live in this land. I will pour great troubles upon you, and at last you will feel My anger." ... The shepherds of My people have LOST their senses. They NO longer seek wisdom FROM the LORD. Therefore, they FAIL completely, and their flocks are scattered. ... [Jeremiah prays:] "I know, LORD, that our lives are NOT our own. We are NOT able to plan our own course. So correct me, LORD, BUT please be gentle. Do NOT correct me in anger, for I would die."

Jeremiah 11:15   The LORD said, "WHAT right do My people come to My Temple, WHEN they do so many immoral things? Can their sacrifices prevent their destruction? They rejoice in doing evil!"

Jeremiah 12:1-3, 5-6, 14-17   Jeremiah asks, "LORD, You always give me justice. I bring this complaint: WHY are the wicked so prosperous? WHY are evil people so happy? Your Name is on their lips, but You are FAR FROM their hearts. LORD, You KNOW my heart. You SEE me and TEST my thoughts. Drag these people away to be butchered!"   ... [The LORD answers Jeremiah:] "IF racing against mere men makes you tired, HOW will you race against horses? IF you stumble and fall on open ground, WHAT will you do in the thickets near the Jordan? Even your brothers, members of your own family, have TURNED AGAINST you. They plot and raise complaints against you. Do NOT trust them, NO matter how PLEASANTLY they speak. I will uproot all the evil nations. Afterward I will have compassion on them. IF these nations truly learn the ways of My people, and IF they learn to swear by My Name, saying, 'As surely as the LORD lives' [instead of swearing by the name of Baal], THEN they will be given a place among My people. BUT any nation who REFUSES to OBEY Me will be DESTROYED. I, the LORD, have spoken!"

Jeremiah 13:11, 22, 25, 27   The LORD says, "They WERE to be My people and bring Me fame, praise, and honor. But My people did NOT listen to Me." You may ask yourself, "WHY is all THIS HAPPENING to me?" It is BECAUSE of YOUR many SINS! The LORD says, "You have forgotten Me, putting your trust in false gods. I have seen your adultery and lust, and your disgusting idol worship. What sorrow awaits you!"

Jeremiah 14:13-16   I said, "LORD, their [false] prophets say, 'All is well.'" The LORD said, "These prophets are telling LIES in My Name. I did NOT give them any messages. They speak foolishness made up in their own LYING hearts. Therefore, I will punish these LYING prophets. They say that no war or famine will come, but they themselves will die by war and famine! As for the people to whom they prophesy – they will also be victims of famine and war. I will pour out their OWN WICKEDNESS on them."

Jeremiah 15:1, 4, 16-17, 19-21   The LORD said to me, "Even IF Moses and Samuel stood before Me pleading for these people, I would NOT help them. Away with them! Get them out of my sight! ... Because of the wicked things Manasseh, king of Judah, did in Jerusalem, I will make My people an object of horror to all." ... When I DISCOVERED Your Words, I devoured them for they are my JOY. I never sat with the crowd as they laughed and had fun. I sat alone because of Your INFLUENCE on me. You filled me with ANGER AT the evil around me. ... The LORD responds: "IF you RETURN to Me, I will RESTORE you so you can CONTINUE to serve Me. IF you speak important words rather than worthless words, you will be My spokesman. You must INFLUENCE them; do NOT let them influence you! They will fight against you, but I will make you secure. They will NOT conquer you, for I am WITH you to PROTECT and RESCUE you. I, the LORD, have spoken! I will certainly KEEP you SAFE from these evil people."

Jeremiah 16:12-13, 17-18 The LORD says, "You are even WORSE than your ancestors! You stubbornly FOLLOW your own EVIL desires and REFUSE to listen to Me. So I will throw you out of this land and send you into a foreign land. There you can worship idols day and night – and I will grant you NO favors! ... I am watching them closely, and I SEE every sin. They CANNOT hide from Me. I will DOUBLE their punishment for all their sins, BECAUSE they have defiled My land with lifeless images of their detestable gods and with their evil deeds."

Jeremiah 17:5, 7-10 The LORD says: "CURSED are those who put their TRUST in MERE humans, who RELY on human strength and TURN their hearts AWAY from the LORD. ... Blessed are those who TRUST in the LORD and have made the LORD their HOPE and CONFIDENCE. ... They NEVER stop producing fruit. ... The human HEART is the most DECEITFUL of all things, and desperately WICKED. Who really KNOWS how BAD it is? ... I, the LORD, SEARCH all hearts and EXAMINE secret MOTIVES. I GIVE all people their due rewards, ACCORDING to WHAT their ACTIONS DESERVE."

Jeremiah 18:11-12 Jeremiah warns them, "The LORD says: 'I am planning disaster for you instead of good. So TURN FROM your evil ways, and DO what is RIGHT.'" But the people replied, "We will CONTINUE to live AS we WANT to, stubbornly FOLLOWING our OWN evil desires."

Jeremiah 19:7-8 The LORD says, "I will upset the careful plans of Judah and Jerusalem. I will allow the people to be slaughtered. I will reduce Jerusalem to RUINS, a monument to their STUPIDITY. All who pass by will gasp at the destruction they see."

Jeremiah 20:11-13   The LORD stands beside me like a great warrior. Before Him my persecutors will stumble. They cannot defeat me. They will fail and be thoroughly humiliated. LORD of Heaven's Armies, You TEST the righteous. You EXAMINE the deepest THOUGHTS and SECRETS. Praise the LORD! For though I was poor, ... He RESCUED me from my oppressors.

Jeremiah 21:8-10, 12, 14   The LORD says: "Take your CHOICE of LIFE or DEATH! Everyone who stays in Jerusalem will die from war, famine, or disease, but those who surrender to the Babylonians will live. I have decided to bring disaster and it will be handed over to the king of Babylon, and he will reduce it to ashes. ... GIVE justice each morning to the people you judge! HELP those who have been robbed; RESCUE them from their oppressors. ... Otherwise, My anger will burn as an unquenchable fire because of all your sins. I will burn up everything around you."

Jeremiah 22:3, 5, 8-9, 15-17, 19   The LORD says: "Be FAIR and JUST. DO what is RIGHT! QUIT your EVIL deeds! Do NOT mistreat foreigners, orphans, and widows. STOP murdering the innocent! ... IF you REFUSE to pay attention to this warning, I swear by My Name that this palace will become a pile of rubble. People from many nations will pass by the ruins of this city and say, 'WHY did the LORD DESTROY such a great city?' The answer is, 'BECAUSE they violated their covenant with the LORD their God by worshiping other gods.' ... A beautiful cedar palace does NOT make a great king! Your father, King Josiah, was just and right in all his dealings. That is why God blessed him. He gave JUSTICE and HELP to the POOR and NEEDY, and everything went well for him. Is that not WHAT it MEANS to KNOW Me? But you! You have eyes ONLY for GREED and DISHONESTY! You MURDER the innocent, OPPRESS the poor, and reign RUTHLESSLY. Therefore, King Jehoiakim will be buried like a dead donkey – dumped outside the gates!"

Jeremiah 23:11, 13-19, 22-24, 26-27, 29, 31-32   "The priests and prophets are ungodly, WICKED men. I have seen their DESPICABLE acts right IN My Temple," says the LORD. "The prophets of Samaria were terribly EVIL for they prophesied IN the name of Baal and LED My people of Israel into sin. Now the prophets of Jerusalem are EVEN WORSE! They COMMIT adultery and love DISHONESTY. They ENCOURAGE those who are DOING EVIL so that no one turns from their sins. These prophets are as wicked as the people of Sodom and

Gomorrah were. I will feed them with bitterness. ... For it is BECAUSE of Jerusalem's prophets that WICKEDNESS has filled this land. Do NOT listen to these prophets when they prophesy to you, filling you with FUTILE hopes. They are MAKING UP everything they say. They do NOT speak for the LORD! They keep saying to those who DESPISE My Word, 'Do NOT worry! The LORD says you will have peace!' And to those who stubbornly FOLLOW their OWN desires, they say, 'No harm will come your way!' Have any of these prophets been IN the LORD's Presence to HEAR what He is REALLY saying? Has even one of them CARED enough to LISTEN? Look! The LORD's anger bursts out like a whirlwind that swirls down on the heads of the wicked. IF they [false prophets] had listened to Me, they would have spoken My Words, and they would have TURNED My people FROM their evil ways and deeds. Am I a God who is only close at hand? No, I am far away at the same time. Can anyone hide from Me in a secret place? I, the LORD, am EVERYWHERE in all the heavens and earth! They are prophets of DECEIT, inventing everything they say. By telling these FALSE dreams, they are trying to get My people to FORGET Me, just as their ancestors did by worshiping the idols of Baal. LET these false prophets tell their dreams, BUT let My true messengers faithfully PROCLAIM My every Word. There is a DIFFERENCE between straw and grain! Does not My Word burn like fire? Is it not like a mighty hammer that smashes a rock to pieces? I am AGAINST these SMOOTH-TONGUED [flattering] prophets who say, 'This prophecy is from the LORD!' I am AGAINST these FALSE prophets. Their imaginary dreams are flagrant LIES that LEAD My people INTO sin. They have NO message at all for my people. I, the LORD have spoken!"

Jeremiah 29:1, 7-13 Jeremiah wrote a letter from Jerusalem to the elders, priests, prophets, and all the people who had been exiled to Babylon. Work for the PEACE and prosperity of the city where I sent you into exile. PRAY to the LORD for it, for its welfare will DETERMINE your welfare. The LORD of Heaven's Armies, says: "Do NOT let your prophets and fortune-tellers who are with you in the land of Babylon TRICK you. Do NOT listen to their dreams, because they are telling you LIES in My Name. I have NOT sent them. You will be in Babylon for 70 years. THEN I will bring you home again. I know the plans I have for you, for good and not for disaster, to give you a future and a hope. When you pray, I will listen. IF you LOOK FOR Me wholeheartedly, you will FIND Me."

Jeremiah 30:22, 24 The LORD says, "You WILL be My people, and I WILL be your God." ... The fierce anger of the LORD will NOT diminish UNTIL it has finished all He has planned. In the days to come you will understand all this.

Jeremiah 31:15, 19, 25, 30, 33-34 The LORD says: "A cry is heard in Ramah – deep anguish and bitter weeping. Rachel weeps for her children, refusing to be comforted – for her children are gone." ... I TURNED FROM God, BUT then I was sorry. I kicked myself for my STUPIDITY! I was thoroughly ASHAMED of all I did in my younger days. ... The LORD says, "I have given REST to the weary and JOY to the sorrowing. ... All people will die for their own sins. ... This is the NEW covenant. I will put My instructions within them. I will write them on their hearts. I WILL be their God, and they WILL be My people. They will not need to teach their neighbors saying, 'You should know the LORD.' For everyone, from the least to the greatest, will KNOW Me already, and I will FORGIVE their wickedness."

Jeremiah 32:17, 19, 27, 33-35 Jeremiah prayed, "Sovereign LORD! You made the heavens and earth. NOTHING is too hard for You! You have ALL wisdom and do great and mighty miracles. You SEE the conduct of all people, and You GIVE them WHAT they DESERVE." ... Then the LORD said: "I AM the LORD, the God of all the peoples of the world. Is anything too hard for Me? ... My people have TURNED FROM Me and have REFUSED to return. Even though I diligently taught them, they would NOT receive instruction or obey. They have their abominable idols IN My Temple, DEFILING it. They have BUILT pagan shrines to Baal, and they SACRIFICE their sons and daughters to Molech. What an incredible EVIL, causing Judah to sin so greatly!"

Jeremiah 33:1, 3, 5-11 While Jeremiah was confined in the guard's courtyard, the LORD said: "ASK Me and I will TELL you secrets you do NOT know about things TO COME. ... You expect to fight the Babylonians, but the men of this city are as good as dead, for I have determined to destroy them. I have ABANDONED them BECAUSE of all their WICKEDNESS. ... Nevertheless, I will RESTORE Judah and Israel and rebuild their towns. I will FORGIVE all their sins of rebellion. Then this city will bring Me joy, glory, and honor before all the nations of the earth! There will be heard once more the sounds of JOY and LAUGHTER. They will sing, 'Give THANKS to the LORD of Heaven's Armies, for the LORD is GOOD. His faithful LOVE endures forever!'"

Jeremiah 34:16-17   The LORD says, "You have broken your oath and defiled My Name by taking back the people you had freed, forcing them to be slaves again. Since you have NOT obeyed Me by setting your countrymen free, I will set you FREE to be DESTROYED by war, disease, and famine."

Jeremiah 39:6-8   King Nebuchadnezzar made Zedekiah watch as they slaughtered his sons and all the nobles of Judah. Then they gouged out Zedekiah's eyes, bound him in bronze chains, and led him away to Babylon. The Babylonians burned Jerusalem and tore down the walls of the city.

Jeremiah 42:3, 6-7, 10-11, 13, 15, 22   They said, "PRAY that the LORD your God will SHOW us WHAT to DO and WHERE to GO. Whether we like it or not, we will OBEY the LORD our God. For if we obey Him, everything will turn out well for us." Ten days later the LORD gave this reply: "… Stay here in this land. IF you DO, I will build you up and not tear you down. Do NOT fear the king of Babylon anymore, for I am with you and will rescue you from his power. … But IF you REFUSE to OBEY the LORD your God, and if you … go to Egypt, … you can BE SURE that you will DIE from war, famine, and disease in Egypt, WHERE you INSIST on GOING."

Jeremiah 44:7-10, 16-17   The LORD God of Heaven's Armies asks: "WHY DESTROY yourselves? WHY provoke My anger by burning incense to the idols you have made here in Egypt? You will only DESTROY yourselves. You have shown NO remorse OR reverence." … They replied, "We will NOT listen to the LORD! We will DO WHATEVER we want. We will burn incense and pour out liquid OFFERINGS to the Queen of Heaven just AS MUCH AS we LIKE."

Jeremiah 51:17-19   The human race is FOOLISH and has NO knowledge! The people are DISGRACED by the idols they make, for their idols are a FRAUD, having NO breath or power. Idols are WORTHLESS; they are ridiculous LIES! On the Day of Judgment they will all be DESTROYED. But the God of Israel is NO idol! He is the Creator of EVERYTHING that exists, including His people, His own special possession. The LORD of Heaven's Armies is His Name!

Lamentations 2:14   Your [false] prophets said so many FOOLISH things, FALSE to the core. They did NOT save you from exile BY

pointing out YOUR sins. Instead, they painted FALSE pictures, filling you with FALSE hope.

Lamentations 3:21-27, 32-40   I still dare to HOPE when I remember this: The faithful LOVE of the Lord never ends! His MERCIES are NEW each morning. The Lord is my inheritance; therefore, I will HOPE in Him! The Lord is GOOD to those who DEPEND on Him, to those who SEARCH for Him. So it is good to WAIT quietly for the Lord. It is good for people to SUBMIT at an early age to His discipline. ... Though God brings grief, He also shows compassion because of His unfailing love. IF people DEPRIVE others of their rights in defiance of the Most High, IF they TWIST justice in the courts, does not the Lord SEE all these things? Who can command things to happen WITHOUT the Lord's permission? WHY should we, mere humans, complain WHEN we are punished for our sins? Instead, let us test and EXAMINE our ways. Let us TURN BACK to the LORD.

Lamentations 5:21   RESTORE us, LORD, and bring us BACK to You again! Give us back JOY!

Ezekiel 1:27-28
He looked like gleaming amber, shining with splendor. All around Him was a glowing halo, like a RAINBOW shining in the clouds on a rainy day. This is what the GLORY of the LORD looked like to me. When I saw it, I fell face down, and I heard a Voice speaking to me.

Ezekiel 3:5-11, 18-19   The LORD says: "I am NOT sending you to a FOREIGN people whose language you cannot understand. IF I did, they would LISTEN! But the people of Israel will NOT listen to you any more than they listen to Me! For the whole lot of them are hard-hearted and stubborn. But look, I have made you as obstinate and hard-hearted as they are. So do NOT be afraid of them NOR fear their angry looks, even though they are rebels. Son of man, LET all My Words sink DEEP into your OWN heart FIRST. Listen to them carefully for yourself. Say to them, 'This is what the Sovereign Lord says!' Do this whether they listen to you or not. ... IF I warn the wicked, saying, 'You are under the penalty of death,' BUT you fail to deliver the warning, they will die in their sins. And I will hold you responsible for their deaths. IF you WARN them and they REFUSE to REPENT and keep on sinning, they will DIE in their sins. BUT you will have saved yourself because you obeyed Me."

Ezekiel 5:5-9, 11, 15   The LORD says: "This is an illustration of what will happen to Jerusalem, who I placed at the center of the nations, but she refuses to obey My decrees and is MORE wicked THAN the surrounding nations. You have NOT even lived up to the standards of the nations around you. Therefore, I, the Sovereign LORD, am now your enemy. I will punish you publicly while all the nations watch. ... Because of your detestable idols, I will punish you like I have never punished anyone before or ever will again. I will show you no pity because you have defiled my Temple with your vile images and detestable sins. You will become an object of mockery and horror. You will be a WARNING to all nations. They will see what happens when the LORD punishes a nation."

Ezekiel 8:15-18   The LORD says: "I will show you even more detestable sins!" He brought me into the inner courtyard of the LORD's Temple. At the entrance to the sanctuary, there were 25 men facing east, bowing low, worshiping the sun! The LORD asks: "Is it nothing that they COMMIT these detestable sins, LEADING the whole nation INTO violence, thumbing their noses at Me? Therefore, I will respond with neither pity nor spare them. Though they cry for mercy, I will NOT listen."

Ezekiel 9:9-10   The LORD says: "The sins of the people of Israel and Judah are very, very great. The entire land is full of murder and injustice. They say, 'The LORD does NOT see it!' So I will have no pity on them. I will fully REPAY them for ALL they have DONE."

Ezekiel 11:18-21   The LORD says: "When the people return, they will REMOVE every trace of their vile images and detestable idols. I will give them singleness of heart and put a NEW spirit within them. I will TAKE away their stony, stubborn heart and GIVE them a tender, responsive heart, so they will OBEY My decrees. Then they will TRULY be My people, and I will BE their God. BUT as for those who long for vile images and detestable idols, I will REPAY them FULLY for their sins!"

Ezekiel 13:2-3, 7-9, 18-23   The LORD says: "Son of man, prophesy against the FALSE prophets who are inventing their own prophecies. ... What SORROW awaits the FALSE prophets who are following their own imaginations and have seen nothing at all! ... Can your visions be anything but FALSE if you claim, 'This message is from the LORD,' when I have NOT spoken to you? Because what you say is FALSE and your visions are a LIE, I will stand against you. I will blot their names from Israel's record books. ... What SORROW awaits you women who are TRAPPING the souls of My people. ... Do you think you can TRAP others without bringing DESTRUCTION on yourselves? By LYING to

My people who love to listen to LIES, you kill those who should NOT die, and you promise life to those who should NOT live. I AM against all your magic charms, which you use to TRAP My people. I will tear them from your arms. I will tear off the magic veils and save My people from your grasp. They will NO LONGER be your victims. Then you will KNOW that I AM the LORD. You have DISCOURAGED the righteous [being right, based on God's standard, includes thoughts, words and actions] with your LIES. You have ENCOURAGED the wicked by promising them life, even THOUGH they CONTINUE in their SINS. Because of this, ... I will RESCUE My people from your grasp."

Ezekiel 14:3, 6, 10, 19-20 The LORD says: "These LEADERS have set up IDOLS in their hearts. They have EMBRACED things that will make them FALL into sin. WHY should I listen to their requests? ... REPENT and TURN FROM your idols, and STOP ALL your detestable sins. FALSE prophets and those who SEEK their guidance will all be PUNISHED for their sins. ... Suppose I were to pour out My fury by sending an epidemic, and the disease killed people. ... EVEN IF Noah, Daniel, and Job were there, their righteousness would save NONE BUT themselves."

Ezekiel 16:2, 14-18, 20-21, 24, 27-28, 30-31, 34, 36-37, 39-41, 46-47, 49-57, 60, 63 The LORD says: "Son of man, CONFRONT Jerusalem with her detestable sins. ... Your fame spread throughout the world because of your beauty. I dressed you in My splendor and perfected your beauty. ... But you THOUGHT your fame and beauty were YOUR OWN. So you gave yourself as a prostitute. You used the lovely things I gave you to make shrines for idols, where you played the prostitute. UNBELIEVABLE! You took the jewels, gold and silver ornaments I had given you and made statues of men and worshiped them. This is adultery AGAINST Me! You used the beautifully embroidered clothes I gave you to dress your idols. Then you took your sons and daughters and sacrificed them to your gods. Must you SLAUGHTER My children BY sacrificing them to idols? You put altars to idols in every town square. I handed you over to your enemies, and even they were SHOCKED by your lewd conduct. After your prostitution, you still were NOT satisfied. What a PERVERTED [corrupt, depraved, immoral, lewd] heart you have, acting like a SHAMELESS prostitute. You are opposite of other prostitutes. You pay your lovers, not they pay you! I will gather together all your allies – the lovers with whom you have sinned, and I will give you to these many nations who are your lovers, and they will DESTROY you. They will knock down your pagan shrines. They will stone you and cut you up with swords. They will burn your homes. I will STOP your prostitution. ... Your sisters were Samaria and Sodom. You quickly SURPASSED them in CORRUPTION. Sodom's sins WERE pride, gluttony, and laziness, while the poor and needy suffered outside her door. She committed detestable sins, so I wiped her out. Even Samaria did NOT commit half your sins. Your sins are so terrible that you make your sisters SEEM righteous. ... But someday I will RESTORE Sodom and Samaria, and I will RESTORE you, too. Then you will be TRULY ashamed of everything you have done. In your proud days you held Sodom in contempt. But now your greater wickedness has been EXPOSED to all the world, and you are the one who is scorned. ... I will establish an everlasting covenant with you. ... REMEMBER your sins and COVER your mouth in shame when I FORGIVE all you have done. I, the LORD, have spoken!"

Ezekiel 20:34   The LORD says: "I will reach out … and I will bring you back from the lands where you are scattered."

Ezekiel 22:27, 30   The LORD says: "Your LEADERS are like wolves. They DESTROY people's lives for MONEY! ... I looked for someone to REBUILD the wall of RIGHTEOUSNESS that guards the land. I searched for someone to STAND IN the GAP in the wall so I would NOT have to DESTROY the land, but I FOUND no one."

Ezekiel 28:2, 5-7, 9-10, 12, 14-17   The LORD says to Tyre: "In your great PRIDE you CLAIM, 'I am a god!' But you are ONLY a man and NOT a god, though you boast that you are a god. Your wisdom has made you very rich, and your riches have made you very proud. Because you think you are as wise as a god, I will now bring against you a foreign army, the terror of the nations, and defile your splendor! Will you then boast, 'I am a god!' to those who kill you? To them you will be NO god but MERELY a man! You will die like an outcast. I, the Sovereign LORD, have spoken!" ... The LORD says: "You [Satan, Lucifer] were the model of perfection, full of wisdom and beauty. I anointed you as the mighty angelic guardian. You had access to the holy mountain of God. You were blameless in all you did from the day you were CREATED until the day evil was found in you. So I BANISHED you in disgrace from the mountain of God. Your heart was filled with PRIDE because of all your beauty. Your wisdom was CORRUPTED by your love of SPLENDOR."

Ezekiel 33:7-9, 11-20, 25-26,28-29,30-33   The LORD says: "I am making you a watchman for the people of Israel. LISTEN to what I say and WARN them for Me. IF I announce that some wicked people are sure to die and you FAIL to tell them to CHANGE their ways, then they will die in their sins, and I will HOLD you RESPONSIBLE for their deaths. But IF you WARN them to REPENT and they do not repent, they will die in their sins, but you will have saved yourself." ... The Lord says, "I take NO pleasure in the DEATH of wicked people. I ONLY want them to TURN FROM their wicked ways SO they can LIVE! TURN FROM your wickedness! WHY should you DIE? ... The righteous behavior of righteous people will NOT save them IF they TURN TO sin, NOR will the wicked behavior of wicked people destroy them IF they REPENT and TURN FROM their sins. ... Again I say, WHEN righteous people turn away from their righteous behavior and turn to evil, they will DIE. IF wicked people turn from their wickedness and do what is just and right, they will LIVE. ... People are saying, 'The Lord is not doing what is right,' BUT it is they who are NOT doing what is right. I will JUDGE you ACCORDING TO your own DEEDS." ... The LORD says: "You eat meat with blood in it, you worship idols, and you murder the innocent. Do you REALLY THINK the land SHOULD be yours? Murderers! Idolaters! Adulterers! I will completely destroy the land and demolish her pride. Her arrogant power will come to an end, because of their detestable sins, THEN they will KNOW that I AM the LORD. ... They say, 'Let's go hear the prophet tell us what the LORD is saying!' So My people come PRETENDING to be sincere before you. They listen to your words, but they have NO INTENTION of doing what you say. Their mouths are full of lustful words, and their hearts seek only money. ... You are very entertaining to them, like someone who sings love songs with a beautiful voice or plays fine music on an instrument. They HEAR what you say, but they do NOT ACT on it! But when all these terrible things happen to them – then they will know a prophet has been among them."

Ezekiel 34:2-22, 31 The LORD says: "Son of man, prophesy AGAINST the shepherds, the leaders of Israel: What SORROW awaits you shepherds who feed yourselves instead of your flocks. You have NOT taken care of the weak, NOT tended the sick or bound up the injured. You have NOT gone looking for those who have wandered away and are lost. Instead, you have ruled them with harshness and cruelty. So My sheep have been scattered without a shepherd, and they are easy prey for any wild beast. They have wandered, yet no one has gone to search for them. Therefore, you shepherds, HEAR the Word of the LORD: You abandoned My flock. You did NOT search for My sheep when they were lost. You took care of yourselves and left My sheep to starve. I now consider you shepherds My enemies, and I will hold you responsible for what has happened to My flock. I will stop you from feeding yourselves. I will rescue My flock; the sheep will no longer be your prey. I, the LORD, say: I will SEARCH for My lost ones who strayed away, and I will BRING them safely home again. I will bandage the injured and strengthen the weak. But I will DESTROY you who are fat and powerful. I will feed you JUSTICE! I will JUDGE between one and another, SEPARATING the sheep from the goats. Isn't it enough for you to keep the best for yourselves? Must you also trample down the rest? Isn't it enough for you to drink the best water? Must you also muddy the rest with your feet? WHY must My flock eat what you have trampled down and drink water you have fouled? I will rescue My flock, and they will no longer be abused. You are MY people, and I am YOUR God!"

Ezekiel 36:26-27 The LORD says: "I will TAKE out your stony, stubborn heart and GIVE you a new, responsive heart. I will put My Spirit in you so that you will FOLLOW Me and be careful to OBEY Me."

Ezekiel 37:3-5, 21, 23-25, 27 The Lord asked me, "Son of man, can these bones become living people again?" I replied, "You alone know the answer to that." He said, "Speak a prophetic message to these bones and say, 'Dry bones, LISTEN to the Word of the LORD! I am going to put breath into you and make you live again!' I will gather the people of Israel and bring them home to their own land from the places where they have been exiled. They will never again pollute themselves with their idols and vile images and rebellion, for I will SAVE them FROM their sinful BACKSLIDING. I will cleanse them. THEN they will truly be My people, and I will be their God. They will OBEY My regulations and be careful to KEEP My decrees. My servant David will be their King forever. I will make My home AMONG them. I will be their God, and they will be My people."

Ezekiel 38:14-16, 19, 22-23 The LORD says: "Prophesy against Gog of the land of Magog: When My people are living in peace, then you will come from the distant north with your mighty army, and attack My people Israel. At that time in the DISTANT FUTURE, I promise a mighty earthquake in Israel on that day. I will punish you and your armies with disease and bloodshed, hailstones, fire, and burning sulfur! I will show My greatness and holiness, and I will make Myself known to all the nations of the world. THEN they will KNOW that I AM the LORD."

Ezekiel 39:6 The LORD says: "I will RAIN down FIRE on Magog and on all your allies who live safely on the coasts. THEN they will KNOW that I AM the LORD."

Ezekiel 43:4, 7, 9 The Glory of the LORD came into the Temple through the east gate. The Lord said to me, "Son of man, this is the place of My throne and footstool. I will live in this place among the people of Israel forever. The family of Israel will NOT ruin My Holy Name again. The kings and their people will NO longer bring shame to My Name by COMMITTING SEXUAL sins OR by BURYING the dead bodies of their kings in this place. Then I will live AMONG them forever."

Ezekiel 45:9-10 The Lord GOD said: "Enough, you RULERS of Israel! STOP being cruel and stealing things from people! BE fair and DO what is right! STOP forcing My people out of their homes! STOP cheating people. Use accurate scales and measures!"

Daniel 1:8
Daniel was determined NOT to defile himself by eating the food and wine given to them by the king. He ASKED the chief of staff for PERMISSION not to eat these unacceptable foods.

Daniel 2:20-22, 27-28, 31-35, 44 Daniel said, "PRAISE the Name of God forever and ever, for He has ALL wisdom and power. He CONTROLS the course of world events. He removes kings and sets up other kings. He REVEALS deep and mysterious things and KNOWS what lies hidden in darkness, though He is surrounded by light." ... Daniel replied [to the king], "There are NO wise men, magicians, or fortune-tellers who can reveal the king's secret. BUT there is a God in heaven who reveals secrets, and He has shown King Nebuchadnezzar what will happen in the FUTURE. ... In your vision, Your Majesty, you saw standing a huge, shining statue of a man. As you watched, a rock was cut from a mountain, but not by human hands. It struck the feet of iron and clay, smashing them to bits. The whole statue was crushed into small pieces of iron, clay, bronze, silver, and gold. Then the wind blew them away without a trace. But the rock that knocked the statue down became a great mountain that covered the whole earth. ... The God of heaven will set up a kingdom that will NEVER be destroyed or conquered. It will crush all these kingdoms, and it will stand FOREVER."

Daniel 3:16-18, 23-25, 28-30 Shadrach, Meshach, and Abednego replied, "We do NOT need to DEFEND ourselves before you. IF we are thrown into the blazing furnace, the God whom we serve is ABLE to

SAVE us. He will rescue us from your power. But EVEN IF He does NOT, we want to be clear to you, that we will NEVER SERVE your gods." ... So Shadrach, Meshach, and Abednego, securely tied, fell into the roaring flames. Suddenly, Nebuchadnezzar jumped up and exclaimed, "Didn't we tie up 3 men and throw them into the furnace? Look! I see 4 men, unbound, walking around in the fire unharmed! The fourth looks like a god!" ... Then Nebuchadnezzar said, "Praise to the God of Shadrach, Meshach, and Abednego! He sent His angel to RESCUE His servants who TRUSTED in Him. They DEFIED the king's command and were WILLING to DIE rather than serve or worship any god except their own God. There is NO other god who can rescue like this!" Then the king promoted Shadrach, Meshach, and Abednego to even higher positions in Babylon.

Daniel 4:34-37 My [Nebuchadnezzar] sanity returned, and I praised and worshiped the Most High and honored the One who lives forever. His kingdom is eternal. All the people of the earth are nothing compared to Him. He does as He pleases. No one can stop Him. All His acts are JUST and TRUE, and He is able to HUMBLE the proud.

Daniel 5:22-24, 30 Daniel replied to the king, "... O Belshazzar, you KNEW all this, yet you have NOT humbled yourself. You PROUDLY DEFIED the LORD of heaven and had these cups from His Temple brought before you. You and your wives and concubines have been drinking wine from them while praising gods of silver, gold, bronze, iron, wood, and stone – gods that neither see nor hear nor know anything at all. You have NOT honored the God who GIVES you the breath of life and controls your destiny! So God sent this hand to write this message." ... That very night Belshazzar, the Babylonian king, was KILLED.

Daniel 6:10-27 When Daniel learned that the law had been signed, he went home and knelt down as usual in his upstairs room, with its windows open toward Jerusalem. He PRAYED 3 times a day, just AS he had ALWAYS done, giving THANKS to his God. Then the officials went to the king and reminded him about his law. "Did you not sign a law that any person who prays to anyone, except to you – will be thrown into the den of lions?" Then they told the king, "That man Daniel is IGNORING you and your law. He still prays to his God 3 times a day." The king was deeply troubled, and he tried to think of a way to save Daniel. He spent the rest of the day looking for a way to get Daniel out of this predicament. In the evening, the king gave orders for Daniel to be thrown INTO the DEN of LIONS. The king said to him, "May your God, whom you serve so faithfully, rescue you." Then the king returned to his palace and spent the night fasting. Very early the next morning, the king got up and hurried out to the lions' den. He called out in anguish, "Daniel, servant of the living God! Was your God, whom you serve so faithfully, able to rescue you from the lions?" Daniel answered, "Long live the king! My God sent His angel to SHUT the lions' mouths so that they would not hurt me, for I have been found innocent in His sight, Your Majesty." The king was OVERJOYED and not a scratch was found on Daniel, for he had TRUSTED in his God. Then the king gave orders to arrest the men who had MALISCIOUSLY accused Daniel. He had them thrown INTO the lions' den. The lions leaped on them and tore them apart before they even hit the floor of the den. King Darius sent this message: "Peace and prosperity to you! I decree that everyone throughout my kingdom should tremble with fear before the God of Daniel. For He is the LIVING God, and His kingdom will never be destroyed. He has rescued Daniel from the power of the lions."

Daniel 7:13 AMP, 14, 17-18 I saw someone like a Son of Man coming on the clouds of heaven. He approached the Ancient One and was led into His Presence. He was GIVEN authority, honor, and sovereignty over all the nations, so people of every race and nation and language would obey Him. His rule is ETERNAL. … These 4 huge beasts represent 4 kingdoms that will arise. But in the end, the holy people of the Most High will be given the kingdom, and they will rule forever.

Daniel 9:4-7, 9-14, 17-20, 25-26 I PRAYED to the LORD my God and CONFESSED: "O Lord, you are a great and AWESOME God! You always KEEP Your PROMISES of unfailing love to those who LOVE You and OBEY your commands. But we have sinned and done wrong. We have rebelled against You and scorned Your commands. We have refused to listen to Your prophets. Lord, You are RIGHT, our faces are covered with shame. But the Lord our God is merciful and forgiving. We have NOT obeyed the LORD, for we have NOT followed the instructions He gave us. So NOW the curses and judgments written in the Law of Moses have been poured down on us BECAUSE of our sin. You have KEPT Your Word and DONE to us and our rulers EXACTLY as You warned. Every curse written against us in the Law of Moses has come TRUE. Yet we have REFUSED to SEEK mercy from the LORD our God by TURNING FROM our sins and RECOGNIZING His TRUTH. The LORD our God was RIGHT to DO all of THESE things, for we did NOT obey Him. We make this plea, NOT because we deserve help, BUT because of Your MERCY. O Lord, forgive, listen and act! For Your own sake, do not delay for your people." I went on PRAYING and CONFESSING my sin AND the sin of my people. ... [The angel Gabriel said:] "Listen and understand! Jerusalem will be rebuilt with streets and strong defenses, despite the perilous times. The Anointed One [Jesus] will be killed, APPEARING to have accomplished NOTHING, and a ruler will arise whose armies will destroy the city and the Temple. War and its miseries are decreed FROM that time TO the VERY END."

Daniel 11:29-38, 44-45 At the APPOINTED TIME he will vent his anger against the people of the holy covenant and reward those who forsake the covenant. ... His army will take over the Temple fortress, pollute the sanctuary, and set up the sacrilegious object that causes desecration. He will FLATTER and win over those who have violated the covenant. BUT the people who KNOW their God will be STRONG and will RESIST him. Wise leaders will give instruction to many, but these teachers will die by fire and sword, or they will be jailed and robbed. During these PERSECUTIONS, little help will arrive, and MANY who JOIN them will NOT be SINCERE. Some of the wise will fall victim to persecution. In this way, they will be refined and cleansed and made pure until the time of the end. The king will do as he pleases, exalting himself and claiming to be greater than every god, even blaspheming the God of gods. He will SUCCEED, but only UNTIL the time of wrath is COMPLETED. For what has been determined will surely take place. He will boast that he is greater than all gods. He will WORSHIP the god of fortresses. ... He will set out in great anger to destroy and obliterate many. He will stop between the glorious holy mountain and the sea. While he is there, he will meet his end, and NONE will HELP him.

Daniel 12:1-2, 4, 10, 13 At that time every one of you whose NAME is WRITTEN in the BOOK will be RESCUED. Many of those whose bodies lie dead and buried will RISE up, SOME to everlasting life and SOME to shame and everlasting disgrace. At the TIME of the END, many will rush here and there, and knowledge will increase. ... MANY will be PURIFIED and refined by these trials. But the WICKED will CONTINUE in their wickedness, and NONE of them will understand. ONLY those who are WISE will KNOW what it MEANS. ... As for you, you will rest, and then at the end of the days, you will rise again to receive the inheritance set aside for you.

Hosea 2:23 The LORD says, "I will show love to those I called 'Not loved.' And to those I called 'Not My people,' I will say, 'Now you are My people.' And they will reply, 'You are our God!'"

Hosea 4:4, 6 The LORD says, "Do NOT point your finger at someone else and try to pass the blame! My complaint, you priests, is WITH you. My people are being DESTROYED because they do NOT know Me. Since you priests REFUSE to know Me, I REFUSE to recognize you as My priests.

Hosea 6:3, 6 Press on to KNOW the LORD! ... The LORD says, "I want you to SHOW love. I want you to KNOW Me more than I want burnt offerings."

Hosea 14:9 Let those who are WISE UNDERSTAND these things. Let those with DISCERNMENT LISTEN carefully. The WAYS of the LORD are TRUE and RIGHT, and righteous people LIVE by WALKING in them. BUT sinners stumble and fall.

Joel 2:12-13, 28, 32

The LORD says, "TURN to Me now, WHILE there is STILL TIME. Give Me your hearts. Come with fasting, weeping, and mourning. Do not tear your clothing in your grief, but tear your hearts instead." RETURN to the LORD your God, for He is merciful and compassionate, slow to get angry and filled with unfailing love. He is EAGER to RELENT and not punish. ... The LORD says, "After doing all those things, I will POUR out My Spirit upon all people. Your sons and daughters will prophesy. Your old men will dream dreams, and your young men will see visions. ... Everyone who CALLS ON the Name of the LORD will be SAVED."

Amos 3:3 Can 2 people walk TOGETHER without AGREEING on the direction?

Amos 5:7, 11-15 You WICKED people! You TWIST justice, making it a BITTER pill for the poor and oppressed. ... Righteousness and fair play are MEANINGLESS to you. You TRAMPLE the poor, stealing their grain through taxes and unfair rent. ... You OPPRESS good people by taking BRIBES and deprive the poor of justice in the courts. So those who are SMART keep their mouths SHUT, for it is an evil time. DO good and RUN FROM evil SO that you may LIVE! Then the LORD will be your helper. HATE evil and LOVE what is good; turn your courts into

TRUE halls of JUSTICE. Perhaps even yet the LORD will have mercy on the remnant of His people.

Obadiah 1:21   Those who have been RESCUED will have the LORD Himself be their KING!

Jonah 1:17   The LORD had arranged for a great fish to swallow Jonah. And Jonah was inside the fish for 3 days and 3 nights.

Jonah 2:9   I offer songs of praise. ... My SALVATION is FROM the LORD ALONE.

Jonah 3:5, 7-10   The people of Nineveh BELIEVED God's message, and from the greatest to the least, they declared a fast and put on burlap to show their sorrow. The king sent this decree: "People must be in mourning, and PRAY earnestly to God. They must TURN FROM their evil ways and STOP all their violence. Perhaps even yet God will change His mind and hold back His fierce anger from destroying us." When God SAW how they stopped their evil ways, He did NOT destroy them.

Micah 6:8   The Lord has TOLD you what is GOOD. The Lord REQUIRES that you do JUSTICE [be fair to others], be KIND, love MERCY [compassion, forgive, generous], and WALK HUMBLY [gentle, teachable, trusting God, not pridefully depending on self] with your God.

Micah 7:8   Do NOT gloat over me! Though I fall, I will RISE again. The LORD is my LIGHT.

Nahum 1:7   The LORD is GOOD, a strong fortress, and CLOSE to those who TRUST Him.

Habakkuk 1:2-5   I cry, "VIOLENCE is everywhere! I am surrounded by people who love to ARGUE and FIGHT. There is NO justice in the courts." The LORD replied, "Look around at the nations; look and be AMAZED! For I am doing something in YOUR own day, something you would NOT believe even IF someone TOLD you about it."

Habakkuk 2:2-6, 12-13, 20   The LORD said to me, "This vision describes THE END, and it will be fulfilled. IF it seems slow in coming, WAIT patiently, for it will surely take place. The PROUD TRUST in

THEMSELVES, and their lives are crooked. But the RIGHTEOUS will LIVE by their FAITHFULNESS [trust, loyalty] to God. Wealth is treacherous, and the arrogant are NEVER satisfied. What SORROW awaits you thieves! NOW you will GET WHAT you DESERVE! ... What SORROW awaits you who build big houses and build cities with money gained through murder and corruption! The LORD of Heaven's Armies has PROMISED the wealth of nations will TURN TO ashes! ... Let ALL the earth be SILENT before the LORD."

Habakkuk 3:17-19 Even though the fig trees have NO blossoms, and there are NO grapes on the vines; even though the olive crop FAILS, and the fields lie EMPTY and barren; even though the flocks DIE in the fields, and the cattle barns are EMPTY, YET I will be FULL of JOY in the LORD! I will be JOYFUL in the God of my SALVATION! The Sovereign LORD is my STRENGTH!

Zephaniah 3:17
The LORD your God is living AMONG you. He is a MIGHTY Savior. He will take DELIGHT in you with gladness. With His love, He will CALM all your fears. He will REJOICE over you with joyful songs.

Haggai 1:4-6, 8, 10
The LORD of Heaven's Armies says, "WHY are you living in luxurious houses WHILE My house lies in ruins? LOOK at WHAT is HAPPENING to you! You have planted much but harvest little. ... Your wages disappear as though you were putting them in pockets filled with holes! ... Now rebuild My house. Then I will take pleasure in it and be honored. ... It is BECAUSE of YOU that the heavens withhold the dew and the earth produces no crops."

Haggai 2:9 "The FUTURE glory of this Temple will be greater than its past glory, and I will bring PEACE," says the LORD of Heaven's Armies.

Zechariah 1:3
The LORD says: "RETURN to Me, and I will RETURN to you."

Zechariah 4:6, 10 The LORD of Heaven's Armies says: "It is NOT by force NOR by strength, BUT by My SPIRIT. ... Do not despise small beginnings, for the LORD rejoices to see the work begin."

Zechariah 8:16-17 "This is what you must do: Tell the TRUTH to each other. Render verdicts in your courts that are JUST and that lead to

PEACE. Do NOT scheme against each other. STOP your love of telling LIES that you swear are the truth. I HATE all these things," says the LORD.

Zechariah 9:9 Rejoice, your King is coming to you, humble, riding on a donkey's colt.

Zechariah 14:9, 12-13 The LORD will be King over ALL the earth. On that day there will be ONE LORD – His Name ALONE will be worshiped. … The LORD will SEND a plague ON ALL the nations that fought AGAINST Jerusalem. Their people will become like walking corpses, their flesh rotting away. Their eyes will rot in their sockets, and their tongues will rot in their mouths. On that day they will be terrified, stricken with great panic. They will fight their neighbors hand to hand.

Malachi 1:12-13
The LORD says, "You DISHONOR My Name WITH your ACTIONS. You say, 'It is too hard to serve the LORD,' and you turn up your noses at My commands."

Malachi 2:7-9, 14-17 The LORD says, "The words of a priest SHOULD preserve knowledge of God, and people SHOULD go to him for instruction. BUT you priests have LEFT God's paths. Your instructions CAUSED many to STUMBLE into sin. So I have made you DESPISED and HUMILIATED in the eyes of all the people. For you have NOT obeyed Me but have SHOWN favoritism in the way you carry out My Instructions." … You cry out, "WHY does the LORD NOT accept my worship?" … BECAUSE the LORD witnessed the vows you and your wife made. … You have been UNFAITHFUL to her, THOUGH she remained your faithful partner. Didn't the LORD make you ONE with your wife? In body and spirit you ARE His. WHAT does He want? Godly [committed to obeying God] CHILDREN from your union. So GUARD your heart: REMAIN loyal to your wife. The LORD says, "I HATE divorce! To divorce your wife is to OVERWELM her with cruelty. So GUARD your heart, do NOT be unfaithful to your wife." You have wearied the LORD with your words. "HOW have we wearied Him?" you ask. You have wearied Him by SAYING that all WHO do EVIL are GOOD in the LORD's sight, and He is pleased with them.

Malachi 3:5-10, 13-16, 18 The LORD of Heaven's Armies says, "I will put you on trial. I am eager to WITNESS AGAINST all sorcerers, adulterers, and liars. I will SPEAK AGAINST those who cheat employees of their wages, who oppress widows and orphans, or who deprive foreigners of justice, for these people do NOT fear [reverential awe, honor, respect] Me. I AM the LORD, and I do NOT change. That is why you ... are not already destroyed. ... You have scorned My decrees and failed to OBEY them. Now RETURN to Me, and I will RETURN to you. But you ask, 'HOW can we return when we have never gone away?' Should people CHEAT God? Yet you have cheated Me! But you ask, 'WHEN did we ever cheat You?' You have CHEATED Me of the tithes and offerings due to Me. You are under a curse, for your whole nation has been cheating Me. Bring all the tithes into the storehouse. ... IF you DO, ... I will pour out a blessing so great you will not have enough room to take it in! TRY it! Put Me to the test! ... You have said TERRIBLE things about Me. But you say, 'What have we said against you?' You have said, 'What is the use of serving God? What have we gained by obeying His commands or by trying to show the LORD that we are sorry for our sins? From now on we will call the arrogant blessed. For those who do evil get rich, and those who dare God to punish them suffer no harm.'" ... A BOOK of REMEMBERANCE was written to RECORD the NAMES of those WHO feared [honored, respected] the LORD. ... The LORD says, "On Judgment Day, you will see the DIFFERENCE between the righteous [being right, based on God's standard, includes thoughts, words and actions] and the wicked, BETWEEN those WHO serve God and those WHO do NOT serve Me."

Malachi 4:1-2 The LORD of Heaven's Armies say, "The Judgment Day is COMING, burning like a furnace. On that day the ARROGANT and the WICKED will be BURNED UP like straw. They will be consumed – roots, branches, and all. BUT for you WHO fear [respect God's power and authority, because we desire to please] My Name will go FREE, leaping with JOY."

===== 11/26/2023 =====

AFTERWORD

Thank you for reading, Glimpse the entire Bible through my Favorite Bible Verses, which includes less than 9% of the words of the entire Bible. You may want to continue reading the full Bible to catch up on the many details you are missing.

To assist you on your journey to understand what God may be telling you through His Bible, you may want to go to a church that preaches from the Bible (not all churches do, some are too selective in what they preach – omitting anything controversial, others distort what the Bible actually says) where you can also attend a Bible study class or attend a small group with other interested people, in addition to listening to a Bible based sermon.

Consider these **link**s:
    Find a Church in the United States
        https://churches.goingfarther.net/
    Find a Church in US and world
        https://www.jesuscares.com/find-a-church

For those who want to **chat online** about questions you may have, consider these **links**:
    Jesus Cares   https://www.jesuscares.com/
    Do I Matter   https://www.doimatter.chat/
    When Life Hurts   https://www.whenlifehurts.com/

For people who want someone to **pray** with them on the phone. Here are 3 ministries that may fill this need:
        www.prayandhope.org   1-866-599-2264 **Prayer and Crisis Line**
        https://faithprayers.org   1-866-515-9406
        https://www2.cbn.com/prayer   1-800-700-7000

For those who may be considering following Jesus, but still have questions as to what that means, or why that is necessary, consider these links:

God's Rescue Plan is wonderfully illustrated using the EvangeCube as a 4 minute video on YouTube you can watch here:
        https://www.youtube.com/watch?v=zETUh50u8Vs

3 Circles gospel presentation, 3 minutes on YouTube
        https://www.youtube.com/watch?v=5W8ynRMr59k&t=1s

Many people appreciate songs to help them think about key ideas, some of my **favorite songs** are:

1) Jesus loves me, this I know – written by Anna Warner, 1859
https://hymnary.org/text/jesus_loves_me_this_i_know_for_the_bible

2) Trust and obey, for there's no other way – John Sammis, 1887
https://hymnary.org/text/when_we_walk_with_the_lord

3) 25 Easy Christian Worship Songs to Play on Guitar
https://sandymusiclab.com/25-easy-christian-worship-songs-to-play-on-guitar/

4) 25 Kids' Worship Songs
https://www.playlister.app/blog/25-kids-worship-songs-to-teach-in-your-kids-ministry

May your mind and heart continue to be open to what God may want you to know about Him! May you enjoy your journey as you **continue experiencing the Bible as a love story about God's pursuit of us**. There are many stories of redemption – in both the Old and New Testaments – and you could be next!

Made in the USA
Columbia, SC
06 December 2023